Self-Defense Finance

WILEY SMALL BUSINESS EDITIONS

Self-Defense Finance

FOR SMALL BUSINESSES

Wilbur M. Yegge, CBC, Ph.D.

NAM/Wiley Series in Manufacturing

John Wiley & Sons, Inc.
New York ◆ Chichester ◆ Brisbane ◆ Toronto ◆ Singapore

Copyright © 1995 by Wilbur M. Yegge
Published by John Wiley & Sons, Inc.

Library of Congress Cataloging-in-Publication Data

Yegge, Wilbur M.
    Self-defense finance for small businesses / Wilbur M. Yegge.
        p.   cm.
    Includes bibliographical references.
    ISBN 0-471-12294-7 (cloth : alk. paper). — ISBN 0-471-12295-5
(pbk. : alk. paper)
    1. New business enterprises—Finance.   2. New business
enterprises—Planning.   3. Small business—Finance.   4. Small
business—Planning.   I. Title.
HG4027.6.Y44   1995
658.15′92—dc20   95-11737

10   9   8   7   6   5   4   3   2   1

Dedication

There are over ten million nonagricultural small businesses in the United States, and they represent over 95% of the nation's total businesses. Irrespective of the magnificence of their larger counterparts, small businesses account for nearly 60% of all private employment and almost one-half of total business output. Small business contributes over half of all industrial innovation, which is produced at substantially less cost than that which is incurred by large business. Employment growth coming from the small-business sector is nearly nine times greater than that coming from other sectors. The effect brought about by small business on the total U.S. economy is of major importance to us all.

Although these data paint a land-of-opportunity picture, according to the U.S. Small Business Administration (SBA), it must be noted that over 80% of all businesses fail in their first ten years of operation. Fifty-three percent of these businesses will fail by the end of their fifth year, while fewer than 20% fail after ten years in operation. Overwhelmingly, the major cause of this failure is weak management. Individuals usually go into business because of an acquired skill in production or sales and seldom possess the knowledge necessary to manage all aspects of the business. This is especially true in the critical area of finance. Financial management need not be complicated. It is the goal of this handbook for you to immediately begin using these tools in your business.

This handbook is dedicated to the millions of small-business owners who struggle, work, and survive in what sometimes appears to be a hostile environment, always courting the word NO.

Acknowledgments

The scope of experience reflected in this handbook is the result of many years of education, applied practice, and accumulated contributions from many business and professional individuals (who, by passage of time, leave their mark rather than name) to be acknowledged. Six persons, however, deserve special recognition. I thank Christopher Micklatcher, Attorney and C.P.A., and Thomas F. Dobens, C.P.A., for their willingness to review concepts and mechanical application. I thank Richard Nass, BS Mathematics, MBA Accounting, and James Whitney, BSBA, MBA, MS Education, course work completed DBA studies, for their willingness to review both text and mechanical presentation. All four have had many years of experience in working with small, privately owned businesses. A special thanks to Mary Rich, whose aid and assistance were given freely in proofreading my manuscript. It is a pleasure to acknowledge Michael Hamilton, senior editor at John Wiley & Sons, Inc., whose thoughtful suggestions and enthusiasm for the manuscript were invaluable. Michael also taught me something about the publishing world that no book or seminar has been able to teach. I owe him a deep debt of gratitude.

About the Author

Nineteen ninety-four marks the passage of ten years in the field of small-business consulting and 15 years in other small-business ownership for me. This, I believe, is a relatively long time for a man to survive without the trappings and, yes, the safety of the corporate cocoon, where I spent the previous years of my business life. Somewhere along the line, I found time to acquire graduate degrees in both psychology and business. Without the blending of these two disciplines, I might still be in the corporate environment.

My first and second adventures into small-business ownership were start-up situations and successful by both then and today's standards. The first was an automatic letter writing and data processing business, which when sold in 1968 was producing nearly four hundred thousand dollars of sales. Today, that business has sales in excess of 15 million dollars and provides jobs for 50 people. A second venture was the establishment of a management consulting firm in Boston, Massachusetts. During graduate school, I worked part-time in a consulting firm, and through both college and work experience, I learned not only the value of "cramdown" scheduling for achievement during 16-hour days but also the framework for building a consulting practice of my own. Three years after its inception, and one year after graduation from college, my consulting practice was profitably sold. Offices of this company were operating in Boston, Houston, and Los Angeles. We were 20 professionals in all and had annual billings of six hundred thousand dollars for our services. My bright, shiny, and new Master's in business told me to move on when I was invited into the exciting prospect described through my education for the large, multinational corporate life.

Six-plus years at this corporation introduced me to many wonderful experiences, among which was their mergers and acquisitions department, where I worked under the toughest boss in my career. He was also the best of all those before and after him. Much of my present day entrepreneurial belief system was molded during these "high-flying," leverage buy-out times of the late 1960s and early 1970s. I progressed to the head of the acquisition team before this corporation was acquired by still a larger giant. This, too, was a valuable education, but one best left to tell at another time. When my boss fell under the proverbial ax customarily wielded on those at the top of acquired companies, I realized that it was time to move on again.

My third and fourth business purchases were not as successful. These occurred after tenure in the corporate world and, perhaps, after decision making on my part became too molded by those stratified corporate philosophies. The third adventure was the purchase of a bankrupt company. Short on personal capital, I leveraged and put too much of my personal self on the line. I learned from my mistakes, however, and made the next leverage purchase from bankruptcy proceedings, before returning to the consulting field once again. No loss, or real profit for that matter, was made in either venture, but I clearly learned the value of planning for financial control. Entrepreneurs, it is said, are made when, because of business conditions, they miss their first payroll. With commonsense planning and through appropriate control, it is not necessary to get this close to failure. Andrew Carnegie said, "Concentrate. Put all your eggs in one basket, and watch that basket."

Operating a business is not easy, nor is the task of buying or selling a business. My father, during the 1940s and 1950s, who always paid cash for what he bought in his restaurant business, had a simple philosophy about accounting: "If I start the day with x dollars in cash, pay my bills in cash as I go along, and then end up with x plus y dollars of sales in cash, what's left over is the profit for the day. Applied and managed thus daily, this is all the accounting I need." He had only an eighth grade education, but he succeeded in providing for his family throughout his life.

"Shoebox" record keeping still exists today, but there are so many more variables that now come into play. Through the years, buyers, sellers, lawyers, accountants, and middlemen perpetuate a need to add value, justifying the expense of their time. Legislators passed into law complex rules that exacerbate even the simplest of business operations. Out-of-control spending on the part of government led to complex tax structuring schemes to fund government expansion. Small business has been forced into applying big-business principles for small-business survival.

Overall, it is a picture that reminds me of an ancient battle and the poor judgment of two generals. Perhaps you will recall from Roman history the battle strategy referred to as the "Phalanx." Opposing legions faced each other in closely formed wedges, appearing much like the pins at a bowling alley. The intended purpose was to advance and confront each other, point to point. Weapons of that day were comprised largely of shield and sword, carried by a foot soldier. With only a shield on the left hand and sword on the right, you might imagine the feeling of bodily exposure for men at the point and all along the wedge to the right-hand side. A natural tendency was for each phalanx to "shift" left with distance, each seeking the safety and comfort of shield. A successful strategy of generals was found in the skillful positioning of their armies in proximity close enough to engage each other before a significant shift was to occur. History records at least one great battle where two generals misjudged the distance and their armies passed without either striking a blow. So much confusion existed between the two sides that the battle was ultimately put off to be fought on another day.

I often think of this story when working for the small-business owner, where too many generals seem to be present in the decision-making process. The only generals who count are the ones with their bucks on the line. President Harry S. Truman made famous the saying, "The buck stops here!" He rose from the bankruptcy of his small Missouri haberdashery business to statesman and, finally, to president of the United States. Throughout his life, he collected information, learned from this information, made *his* decisions, and stuck by *his* guns.

It is my hope that this text brings credible logic to the arduous *process* that some of us go through while deciphering various elements of business finance. It is also my hope that the suggestions offered herein will lend strength to the business owner when confronted by the opinions of accountants, lawyers, buyers, sellers, business brokers, mothers, fathers, mothers-in-law, and fathers-in-law. I add the last four categories to emphasize the very real possibility in small business for the "blue-sky" dilemma, presented in an old real estate story, to occur—the one where a consulted father-in-law, a self-ordained expert, kills the proposed deal. After all, many of us finance some of our ventures through the benefit of family owned capital.

It is my further hope that you will send comments, thoughts, constructive criticisms, or other ideas that may improve the quality of this handbook for others and for future editions. Also, I would like to hear about your experiences in using this text.

WMY

Preface

As most of our careers advance, we eventually steer a course into the mature and hopefully growing field that reflects our previous training. Some of us take charge in our jobs and contribute significantly to the management style, creative aspects, and/or the technical elements in our chosen fields, while others may feel more secure in following the footsteps provided by others who went before them. Only a few persons will strike out each year into unproven ventures, such as the purchase of a small business of their own. The task before these few is large and requires all the tenacity, intelligence, and common sense they can muster for eventual success.

There are some very good reasons why private business ownership is not for everyone. Among the chief reasons are security and peace of mind. The stress generated by starting, owning, and operating a small business is unparalleled by that in most of life's adventures. Regardless of one's strength of conviction, that business-related stress will eventually carry over into family life, and the existence of strong family relationships is essential to appropriately handle those inevitable times when the business puts our survival at risk. It is important to consider well our marital situations and make appropriate time for family life.

Work loads, although we may have unfinished business at the end of a day, are traditionally *scheduled* for us in the corporate environment. Bottlenecks in assignments can be distributed to others to even out the work flow. Small-business owners more often find themselves in the roles of "chief cooks and bottle washers," when they must unilaterally wear the corporate hats of CEO and CFO and perform management, marketing, sales, purchasing, stocking, and accounting tasks without the benefit of assistants. It is not uncommon for many business owners to attire in janitorial regalia when the business day has ended. A business life for most owners is usually not at all what was first envisioned and clearly less than those carefree allusions to quiescent business drama as seen in the movies.

Mr. Kenneth Olsen founded Digital Equipment Corporation in the garage of his home. I'm confident that in earlier years he missed the community found in working with others. With the aid of venture capital and his university ties, we, today, know the magnitude of his achievements. This is one example of fulfilling dreams envisioned by many entering private enterprise. Some people will achieve similar lofty goals, but many more will be content and happy with their company remaining small . . . to continue in their roles of sole proprietor, performing as much as they can, and then agonizing over what is left undone.

This text is directed to those several million independent businesspeople who market products or services and who are without the benefit of a chief financial officer in their employ. It incorporates personal experiences derived from assignments during ten years of small-business consulting, the adventures from 15 years of ownership and sale of small businesses, and the thoughts and comments from other business owners and their advising professionals. It is tempered by knowledge gained from the unfortunate drama played out in nearly 40 bankruptcy proceeding assignments. And it provides insight into the traditional roles played by bankers, accountants, attorneys, buyers, and sellers, whenever these parties are facilitating or affecting aspects of the economic cycle of the small business.

My hope is that, as you read this handbook, you will find guidance in resolving issues surrounding management finance, which have been difficult in handling alone. My further hope is that, through studying the text, you will be better prepared to know *when* to seek professional assistance while a problem is still malleable. It takes courage to ask for help, but courageous men and women enjoy the most success.

Wilbur M. Yegge, CBC, Ph.D.
W. M. Yegge & Company

Wells, Maine

Contents

Introduction

A preordained logic to organization of chapters in this handbook may not at first seem readily clear. There is, however, a certain specific purpose. Every service or product, to include the writing of books, begs creation of a *marketing and financial plan*. We each need and deserve some form of compensation for our work. This can come in the form of emotional and financial reward. Frankly, I expect to receive both through writing this handbook. From elementary SBA publications to scholarly works, I have not yet found a text that truly addresses the *average* of problems incurred by nontech, "mom and pop," or "lifestyle"-type businesses. Publications tend to be either too simple for any real use or too academic to fit in with constant time demands placed on the owner of the small and, perhaps, lifestyle-type business. For the purpose of this handbook, I define lifestyle ventures as "businesses that are restricted in sales by the size of the local economy and population." Examples might be the corner grocery store, restaurant, small motel, retail store, accountant, lawyer, doctor, therapist, etc., or businesses that would be owner run, often from a single location. Further definition might be "businesses that encompass the previous statement, and that to substantially grow beyond these conditions would require *cloning* the business at other locations." With some exceptions, these businesses often have sales of three million dollars or less and seldom have a stable year-round work force of more than 15 employees. Examples of lifestyle manufacturing or distribution businesses might be those with products or services where transportation or a predominance of similar-type competitors prevent serious entry into more distant markets. Some businesses with five, ten, or more million dollars of sales also fit into this lifestyle category. For a business to be lifestyle in nature does not mean that handsome profits cannot be made.

Other texts about closely held business generally use case examples from the larger and better-established small businesses. Most address their subject well but miss elements that are directly related to the much smaller entrepreneur. For example, this handbook, while it does not violate established principles of finance and accounting, is *written* from a *business owner's* point of view. The sample cases of XYZ and ABC companies make use of **positive cash flow** examples to emphasize salient points. *Many text* examples will *use the negative* income and balance sheet to highlight the author's application of financial tools. Perhaps this is simply the psychologist coming out in me. I like to think positively and be around positive-thinking people.

Chapters in this handbook are organized along the line of their usefulness, as described to me by clients, students, and beginning entrepreneurs. For example, some people, because of an existing skill level, require no more than the overview on writing business plans, which is provided in Chapter 1. Even if this is the case, then in view of my "Marketing and Monetary Logic," I still want my handbook to be purchased. If Chapter 1 is insufficient guidance for meeting previously acquired skill, then Chapter 2 provides details on financial statement analysis and could represent all that is required. (Of course, I still want my handbook to be purchased.) Subsequent chapters are thus arranged along lines of their possible and sequential useful need.

My "mission statement" or purpose for this handbook reads as follows: "To write a book, not necessarily a scholarly rendering, but one that is completely educational, which provides guidelines to address issues surrounding the major reason why so many small businesses fail. A handbook that relates to the needs of persons who want to be in business for themselves and want also to take personal control of their business's direction. Finally, to write in a *user-friendly* manner."

My "target market" is a large sector of nonagricultural small-business owners who operate grocery stores, restaurants, small motels, smaller-sized manufacturing, single-store retail, small group or single professional practices, nontech start-up businesses, etc. This segment is often overlooked in publications due to their size and insignificant, singular role in the more global economy. Additionally, this text is for those people who themselves are from lifestyle businesses and who provide accounting, financial, and legal advice to independent owners. This text is also directed to commercial bankers who analyze and provide capital to smaller enterprise. Without them, many more small businesses would not survive. Finally, this text is directed to would-be business owners contemplating their first purchase.

1

Writing *Business Plans* That Work

PREVIEW

Throughout all the business plans that I have developed and presented to banks for financing personal business ventures, *not once* has the strength of my marriage been questioned. I have raised this question with countless numbers of persons contemplating private ownership for the first time. Responses ranged from downright outrage to puzzlement over my query. The facts make the answer to a first and basic question about being in business for yourself quite simple: private business ownership *increases* the stress in your life. Elementary logic suggests that a weak marriage will just get weaker, whether the spouse is involved in the business or not. Partners who are focused on and considerate of each other's wants and needs stand a better chance for long-term success in the world of private enterprise. This applies to nonmarital partnerships as well.

During our lives we purchase homes, automobiles, and other major items for shelter, transportation, and comfortable surroundings. No business plan is required of us to meet these objectives. And then, after frustration with our jobs, or for whatever reason, we develop an idea of how good it might be to be self-employed. After all, the most common American dream is to be a private business owner.

We find a business to purchase, or conceptualize the idea for a new business, and approach the *bank*. They like our verbal plans, but . . . but, now they want us to submit a *business plan* in writing. Beyond history and

1

projected thinking, they want financials—historical financials, projected financials, and comparative financials of similar businesses. Where do we turn? How do we obtain this type of information? Who can help? *Not the bank!* However, they do have much of this information available to them and will use these data to evaluate the merit of our individual plans. The following is a broad overview of the planning process and business plan format. Succeeding Chapters 2 through 9 provide detail in areas where the reader may desire more complete reference material.

Guide to Planning Your New Enterprise

Any company, regardless of its size, faces two common problems. First, it routinely functions with limited resources—just so much money and so many people available. Second, it has certain objectives, such as a desire to increase sales by 10%, to introduce new products or services, or to expand in other ways. Matching a company's objectives with its resources is an important task. Ensuring that the objectives are realistically achieved is an even greater undertaking. The purposes of the business plan are to guide the accomplishment of these tasks and, further, to serve as an instrument to secure financing where such is required.

Some specific advantages of formulating a business plan are as follows:

1. The *process* forces the planner to think carefully, to be disciplined, and to focus.

2. The *process* helps identify which factors success depends upon and highlights critical elements that are essential to achieve a planned goal.

3. The *plan* provides a clear idea of *what* the organization or individual is attempting to do and *how, when,* and *why* they plan to do it. This represents the essence of the business plan.

4. The *plan* can enable management to measure progress toward objectives. In some instances, banks review the progress of their loan in light of the original business plan.

Are there objections to developing a business plan? Surprisingly, yes. Not everyone is convinced of their value, often for good reasons. Like anything else, the plan can be misused. Some critics argue that it takes too much time to develop and culminates in generating a lot of paperwork that is often shelved and not really used.

The plan must be a living document. The plan can be a vital part of thinking and actions contemplated, or actions taken, and may represent a business road map for successful growth and increased profit. Unfortunately for some owners, the business plan turns into a historical bundle of papers used only to secure a loan, and its neglect, perhaps, becomes one additional reason why some business persons ultimately lose control.

The Business Plan

The format and content of business plans will be as varied as the nature of their creators. Often, the owners turn to their accountant, or a consultant, for help in preparing the plan. The responsibility for conceptual elements and the plan's ultimate contents cannot, however, be delegated. It is the business owners who have their chips on the line.

The task of obtaining comparative data is among the more difficult problems faced by the small-business owner. Privately held businesses are not required to publicize their financial conditions, and larger corporate information is not germane to the smaller operation. Further complicating the data interpretation is the profit mission of management in public versus privately owned enterprise. The job of the public company manager is to show a profit for stockholders, whereas the job of the private company manager more often becomes one of operating to minimize personal taxes. This discerning difference in the private company exacerbates intelligent understanding of information, even when obtained.

For years it had been general practice for individuals to own real estate separate from the business itself. The terms of leaseback to the business were often determined by the condition of the mortgage, rather than established by prevailing rental rates in the community where located. Salaries of owners do not necessarily track with rates paid to employees performing equivalent work, and a plethora of other expense items is similarly adjusted to fit the needs of an owner. Subsequently, operating statements must often be *reconstructed* to reflect the true picture of the privately owned company's financial position. When business owners do not understand this reconstructive task, engagement of an accountant or specialized consultant is encouraged.

National comparative information, by business type, can be obtained from the *Annual Statement Studies,* produced by Robert Morris Associates in Philadelphia, and from *Financial Studies of the Small Business,* produced by Financial Research Associates in Winter Haven, Florida. The libraries of business schools and the business section of public libraries can shed more light on the financial aspects of small-business operation.

The business plan requires much time, attention, and detail—but so does continual operation of the business for which the plan is developed. Perhaps a business idea needs additional thought when the invested time in developing a plan seems to be too much work.

The following list is an outline of elements and types of information common to all comprehensive business plans:

1. The loan request
   a. Names, addresses, and telephone numbers of persons requesting the loan.
   b. Stated purpose of loan request.
   c. Stated amount of loan request.
   d. Terms requested.
   e. Detail of collateral offered.
2. Introductory material
   a. Background and history of existing business or the concept detail of the new idea.
   b. Description of product or service.
   c. Role that product or service will play within an industry, the need it will fill, and how it will relate to existing products or services performing a similar function.
   d. Summarization of general industry background.
3. Market research (Include both positive and negative factors about product, industry, potential customers, and competition.)
   a. Research and detail all factors, paying particular attention to past and future activity in the industry and with competitors.
   b. Research pending legislation that might affect continuing or future operation.
   c. Research the particular business under consideration or the new idea. Provide evidence of why it exists and detail what features and benefits your presence brings into the operation. Explore how, when, and why sales have been achieved and *all* expenses

incurred by the operation. Trust what you can see and prove, and discard most of what you hear. Understand the business fully before you proceed with the plan.

4. The business or new idea

   a. Provide statement of events expected to be accomplished, including financial forecasts, during various future time periods.

   b. Show by example how the business will grow internally in response to projected sales growth. Be realistic in projections. The resources of funding, staffing, and employee training are not easily obtained and directly affect the reality for growth. Financial institutions understand, and will often reject on common sense merit, those business plans that are overly optimistic in their forecast performance.

   c. Detail the effect of growth on the business and its financial and personnel requirements. Provide a current and future plan to handle financial needs and staffing considerations. Plan for the unexpected because it usually does occur.

   d. Don't neglect planning for line-of-credit and other short-term capital requirements. Request line-of-credit financing together with original financing requirements.

   e. Provide historical operating information: three to five past years.

   f. Detail accounts receivable, accounts payable (include aging of accounts), work in progress, and backlog of orders.

   g. Detail assets available for purchase, and affix approximate values to each.

   h. Provide detail of forecasts for future operation (at least three years out).

   i. Provide a management plan for the operation, and explain why you can operate, retain what exists, and grow.

5. Organization

   a. Include résumés of the principals of the company.

   b. Show that prior experience, training, and educational backgrounds of each will contribute to success of the company.

6. Personal financials (on each principal)

   a. Complete and include loan application forms for each bank.

    b. Include copies of at least two past years of personal tax filings. *Be sure to sign these copies.*

7. Sign the business plan report (provide for signature page toward end of report).

The Marketing Plan

A marketing plan is simply a statement of *what* the business is going to do during a certain period of time, *how* it is going to do this, and *who* is going to do what. When the entrepreneur answers each of these questions with respect to the sale and distribution of the product or service, he or she has the essence of a marketing plan. Unless management knows exactly how and what it wants to do, it is unlikely that success will be achieved. In joint ownership situations, the particular responsibility for executing various elements of the plan must be clear to all parties.

What Should a Marketing Plan Contain?

A marketing plan should contain the following:

1. Statement of goals. These goals should be quite specific and stated for at least the period of one year. Bear in mind that the concept of what will be accomplished two and three years out will be necessary to form the "future" sales aspect of the financial plan.

2. Background material on each product or service and markets served. A business owner cannot know too much about his or her marketplace.

3. Description of the program to achieve goals. Care should be exercised to consider each of the possible alternative programs, how much each will cost, and how likely each is to succeed.

4. Statement on timing. The resultant marketing plan, as with the general business plan, should include specific statements about when the planned events are to take place. A statement such as "we shall commence marketing on July 1st, have the machinery and people in place by August 1st, and start delivery by September 1st," is one example of describing the time frame involved.

5. Statement describing who is responsible for what action. This includes a forecast for additional staff required to achieve certain

goals. Unless responsibilities are clearly assigned, and understood, it is unlikely that the planned actions will take place.

6. Evaluation plan. The marketing plan, like the general business plan, must be a "living" document. Re-evaluation must be built in to measure progress against the plan. It should be reviewed and updated at least *quarterly*. Much can and usually does happen in a three-month period, and one must adjust contemplated actions accordingly.

The marketing plan is developed in conjunction with the general business plan, and both are tied together with the forecast cash requirements projected in the financial plan.

The Financial Plan

Financial institutions expect not only to understand how much money you request but also clearly *when* and in what amounts you will need it. Perhaps a little reminder from family parenting experiences will best explain this issue. Most of us have had experience with children asking for "pen" money. Usually this request occurs without much planning or forethought. In the beginning the request seems okay, and we accommodate our children's need. But as time wears on, these unexpected requests get old and very tiresome to most of us. So it is with banks, particularly when as businesspeople we are *expected* to anticipate and to plan for our needs in *advance*.

Funds to a business come from a variety of sources: the business owner, outside investors in the company, banks, creditors who lend the company money, and from past earnings that the company retains. These funds have been committed to fixed assets, i.e., real estate, furniture, fixtures, etc.; to inventories in the forms of loans, lines of credit, and asset-based lending arrangements; to accounts receivable, which are occasionally sold to "factoring" houses; and to working cash or marketable securities. Over time, the pool of funds change. These changes are known as *funds flow* or cash flows. In an ongoing business, these funds continually flow throughout the enterprise. The term financial management indicates that these flows are *directed* according to some preconceived plan. Advance planning for future cash needs is essential to sustaining and growing a business.

Financial planning falls into two broad areas of *planning for liquidity* and *planning for profit:*

1. Planning for liquidity. In essence this is simply planning the company's cash flow. A principal tool for short-term planning is the *cash budget,* which more often assists best as a *written* plan detailing the amount and timing of expected inflows and outflows of cash. It is commonly prepared on a month-to-month basis, for the period of one year at a time. Effectively applied, the cash budget will forecast the *critical path* of *critical elements:*

   a. Identifies periods when cash inflows do not meet cash outflow requirements.

   b. Identifies timing and magnitude of cumulative effect of "shortages" and/or cash excesses produced by the business.

   Armed with this knowledge, the business owner knows how much financing will be needed, when it will be required, how long it will be used, and how it can be repaid.

2. Planning for profit. This usually involves a longer-range projection of the company's status, its future income, the assets required to generate this income, and the sources and amounts of funds that will be necessary to finance its growth. Planning for profit generally requires extending the one-year plan out into the future for three to five years of expected performance. The principal means of accomplishing this task is to project the company's income statements and balance sheets into these future periods. In making these projections, it is necessary to make explicit, realistic assumptions, many of which are based on aspects of the marketing plan. These assumptions should be clearly stated within the context of the financial plan.

The market research effort and the marketing plan provide significant inputs to these long-range financial plans. The single most important variable influencing future financing requirements is sales. Sales volume, of course, directly influences the level of operations, real estate, and equipment required; inventories; and accounts receivable and payable. One prime purpose of preparing long-term financial plans is to identify the extent and timing of additional capital needs. In many cases, the business owner will do an excellent job of planning for funds to accomplish an initial task but will fail to plan for lines of credit to fund the slack periods that occur in most businesses. Lines of credit should be requested concurrently with primary funding needs.

Planning allows management to view a wide range of possible outcomes with little or no cash impact on the current operation. The process encourages continuous planning and, at times, may suggest the most appropriate course of action for responding to unexpected changes within a given market. The business plan is a tool to help business owners get to where they want to be and serves to communicate objectives to company employees.

While small-business owners traditionally dream of and, yes, visualize growing their enterprise into something larger, many are unable to produce in writing the various requirements for that growth. Some elements affecting growth are beyond the efforts of owners, and some are within their control. Regardless of personal background and experience, it is always useful to have your accountant or consultant review and comment on short- and long-range financial plans. By the nature of their practice, they regularly work with businesses experiencing similar problems and may add particular merit into the reliability of expected events to occur. Minimally, these professionals can help to solidify the owners' conviction in their proposals.

SUMMARY

The business plan incorporates and exists through the features and benefits of both the marketing and the financial plans. The resources of money and personnel, when coupled with human engineering, become the telltale elements to future success. Historical information about the business, the competition, the industry, the local and national economy, the existing and pending legislation, and the background of individuals involved must all be examined in detail to determine what realistically can be achieved in both continuing and future markets. The *process* is educational and becomes convincing evidence that the project or idea has real merit. The *plan* becomes the word picture of the past, present, and future and the document for financing and for continuing management. Each business possesses unique characteristics that differ from similar businesses within their industry. These characteristics often provide niche marketing strengths for the small business and can become key to future growth.

GUIDE TO BORROWING FROM LENDERS

The first job of the lenders is to assess the degree of RISK in each proposed loan and to be satisfied that every loan will be repaid according to its terms. They do this by analyzing, among other things, the following guide (also see Chapter 9):

1. The nature and history of a business.
2. The purpose of the loan.
3. The amount requested.
4. The collateral offered.
5. The source of repayment.
6. The owner's personal background and credit history.

Debt to net worth ratios are often among the first criteria examined. Financial institutions, by their conservative nature, do not like highly leveraged deals. They want to see that an owner has personal funds on the line. The SBA and other financing authorities can reduce a bank's risk through guarantees; however, these authorities also seek safety in the principal amount guaranteed. When a company's "hard" asset base is low, in comparison to a loan request, and/or debt is high, in comparison to an owner's personal investment (net worth), be prepared to explain . . . explain . . . explain! Fine work done on the business plan at this juncture may be a deciding factor in securing the loan.

A credit request will get the best analysis and response when information is complete and well organized and when submission allows enough time for proper consideration by the commercial loan officer and the loan review committee. It is to the lender's best advantage to obtain as much information as possible to make a sound credit decision. Procrastination in filling the lender's requests can both add suspicion and delay the decision process.

There is an important side benefit to you from these proceedings. The process of detailing complete financial information on your business, in an orderly fashion, highlights your firm's strengths and weaknesses and allows you to identify potential areas needing attention. The initial loan process is essentially free, and the applicant gains the benefit of "outsider" questions they might not otherwise ask themselves.

The following outline is one commercial bank's suggested guide for preparing a loan request:

1. Cover letter
   a. Business name, address, and telephone number.
   b. Amount and purpose of loan.
   c. Terms and source of repayment.
   d. Security or collateral offered.
2. Business history
   a. Business legal structure.
   b. Date established—when purchased by present owner.
   c. Number of employees.
   d. Nature of business.
   e. Describe real estate—owned/leased.
3. Marketing plan
   a. Industry background.
   b. Explain role of competition and influence on business requesting loan.
   c. Goals of business requesting loan.
   d. Description of products or services.
   e. Describe how goals will be achieved.
4. Supporting financial data and financial plan
   a. Balance sheets (for past three years).
   b. Profit and loss statements (for past three years).
   c. Cash flow projection (at least one future year, by month—best if one or two additional years can be forecast realistically).
   d. Be sure to answer the question, Does the amount requested make suitable allowance for unexpected developments?
   e. Trade references.
5. Personal information on owners (complete for each owner)
   a. Personal and family data.
   b. Responsibilities (outline where and why your particular experience will benefit the enterprise).
   c. Education and work history.

    d. Personal financial statement.

    e. Personal tax returns (at least past two years—*be sure to sign the copies*).

    f. Credit references.

For those who possess a good understanding of the principles and techniques of financial management, the process of writing a business plan can possibly end with the guidelines provided in Chapter 1. However, based on government statistics on why businesses fail, I suspect that there are many more who might want to gain additional insight into the formidable elements that comprise the backbone of essential records necessary to creating the business plan. Chapters 2 through 9 provide reasonably straightforward reviews of each of the financial documents that are traditionally expected, and often required, to be included in the business plan of the smaller-sized company. The processes of accounting and financial planning, much like the subject of mathematics, have been difficult for many of us to fully grasp. This was initially a problem for me with early accounting classes, when the case studies involved very large businesses and the size of the numbers seemed always to get in the way. As with the study of mathematics, to learn and retain the processes, one needs continual practice. A simple technique that I used in those early studies was to *think* of each equation as a *loop* requiring *closure,* sort of resembling an electrical circuit, where to provide current to a certain point, the circuit must be closed. In an overall example of the accounting "circuit," cash or other forms of investment are put into the company by the owner who, in turn, purchases a work force and machines to produce a product or service that is marketed to the public for profit. That profit is used to pay operating expenses, debt, and a return, which is often paid back in the form of salary to the owner. So long as the company makes a profit that is consistent with debt load and expected returns, the circuit remains closed, and the owner, company, customers, and employees prosper. This circuit of profitable events can be interrupted by any number of causes, which will be outlined as we proceed in the text.

There are many texts written on accounting and financial control. For additional reference, one textbook tends to stand out as particularly useful to the small-business owner, *Accounting: The Basis for Business Decisions,* Walter B. Meigs, Ph.D., C.P.A., and Robert F. Meigs, D.B.A., published by McGraw-Hill Book Company. This is the text used in many colleges and universities by beginning students of accounting or business. Its case studies are comprised of small-business scenarios.

2

Financial Statement Analysis

The backbone and the element most noticed by financial institutions in a business plan are the financial statements. These documents are studied not only for their historical significance but, more importantly, for the telltale secrets they hold, and can reveal, about the likelihood of some forecasted event to occur. Although financial statements traditionally record what has taken place between specific periods of time, their comparison to several past periods reveal the financial *trends* taking place within the organization.

On the balance sheet, for example, accounts receivables are often compared with accounts payables for their balance between each other. Cash on hand becomes a particularly important element of the comparison when payables outdistance receivables. If payables are two or more times greater than receivables, then how much cash on hand is available to pay the difference? If not through available cash, then how can the payables be cleared and the business continue operation? On the other hand, when receivables, which are current, exceed payables by some margin, the question of available cash may not be quite so critical to the analysis.

Another important element in the examination of payables and receivables is a review of their *aging*. How many and what dollar amount is beyond the *normal* payment or collection period? What component of each is 30, 60, 90, or more days beyond customary? Are there units from receivables that are uncollectable or bills in payables that cannot be paid?

Questions to be raised during examination of financial statements are well documented in texts of accounting procedures. Many times, answers to questions will lead to other questions that need a response. In the business plan, whether designed for achieving loans or for management controls, customary inquiry must be *anticipated* in advance, and all questions must be answered honestly, to the best of the entrepreneur's knowledge. Not doing so invites skepticism from the reviewer. If there is a problem occurring, identify it, and suggest a practical solution to handling the problem! After all, if the business is operating smoothly, perhaps the need for a *written* business plan is of less importance.

In the ensuing part of this chapter, we will work through a simple examination of a balance sheet and then a profit and loss statement. These two documents are inseparable in the preliminary examination process but do not necessarily comprise the full picture. Industry ratio comparables used were those published, by industry, in each applicable year, through the *Annual Statement Studies,* produced by Robert Morris Associates of Philadelphia. Other helpful information may be obtained through *Financial Studies of the Small Business,* which is published by Financial Research Associates of Winter Haven, Florida. The libraries of business schools and the business section of public libraries can shed more light on the financial aspects of the small-business operation. Significant local economic information may only be available through your own accountant or financial consultant, where present or recent past experience data may solidify reliability of ratio building on a local level. Following chapters will describe additional elements of the review.

In our first of two examples, the case we will use is an actual business that was formed five months ago. As one might assume, the business is cash starved and in need of additional funding. The business enjoys a developing marketplace niche and enjoys what appears to be a good future for increasing sales and profits. The second example is a manufacturing business. To protect the privacy of the owners, much of these companies' data and product history are withheld.

CASE #1—A START-UP BUSINESS

The Balance Sheet

By definition, the balance sheet (*in reality, a "snapshot" of one day*) reflects the financial condition of a business at a particular point in time. It summarizes what the business owns, called **assets;** what the business has for debt, called **liabilities;** and the *difference* between assets and liabilities, called **owner's equity** or the investment of the owners. The difference between assets and liabilities can be a positive or negative number and is commonly referred to as either *positive net worth* or *negative net worth*. In a balanced accounting equation, total assets equal the total of liabilities and owner's equity. Stated in the reverse, total liabilities plus owner's equity equals the total of assets.

XYZ Company
Balance Sheet
As of May 31, 1994

ASSETS
Current Assets

Cash in Bank	$ 15,720
Total Cash	$ 15,720

Other Current Assets

Accounts Receivable	$ 36,420
Inventory at Cost	$ 18,500
Total Other Current Assets	$ 54,920
Total Current Assets	$ 70,640

Equipment, Vehicles, Furniture

Equipment	$529,000
Vehicles	116,000
Furniture & Fixture	17,000
Subtotal	$662,000
Less: Accum. Depreciation	32,135
Total Equip./Veh./Furn.	$629,865

TOTAL ASSETS	**$700,505**

LIABILITIES
Current Liabilities

Current Portion of Long-Term Debt	$ 86,177
Notes Payable—Bank	79,944
Accounts Payable	15,433
Total Current Liabilities	$181,554

(continued)

XYZ Company
Balance Sheet
As of May 31, 1994 *(continued)*

Noncurrent Liabilities	
Long-Term Debt, Net Of Current Portion	$411,221
Notes—Bank	—
Notes—Owner	28,500
Total Noncurrent Liabilities	$439,721
TOTAL LIABILITIES	**$621,275**
OWNER'S EQUITY	
Capital	$107,126
Net Income or (Loss)	($ 27,896)
Total Owner's Equity	$ 79,230
TOTAL LIABILITIES & OWNER'S EQUITY	**$700,505**

Once the balance sheet has been constructed, an initial and useful task is to visually compare the relationship of some accounts to others. In our balance sheet on the XYZ Company, components of the current assets and liabilities, namely, the accounts receivables, are greater than twice that of accounts payables, which appears relatively healthy. However, when viewing the whole of the account, total current liabilities are more than two and one-half times greater than total current assets and signify the possibility of a beginning *trend* toward a cash-starved position. These conditions can be more aptly viewed through the process of calculating *ratios*. Ratios will help diagnose the financial condition of the business. The relationship of a particular business's ratios to those of its industry can add further insight to the overall picture. Start-up businesses, such as is used in this example, often are distorted in their ratio relationship to published industry comparison studies involving more established companies. However, the *key balance sheet ratios* for *solvency* and *safety* are always important to the evaluation. Simply defined, solvency is the ability of a company to pay its bills and is measured by the **current ratio** and by the **quick ratio.**

The current ratio is a test for solvency and indicates how much money is in current assets (*assets that can be converted to cash in one year*) to pay current liabilities (*debt that is due within one year*). It is calculated as follows:

$$\textbf{Current Ratio} = \frac{\text{Total Current Assets}}{\text{Total Current Liabilities}}$$

or, in the case of XYZ Company,

$$\text{Current Ratio} = \frac{\$70,640}{\$181,554} = .4$$

Generally, the higher the current ratio, the greater the company's ability to pay current obligations. Published information for similar-sized firms in this particular industry show the current ratio ranging from a high of 1.7 down to .5. Calculated at .4, this firm is at the low end of the range and pointedly reveals a need for cash infusion or a reworking of current-term debt to remain solvent.

The quick ratio is a more confining test for solvency and is a good indicator of the *liquidity* of a company. It measures the *very* liquid assets of cash plus accounts receivables to the total current liabilities.

$$\textbf{Quick Ratio} = \frac{\text{Cash \& Equivalents} + \text{Accounts Receivables}}{\text{Total Current Liabilities}}$$

For our sample company,

$$\text{Quick Ratio} = \frac{\$15,720 + \$36,420}{\$181,554} = \frac{\$52,140}{\$181,554} = .3$$

This test is also known as the "ACID TEST" ratio. It is a refinement of the current ratio and a more conservative measure of liquidity. Generally, any value of less than 1 suggests that a company must rely on inventory or other current assets to liquidate short-term obligations. Published information for similar-sized firms in this industry show the quick or acid test ratio, ranging from a high of 1.4 down to .4. Calculated at .3, this again reveals the need for a generous infusion of cash and/or short-term debt restructuring.

The **Safety Ratio** indicates a company's ability to withstand adversity and reflects the degree of **riskiness** attached to a firm's business. It measures the amount of debt against the business net worth of owners. It pinpoints heavily leveraged firms that may be more vulnerable to business downturns. Financial institutions pay particular attention to this ratio in their assessment of safety of principal in such case that liquidation becomes necessary to return their unpaid funds.

$$\textbf{Safety Ratio} = \frac{\text{Total Liabilities}}{\text{Tangible Net Worth}}$$

$$\text{Safety Ratio} = \frac{\$621,275}{\$\ 79,230} = 7.8$$

This ratio determines the extent to which the owner's personal investment has been made in relationship to outside debt. The higher the ratio, the greater the risk that is being assumed by present and future lenders. A company with a low safety ratio generally has greater flexibility in future borrowing. Published information for similar-sized firms in this industry show the safety ratio ranging from a low of 1.2 to a high of 7.4. Positioned at 7.8, this company is highly leveraged and contains little margin of safety for additional debt.

At this point, and if the balance sheet was the only document to be reviewed, this company quite likely would not be granted an additional loan. Balance sheet information and the three key ratios indicate a highly leveraged, cash-starved position and provide very little security for new investment.

Subsequently, compelling and substantiated reasons to justify additional funding must be stated in the business plan. This involves a clearly written description of how the company evolved, how they managed to get to this point, and how they plan to survive and grow. An overview of published industry comparables and how the company will fit in with existing competition will provide more understanding to the plan. A review of customer history, backlog orders, and methods to obtain greater sales are also expected.

The **income statement** measures the company's sales and expenses over a period of time and is the principal supporting document to the balance sheet. The income statement usually covers a period of no more than one year but can be assembled on a shorter period, such as monthly, depending upon the particular business's needs.

XYZ Company
Income and Loss Statement
Five Months Ended May 31, 1994

Sales	$223,847
Expenses	
Payroll & Taxes	$ 64,674
Trucking Expense	93,539
Fuel	23,903
Equipment Repairs	9,500
Parts	13,736
Insurance	9,707
Misc. Expense	7,014
Subtotal	$222,073
Add: Interest Expense	29,670
Add: Owner Salary	None
Total Expenses	$251,743
Net Income or (Loss) Before Deprec. and Payment of Taxes	($ 27,896)

It seems obvious at this point that this company not only is cash starved but also has failed to show a profit in its first five months of operation. Key ratios for comparison of *profitability* are simply not considered necessary since visual observation reveals a clear picture of operation. What is necessary is an examination of their last month of operation. Does the last completed month show evidence of profit? The *progression* toward profitability becomes more of an acute issue than do ratios in the newly formed company. Bear in mind, this company has incurred expenses of $662,000 for start-up capital equipment purchases. One might expect slim operating margins in just five completed months, but there need be *evidence* of improvement in the operating picture for a financial institution or outside investor to consider the infusion of additional funds into this company. *Where patterns of improving conditions exist, all supporting history and detail must be included in the business plan.*

Key ratios for comparison of profitability will be explored in the second case, an established company, which follows the analysis of this start-up business.

Examination of sales and expense by month revealed a steady growth in cash flow. Further, there existed a purchase order confirmed, backlog of work totaling $303,848, and a work-in-progress prospect for an additional $615,630 of sales, much of which represented repeat business. The last completed month, May 31, 1994, showed the following change in the company's financial picture:

XYZ Company
Income and Loss Statement
One Month—May, 1994

Sales	$ 76,592
Expenses	
Payroll & Taxes	$ 9,917
Insurance	3,500
Rent	1,000
Fuel	3,408
Equipment Repairs	2,366
Parts	4,358
Equipment Rental	3,799
Telephone	588
Misc. Expense	162
Subtotal	$ 29,098
Add: Interest Expense	5,934
Add: Owner Salary	None
Total Expenses	$ 35,032
Positive Cash Flow for Month of May	**$ 41,560**

Detail analysis of each month completed to date, work backlog, and work-in-progress accounts suggested that this company might complete one full year of operation, as depicted in the following forecast statement.

XYZ Company
Forecast Income & Loss Statement
For the Period Ending December 31, 1994

Sales	$1,143,325
Less: 20% Contingency	228,665
Net Pro Forma Sales	$ 914,660

Expenses

Payroll & Taxes	$ 169,274
Owner Salary	44,880
Insurance	42,000
Rent	12,000
Fuel	57,367
Equipment Repairs	48,392
Parts & Service	52,296
Telephone	7,056
Equipment Rental	45,588
Misc. Expense	4,044
Subtotal	$ 482,897
Add: Interest Expense	71,208*
Add: 10% Contingency	55,411
Total Expenses	$ 609,516

Forecast Net Profit before Depreciation and Taxes	**$ 305,144**

* The owners of this company borrowed $521,500 from equipment manufacturers at 12% interest, financed over 36 months, and nearly $80,000 from local banks in short-term (90 days) loans. Principal and interest payments amount to $17,743 per month. Restructuring $600,000 into long-term debt would bring their payments down to $12,601 per month. This would represent $5,142 in cash out-flow savings per month and $61,704 in cash out-flow savings per year in a 9.5% interest, 60-month payout scenario. To create a year-end forecast balance sheet, an allocation for depreciation and payment of taxes must be made. This balance sheet draws upon the assumption that new financing is in place.

Return: Net Profit	$ 305,144
Less: Allocation for Deprec.	77,124
Less: Estimated Taxes	63,846
Forecast Cash Flow	**$ 164,174**

XYZ Company
Forecast Balance Sheet
As of December 31, 1994

ASSETS

Current Assets

Cash in Bank	$ 84,026
Total Cash	$ 84,026

Other Current Assets

Accounts Receivable	$149,080
Inventory at Cost	60,257
Total Other Current Assets	$209,337

Equipment, Vehicles, Furniture

Equipment	$529,000
Vehicles	116,000
Furniture & Fixture	17,000
Subtotal	$662,000
Less: Accum. Depreciation	77,124
Total Equip./Veh./Furn.	$584,876

TOTAL ASSETS	**$878,239**

LIABILITIES

Current Liabilities

Current Portion of Long-Term Debt	$104,012
Accounts Payable	62,614
Total Current Liabilities	$166,626

Noncurrent Liabilities

Long-Term Debt, Net of Current Portion	$439,709
Notes—Owner	28,500
Total Noncurrent Liabilities	$468,209

TOTAL LIABILITIES	**$634,835**

OWNER'S EQUITY

Capital	$ 79,230
Net Income or (Loss)	164,174
Total Owner's Equity	$243,404

TOTAL LIABILITIES & OWNER'S EQUITY	**$878,239**

To arrive at the December forecast balance sheet, a detail of the five months completed, plus estimates for the remaining seven months, was constructed on a month-by-month basis. Particular analysis was concentrated on sources and uses of cash, inventory accumulation, and changes in accounts receivables and payables. Coupled with historical practices of the owner and the customers, year-end estimates were compiled. While performance in achieving forecast goals is wholly dependent upon management's skills, *the key elements to believability in this plan were the month of May operating performance, backlog of work, and probable work in progress.* Financial institutions, by obligation to stockholders and regulators, cannot finance wishful thinking. **The business plan must show a constructive and realistic way to pay back a loan, or additional financing is unlikely to be achieved.**

RATIO	At 5 Months	At 12 Months	Range of Industry
Current	0.4	1.8	1.7–0.5
Quick	0.3	1.4	1.4–0.4
Safety	7.8	2.6	1.2–7.4

Folding short-term debt of $80,000 into long-term financing, refinancing equipment purchases at more attractive interest rates with longer terms, coupled with evidence of increasing sales and profitability, all served in allowing this firm to be viewed in a lower risk category by a bank. These data, when added to the personal and business history of the owner, permit a bank to evaluate the full scope of the risk involved.

CASE #2—A SUCCESSFULLY OPERATING COMPANY

In the second case, we look at the financial elements of a reasonably successful, ongoing business, which may be sold. The process of evaluation once again begins with the balance sheet, which should be summarized on a spread sheet covering at least three to five years.

ABC Company
Balance Sheet
As of December 31

	1991	1992	1993
ASSETS			
Current Assets			
Cash in Banks	$ 69,726	$ 9,646	$ 48,744
Accounts Receivable	182,696	303,513	248,976
Allow Doubtful Accts	(5,500)	(10,000)	(6,000)
Advances to Owner	2,619	16,289	—
Cash Investments	25,356	5,000	—
Inventory	185,958	197,668	171,128
Total Current Assets	$460,855	$522,116	$462,848
Property and Equipment			
Leasehold Improvements	$ 12,629	$ 12,629	$ 16,144
Furniture & Equipment	58,606	63,802	86,842
Vehicles	6,350	6,350	6,350
Subtotal	$ 77,585	$ 82,781	$109,336
Less: Accum./Deprec.	52,466	63,628	80,001
Total Property & Equip.	$ 25,119	$ 19,153	$ 29,335
Other Assets			
Cash Value—Life Ins.	$ 4,017	$ 8,477	$ 7,690
Total Other Assets	$ 4,017	$ 8,477	$ 7,690
TOTAL ASSETS	$489,991	$549,746	$499,873
LIABILITIES & EQUITY			
Current Liabilities			
Curr./Por. L.T.D.	$ —	$138,000	$ —
Accounts Payable	183,897	211,610	176,943
Accrued Taxes	33,977	9,331	4,133
Accrued Retirement	—	—	18,136
Total Current Liability	$217,874	$358,941	$199,212
Noncurrent Liabilities			
Note—Owner	$124,965	—	$ 67,599
Total Noncurrent Liab.	$124,965	$ —	$ 67,599
TOTAL LIABILITIES	$342,839	$358,941	$266,811

	1991	1992	1993
STOCKHOLDER EQUITY			
Capital Stock	$ 15,000	$ 15,000	$ 15,000
Retained Earnings	77,135	132,153	175,806
Current Net Income/Loss	55,017	43,652	42,256
Total Equity	$147,152	$190,805	$233,062
TOTAL LIABILITIES & EQUITY	**$489,991**	**$549,746**	**$499,873**

The first exercise is to inspect visually for **trends** that may be occurring. Accounts receivable appear on the increase and raise a question in terms of their collectability. The accounts should be spread out and aged 30, 60, and 90 days-plus outstanding. While appearing relatively stable, accounts payable might also be spread and aged in a similar fashion to determine the payment experience of the owner. The 1992 decrease in available cash in banks, when coupled with cash borrowing of $138,000, raises the question of what was occurring in elevated receivables, payables, and other parts of the company. The booking of $18,136 in accrued retirement may signal the implementation of a company-wide retirement plan that must be examined for future liability by a purchaser. Beyond these elements, the company appears stable but without real growth.

Examination of Ratios (Formulas are not repeated but may be found at the beginning of case #1.) (First-appearing numbers indicate those considered more desirable in industry range.)

	1991	1992	1993
Current Ratio	2.1	1.5	2.3
Industry Range	2.5–1.4	2.0–1.3	2.2–1.2
Quick Ratio	1.2	0.9	1.5
Industry Range	1.2–0.4	1.0–0.5	1.2–0.5
Safety Ratio	2.3	1.9	1.1
Industry Range	0.7–2.9	0.9–3.3	0.8–2.6

The current and quick ratios appear at the high end and within industry comparable range. However, the *downward* trend of ABC Company's safety ratios point to greater long-term financial safety and an ability to borrow during times of adversity. Note the change in the safety ratio from

2.3 in 1991 down to 1.1 in 1993 and the closer proximity to the more desirable end of the range for industry comparables. Further examination of the income and loss statements may shed additional light on what possibly has been occurring to decrease their debt load.

ABC Company
Income and Loss Statement
As of December 31

	1991	1992	1993
Net Sales	$1,482,349	$1,495,464	$1,752,729
Cost of Sales	742,664	851,227	964,080
Gross Profit*	$ 739,685	$ 644,237	$ 788,649
Percent Gross Profit	49.9%	43.1%	45.0%
Expenses			
Salaries and Wages	$ 72,067	$ 85,168	$ 134,660
Payroll Taxes	2,349	6,217	8,843
Advertising and Promo	21,616	53,220	46,096
Auto and Travel	19,899	19,169	35,490
Bad Debt and Collection	10,460	6,711	27,165
Commissions	34,507	55,940	49,241
Contributions/Dues	2,908	2,192	1,719
Insurance	17,394	16,860	11,681
Office/Postage	27,190	30,172	25,429
Professional Fees	5,125	6,392	16,732
Rent—Equipment	—	—	4,086
Repairs/Maintenance	7,629	5,780	8,977
Show Expense	29,412	53,247	50,495
Taxes—Other	4,977	2,099	1,202
Telephone/Electric	9,214	13,388	17,281
Utilities	1,957	3,196	3,654
Misc. Expense	218	2,878	3,742
Subtotal Expense*	$ 266,922	$ 362,629	$ 446,493
Owner's Salary	344,060	133,700	201,628
Payroll Tax	11,246	9,737	13,105
Depreciation	16,127	11,162	16,373
Office Life Ins.	1,096	14,540	16,251
Director Fees	—	10,000	—
Interest Expense	9,813	10,028	8,386
Rent Expense	24,000	30,000	24,000

	1991	1992	1993
Property Tax	—	1,954	4,025
Retirement Plan	—	—	19,324
Total Expenses	$ 673,264	$ 583,750	$ 749,585
Add: Other Income	7,596	1,665	21,192
Net Income before Tax	$ 74,017	$ 62,152	$ 60,256
Less: Income Taxes	19,000	18,500	18,000
Net Income/Loss	$ 55,017	$ 43,652	$ 42,256
*Net Reconstructed Income	$ 472,763	$ 281,608	$ 342,156
As Percent of Sales	31.9%	18.8%	19.5%

To begin with, I should explain the rather unusual layout for the income and loss statement. The accountant-prepared statement was developed in traditional fashion. However, as mentioned several times in this handbook, statements of the privately owned business, when analyzed in customary fashion, do not adequately reflect the true picture of a business operation. Salaries of owners frequently are not established on the basis of comparable worth by comparison to their counterparts employed in industry. Quite often, real estate is owned separate from the business operation. Rents paid frequently track more in line with mortgage payments versus those paid for comparable rents offered elsewhere within the community. On occasion, an owner will use rental payments as another form of compensation to avoid the double taxation aspects of a corporation form of organization. Without belaboring the point again, **reconstructing,** i.e., arraying the income statement as fashioned herein, can clarify the analysis and be used in a business valuation exercise, such as that covered in Chapter 10.

Visual Observations Noted on Income Statement

The following list includes observations noted on the income statement:

1. Sales have increased by 17.4% between 1991 and 1993.
   a. Gross profit, however, is down by 4.5% when compared with 1991/1992. Note the significant drop during 1992.
   b. Subtotal expenses (those less affected by owner compensation and perquisites) are up by 67.2%, whereas total expenses, as traditionally prepared, are up by only 11.3%.

    c. Net income is down by 30% overall, and net "reconstructed" income is down by 38.2%.

2. Employee payroll (not including owner salary) is up by 86.9% overall.

    In 1991, one dollar of payroll produced $20.72 of sales and a profit of 76¢.

    In 1992, one dollar of payroll produced $17.56 of sales, and a profit of 51¢.

    In 1993, one dollar of payroll produced $13.02 of sales, and a profit of 31¢.

3. Professional fees, traditionally accountant, lawyer, or consultant fees, jumped by $10,340 in 1993 over 1992. This adds to questions about the management of the company.

4. The jump to $27,165 in bad debt/collection expense in 1993 raises questions about credit practices and collectability of receivables.

5. Rent expense moved from $24,000 to $30,000 back to $24,000 raises questions, such as who owns the facilities or if there has been a downsizing of operation.

6. A 1993 item of $19,324 booked in retirement plan triggers questions of a legal nature, such as whether the plan meets conditions of federal regulations and what future obligations may be required.

7. Although continuing to benefit by above-average earnings, the company in general may be on the verge of getting out of the owner's control.

Ratio Analysis

In our first case of the XYZ Company, ratio analysis of the income statement was not very realistic due to only five months of actual performance. However, in the ABC Company, we have several years of historical performance where ratio analysis can increase meaningful information to the overall review. The *Annual Statement Studies,* produced by Robert Morris Associates of Philadelphia, and *Financial Studies of the Small Business,* published by Financial Research Associates of Winter Haven, Florida, available at most libraries, were used as the basis for industry ranges.

Financial experts will not always agree as to which ratios are particularly germane to the small and privately owned enterprise. I feel that it is essential to examine the following:

$$\textbf{Ratio for Gross Margin} = \frac{\text{Gross Profit}}{\text{Sales}} \quad \text{or}$$

1991	1992	1993	Published Ind. Range
49.5	43.1	45.0	35.1

This ratio measures the percentage of sales dollars left after manufactured goods are sold. The significant trend in ABC Company appears to be toward erratic and higher cost of manufacturing, although the company does enjoy gross profits of 10% above published industry ranges. Pricing of products, cost of raw materials, labor, and manufacturing cost may be reasons why margins are decreasing.

It should be noted that ratios for net profit, before and after taxes, can be most useful ratios. The fact that private owners frequently manage their business to "minimize" the bottom line often produces little meaningful information from these ratios. Therefore, they are not included.

$$\textbf{Sales/Receivable Ratio} = \frac{\text{(From Income Statement)}}{\underset{\text{(From Balance Sheet)}}{\text{Net Receivables}}} \quad \text{or}$$

1991	1992	1993	Published Ind. Range
8.2	4.9	7.0	11.2–5.7

This is an important ratio and measures the number of times that receivables turn over during the year. In the case of ABC Company, receivables appear to have turned more slowly during 1992 and not to have recovered to 1991 levels by the end of 1993. While the trend is toward the positive, further research into receivable activity is indicated. Where turnover of receivables appears to be slower than industry ranges, it can be helpful to calculate the day's receivable ratio.

$$\textbf{Day's Receivable Ratio} = \frac{365}{\text{Sale/Receivable Ratio}} \quad \text{or}$$

(In Days Outstanding)

1991	1992	1993	Published Ind. Range
44.5	74.5	52.1	36–57

This highlights the average time in terms of days that receivables are outstanding. Generally, the longer that receivables are outstanding, the greater the chance that they may not be collectable.

The cost of sales to payables ratio is used to help indicate the possibility of cash shortages.

$$\textbf{Cost of Sales/Payables Ratio} = \frac{\text{(From Income Statement)}}{\underset{\text{(From Balance Sheet)}}{\text{Payables}}}^{\text{Cost of Sales}} \quad \text{or}$$

1991	1992	1993	Published Ind. Range
4.0	4.0	5.4	18.0–6.9

Generally, the higher their turnover rate, the shorter the time between purchase and payment. Slower turnover, which ABC Company appears to experience, may be due to cash shortages, extended payment terms, or deliberate expansion of trade credit. This ratio does not recognize seasonal fluctuations and can, therefore, be misleading.

Bear in mind that part of the discovery process involves finding out not only why certain things occur but also why a particular company may be for sale. Working capital is a measure of the margin of protection for current creditors and reflects the company's ability to finance current operations. A "squeeze" on working capital could be a possible reason for sale. (Working capital equals current assets minus current liabilities.)

$$\textbf{Net Sales/Working Capital Ratio} = \frac{\text{(From Income Statement)}}{\underset{\text{(From Balance Sheet)}}{\text{Working Capital}}}^{\text{Net Sales}}$$

1991	1992	1993	Published Ind. Range
6.1	9.2	6.6	4.3–19.5

A low ratio may indicate an inefficient use of working capital, whereas a very high ratio often signals a vulnerable position for creditors. The ABC

Company has been below the median, except for the 1992 year, and appears to be suffering under moderate inefficient use of their working capital; however, probably not to the extent of being a priority reason for sale.

To analyze how well inventory is being managed, the cost of sales to inventory ratio and the day's inventory ratio can identify important considerations.

$$\text{Cost of Sales/Inventory Ratio} = \frac{\text{(From Income Statement)} \quad \text{Cost of Sales}}{\text{Inventory} \quad \text{(From Balance Sheet)}}$$

1991	1992	1993	Published Ind. Range
4.0	4.3	5.6	6.2–3.1

A higher inventory turnover can signify a more liquid position and/or better skills at marketing, whereas a lower turnover of inventory may indicate shortages of merchandise for sale, overstocking, or obsolescence in inventory.

The day's inventory ratio measures the number of times that inventory is turned during the year.

$$\text{Day's Inventory Ratio} = \frac{365}{\text{Cost of Sales/Inventory Ratio}}$$

(Days to Turn Inventory)

1991	1992	1993	Published Ind. Range
91.3	84.9	65.2	59–118

This ratio highlights an increasing **trend** toward higher turnover but may still signal developing problems with inventory.

One final ratio that often points to the significant variations existing in privately owned companies is the ratio between owner compensation and sales. I include this ratio to drive home the point that private business owners more often pay themselves in direct relationship to profits and what they **believe** they are worth, rather than any relationship to value established in the employment market. This same belief carries over into the marketplace when they price their business for sale.

$$\text{Owner's Compensation Ratio} = \frac{\text{Owner's Compensation}}{\text{Net Sales}} \quad \text{or}$$

1991	1992	1993	Published Ind. Range
23.0	8.9	11.5	2.1–10.3

Summary of Case #2—ABC Company

From visual inspection and through ratio analysis of the financial statements of ABC Company, it can be reasonably concluded that the company is increasingly under pressure to increase profitability. Simple increases in sales appear not to be adequate alone. Therefore, what can management do? What must a new operator do? Answers to these and many more questions must come from face-to-face discussions with the owner, through examination of various accounts, and finally, from the full chart of accounts. Preliminary financial statement analysis, however, has provided "factual" evidence of difficulty being experienced and has *armed* the reviewer with substantial knowledge of what must be done. This information provides the framework for "intelligent" discovery, a yardstick for assessment of personal operating skill levels required, and later forms the crux of a business plan that **sells** both you and a prospective funding request to a financial institution.

From these data, operating management can decide to focus on areas needing attention and either work through them personally or employ outside help.

Financial statement review and analysis must never be left solely in the hands of the accountant or, for that matter, in the hands of the Chief Financial Officer of the larger corporation. The business of successful *general* management of a large or small company calls upon many diverse skills. Refining each of these skills is the critical task necessary for the general manager of any business.

For the small-business entrepreneur to place himself or herself at risk to the financial skills wholly of another is an invitation to certain distress. One need not *be* an accountant, but one must become a financially inclined manager along with all the other tasks of entrepreneurship. Sales and expenses, without checks and balances, are like a moving automobile without a driver. Both are out of control. Learning fundamental elements of good financial management need not be a complex experience. Although this handbook provides a reasonably simple overview, as with the subject of mathematics, continual study may be a wise choice. Throughout the United States, seminars for nonfinancially trained general managers occur on a weekly basis. Your own accountant, lawyer, or banker can most likely provide information on when they are occurring locally. Periodic involvement at one or two of these type of seminars per year is worthwhile even to the experienced general manager. After all, these are your dollars, and your and your family's future is at stake!

3

Break-Even Analysis

During the late 1970s and again during the mid 1980s, supplier price increases grew in alarming numbers and frequency. After the third or fourth such increase, many businesses resolved that they would just have to absorb some of the increases or else lose customers. Businesses with long delivery times, though constrained to fixed-quote sales, were stuck with one, two, or more supplier increases before they could finish sales. Does this sound familiar?

Break-even analysis will not prevent reccurrence of volatile times; however, it will allow the small-business manager to *understand the madness* in supplier price increase absorption. Break-even analysis will allow time in planning for future increased costs of doing business. Many retailers enjoy the benefit of manufacturers "suggested retail price" criteria but frequently hear sales associates say that competitors regularly sell at $x. At what price can a product or service be sold and still make a reasonable profit or maintain the existing profit margin? Should the product or service be offered if it dilutes existing profit margins? Retail establishments with large numbers of products often face a daily problem of adding or deleting products from their lines. When compared with company overall profit margins, break-even analysis can assist in "weeding" out marginal or less profitable items.

Small-business managers are confronted daily with the constant task of growing or maintaining margins of profit. One test can be found in the more obvious relationship between cost of goods sold, sales, and *gross profit.* Viewed in their percentage relationships to each other, consistent *patterns* or changes can be easily tracked. When using percentages it is, however, important to bear in mind just what each 1% change reflects. For example, 1% of $1,000,000 reflects $10,000 of possible change. "Only a percent or two" thinking can quickly get out of hand.

The following is an example of the more obvious relationship:

Sales	$500,000	100.0%
Costs of Sales	300,000	60.0%
Gross Profit	$200,000	40.0%

But this relationship tells only part of the story. First, it reflects only the *historical* picture in terms of absolutes. Second, it will not pointedly answer questions regarding the effect on gross profits with increases or decreases in future sales. Third, it does not address changes taking place within fixed or variable expenses. For example, if costs go up 10%, 15%, or more, how much of a sales increase is necessary to maintain the past level of profits? At what sales level does the company start losing money? What products contribute the most profit? Which contribute the least? What mix of product or services should the company strive for to gain maximum benefit from sales/profits? Finally, break-even analysis can be particularly useful to the small business that is losing money and that may be in search of ways to regain profitability.

A first step is to determine breakeven on a company-wide basis. To accomplish this task, we must **isolate controllable** and **noncontrollable fixed** and **variable costs.** For reference, examples of controllable fixed costs would be salaries; advertising and promotion; donations and entertainment expenses; and in the case of ABC Company, show expenses. At this point, a good argument could be made for show expenses to be classified as a variable expense. However, while trade show attendance is critical to obtaining sales, including new product introductions, the number of shows attended and the expense of those shows are controllable by management. In some instances, management may want to treat them as variable with sales. In this break-even analysis, they will be considered as fixed costs, because some level of trade show involvement is necessary for ABC to stay in business, but the level of involvement is defined by management.

Noncontrollable fixed cost examples are rent, interest, insurance, depreciation, and some utility expense. Variable costs are those that vary with or track with increasing or decreasing sales/production. Examples are commissions paid on sales, raw material costs, direct product or service labor, freight, and amounts of bad debt.

For purposes of this example, we will return to the ABC Company balance and income statements. To simplify the process, variable costs are $1,040,486, controllable fixed costs are $456,546, noncontrollable fixed costs are $80,345, and sales are $1,752,729 for the 1993 year. For personal practice, you may want to return to the income statement provided in Chapter 2 and experiment with how I arrived at these costs. Hint: For those who wish to try, these costs track with the previous examples.

When fixed and variable costs are isolated, they can be related with each other or sales to create ratios, percentages, and break-even sales volume (BSV). The first step is to calculate the **Variable Cost Percentage** (VCP).

$$\frac{\text{Variable Cost}}{\text{Sales}} = \text{VCP}$$

$$\frac{\$1,040,486}{\$1,752,729} = 59.4\% \text{ (VCP)}$$

The second step is to determine the **Contribution Margin Ratio.**

$$\text{Sales} - \text{Variable Cost \%} = \text{Contribution Margin Ratio}$$

Sales	100.0%
Variable Cost %	59.4%
Contribution Margin Ratio	40.6%

The third step is to determine **Break-even Sales Volume.**

$$\frac{\text{Controllable Fixed} + \text{Noncontrollable Fixed Costs}}{\text{Contribution Margin Ratio}} = \text{BSV}$$

$$\frac{\$456,546 + \$80,345}{40.6\%} = \frac{\$536,891}{40.6\%} = \$1,322,392 \text{ (BSV)}$$

For the mathematically trained individual, the equation can be **proved.**

Break-Even Sales	$1,322,392	100.0%
Variable Cost (59.4) ($1,322,392)	785,501	59.4%
Contribution Margin	$ 536,891	40.6%
Less: Fixed Costs	536,891	
Net Profit	- 0 -	

TARGETING PROFIT OBJECTIVES

When break-even sales have been determined, it becomes relatively easy to estimate a level of sales necessary to meet a certain profit target. For example, we want to attain a 20% return on investment for the ABC Company. Investment in ABC is the net worth of $233,062, as noted in the 1993 balance sheet from Chapter 2. Thus, the profit objective would be $233,062 × .20, which equals $46,612. To calculate sales required to make a profit of 20%, the following formula will be used:

$$\frac{\text{Fixed Cost} + \text{Profit Target}}{\text{Contribution Margin Ratio}} = \text{Sales Required}$$

$$\frac{\$536,891 + \$46,612}{40.6\%} = \frac{\$583,503}{40.6\%} = \begin{array}{c}\$1,437,200 \\ (\text{Sales Target for} \\ 20\% \text{ ROI})\end{array}$$

Proof can again be shown.

New Sales Level	$1,437,200	100.0%
Variable Cost (59.4) ($1,437,200)	853,697	59.4%
Contribution Margin	$ 583,503	40.6%
Less: Fixed Costs	536,891	
Net Profit	$ 46,612	20.0%

Commission sales persons are by nature an independent thinking lot, particularly where 100% of their earnings are derived from personal sales made. On their behalf, it must be recognized that they are *independent businesspeople* to a large degree. A common request is for more of the commission pie. Break-even analysis can be used to evaluate the cost for a company in providing more and/or can show tangible evidence that more is not possible without added sales goals. Assume that a 5% greater commission payout has been requested.

Variable Cost %	59.4%
Add: Proposed Commission Increase	5.0%
Adjusted Variable Cost %	64.4%

Recalculate Contribution Margin Ratio	
Stated at 100%	100.0%
Less: Adjusted Variable Cost %	64.4%
New Contribution Margin Ratio	35.6%

$$\frac{\text{Fixed Costs}}{\text{New Contribution Margin Ratio}} = \text{New Break-Even Sales}$$

$$\frac{\$536,891}{35.6\%} = \$1,508,121 \qquad \begin{array}{c} \text{New Break-Even} \\ \text{Sales with} \\ \text{5\% Higher} \\ \text{Commissions Paid} \end{array}$$

For ABC to pay 5% greater commissions, the breakeven has risen from $1,322,392 to $1,508,121. To maintain the 20% profit margin, the calculation would consider fixed costs at the 20% level, i.e., $583,503 ($536,891 + $46,612), versus the precommission level of $536,891.

$$\frac{\$583,503}{35.6\%} = \$1,639,053$$

All other considerations equal, ABC must reach $1,639,053 of sales to pay 5% more in commissions and maintain the 20% profit margin. The difference, $1,639,053 minus $1,437,200, i.e., $201,853, might then be established as a collective target for bonus commission or a condition under which 5% more commission might be considered.

MARGIN OF SAFETY

The margin-of-safety sales volume is actual sales volume minus the break-even sales volume.

Actual Sales	$1,752,729
Break-Even Sales	−1,322,392
Margin-of-Safety Sales	$ 430,337

Tracking the margin of safety against actual sales to create a margin-of-safety ratio (MSR) will create a useful measurement for some business managers.

$$\frac{\text{Margin of Safety}}{\text{Actual Sales}} = \text{Margin-of-Safety Ratio}$$

$$\frac{\$430,337}{\$1,752,729} = 24.6\% \text{ (MSR)}$$

Like other ratios, the real value in calculating and tracking this number is measuring changes over time. It may also be useful to set pricing and sales goals for new products. If the margin-of-safety ratio is increasing over time, this is an indication of higher profits. On the other hand, a trend of decreasing ratios indicates decreasing profits, which beg for immediate management attention.

PRODUCT-BY-PRODUCT BREAKEVEN

Many small businesses simply do not have the luxury of necessary time required to maintain fixed and variable costs on an individual product basis. A discerning management might, however, keep records of sales and cost of goods sold by product. Unless more detail is known about variable and fixed costs on each product or line, break-even analysis may be limited to *estimating* these variable and fixed costs. For example, if identified sales for product "A" represent 30% of total sales, then perhaps 30% of fixed, variable, and other expenses may be estimated to apply. The business owner will want to adjust, to the best of their ability, based on personal awareness of actual expenses occurring within the product line. As pointed out by the profit philosophy in "factory outlet" or *discount merchandising,* volume is a critical element that must be considered in addition to break-even sales. Product "A" may produce a 60% gross profit but only represent a small percentage of overall sales, while product "B" may provide only 30% toward gross profit but comprise the lion's share of total sales. The multiple-product-line small-business owner may want to minimally track key and high-volume sales items, particularly when overall margins may be dropping. The same formulas for company-wide breakeven can be applied to product-line analysis. In a hypothetical example, units of a particular product come in three sizes:

	Size A	Size B	Size C
Sales Price Per Unit	$2.40	$4.00	$7.20
Less: Variable Cost Per Unit	1.68	2.20	3.60
Contribution Margin Per Unit	$ .72	$1.80	$3.60
Contribution Margin Ratio	30.0%	45.0%	50.0%

Let's assume that fixed costs are $18,000

	Size A	Size B	Size C
Break-Even Sales Volume (assuming that only the one size unit was sold)	$60,000	$40,000	$36,000

The obvious would be to concentrate on selling size C, as breakeven requires 40% fewer sales than that of size A. One hundred units of size C equal $720 of sales, while 100 units of size A equal $240 of sales. Unfortunately, the obvious is not always the best case scenario. Size C may represent a bulk size that consumers purchase only occasionally, while size A may represent the higher demand unit. To effectively sell size C, discounts may have to be offered, and contribution margins may drop to levels no greater than those of size A. Therefore, at what *stocking* levels do we maintain size C, if we choose to stock size C at all?

Break-even analysis assists in selecting products for addition or deletion from overall lines, and internal and external market research becomes the ultimate test used to make final decisions. Bear in mind that inventory is representative of hard-earned, tied-up *cash dollars*—dollars that need to turn over to maintain or increase profits. Perishable consumer-product merchants, such as grocers and restaurateurs, particularly learn the lessons taught from inventory/break-even/volume management quite early in the game. Waste can make a discernible difference between profit and loss.

In 1976 I owned a decorating studio where we stocked a high-grade paint line. Many would not view paint as a perishable product . . . but it is. Shelf life of latex paint is often no more than two or three years—lids and cans rust from the inside after time. Consumers feel cheated when they are sold paint that shows signs of rust or when cans are dented. Even small amounts of container rust transfer into brown spots when applied on the wall. With significant dollars invested in inventory, I quickly learned which lines sold well and which yielded the full retail price. Break-even analysis, combined with customer profile and market awareness, provided information that led to discontinuing all factory-standard colors and offering only custom-mixed colors. Within one year, waste was nearly eliminated, profit margins in the paint department rose by over 8%, and total paint sales volume was not materially affected. Wallpaper, carpet, and custom drapery paint-match counseling was increased, and overall product sales grew by 21% in the following year. I became a *believer* in the benefits possible from break-even studies, applied the concept to all studio lines, and several years later, sold this business for a very handsome profit.

SUMMARY

Many similar break-even studies can be conducted once small-business owners understand how costs relate to sales in their businesses. The larger the contribution margin ratio, the lower the sales volume necessary to cover fixed costs. Thus, sales accorded high contribution margin percentages are referred to as high-quality sales. Shifting from low-quality to high-quality sales, even with sales decreases, can materially increase a company's profit. Moving from high-quality to low-quality sales (discount merchandising) **requires** that sales volume be increased in order to maintain levels of profit. The volume/profit relationship existing within individual product sales must always be a consideration in any break-even study.

Making bold pricing decisions without the aid of break-even analysis can become a disaster waiting to occur. Formulas used are not complex, nor is the process that difficult. For any who still need help, a personal accountant may not be so expensive compared with the price ultimately paid for impromptu decisions.

4

Forecast Statements

Perhaps among the more difficult tasks for many during the production of business plans is financial planning or, in long-range planning, the development of forecast statements.

The word *pro forma* is sometimes confused with **forecast.** In a pure accounting definition, pro forma does not cover a future period but traditionally makes use of *historical* financials for alternative planning. Forecast statements could be described as a "formal, advance description of events likely to occur, when based upon assumptions believed to be reliable."

INCOME AND LOSS STATEMENT

Forecasting Sales

The process of developing forecast statements is not so complex when broken into component parts. To project two, three, or five years of activity into the future, one begins with the present or incomplete year. *The first step of the process involves estimating the sales picture for the remainder of the fiscal or calendar year.* While the process for the start-up operation is much more involved, both start-up and established businesses must begin with much of the same data.

When attempting to forecast remaining sales in any given year, or for that matter, two, three, or five years of future sales, consideration must be given to a number of potential influences that exert positive or negative pressure on achieving those sales, as outlined in the following:

1. **Sales history and sales trends of the specific business.** If, for example, the business in a preceding number of years has not achieved more than 5–10% growth per year, how can a forecast increase of 20% or 30% be realistic? Unless, of course, there are new product or service introductions or changes in other conditions that influence how the business operates.

2. **Existing business capacity and available work force.** It takes time to install new equipment and to fully train new employees. Pro forma statements must take this into account and *reflect stages of progress* toward goals.

3. **Financial strength or weakness of the business.** When a business develops forecast statements for the purpose of additional financing, it can become helpful in selling the need by showing two sets of projections: one that is achievable without financing, and one that depicts the effect on performance when financing is added.

4. **Product availability.** The construction and real estate industries are classic examples of restricted product availability during the mid 1980s. Real estate firms sold their *available* "inventory" as fast as it was obtained. Prices got out of control. Contractors were inundated with new construction requests. Lead time necessary to build increased 3, 6, 9, or 12 months. Sales could clearly be made, but product was unavailable in sufficient quantities for real estate firms to meet demands. Products and services must be obtainable in sufficient quantity, in a timely fashion, and at a middleman price where volume and profits can reasonably be assured.

5. **Effect of competition—both existing and possibly developing.** Along with the advent of any good "mousetrap" there will always be some degree of competition. Competition is healthy for business. Competition sharpens our senses and product or service delivery to the ultimate market. Without competition, quality, price, and service get out of control. Too much competition has the effect of splitting the pie too many times and diluting each competitor's ability to obtain sales and profits. Any business is exposed

to the risk of too many competitors when it is easy for almost anyone to "get on the bandwagon." A large amount of initial capital outlay necessary to enter a particular industry places limiting conditions on new or existing competition. Beyond this condition, most smaller businesses have only *strategy* to defend their position in any given market. The strategies are **pricing, quality of product, or service offered.** Where competition exists, no business can truthfully enjoy more than two out of the three strategies. What is your business's *edge*?

6. **Overall conditions of the economy in which the business operates.** Many small-business owners tend to view only local economies as impacting their businesses. Frequently, the local economy is of major importance; however, don't overlook state or national conditions. The *national picture* often *forecasts things to come* to the *local scene*.

7. **Conditions of the industry in which specific business is a part.** We have all heard terms such as "new industry," "fast growing industry," or "dying industry." Although a particular business may presently be reaping fruits from a solid foundation, industry trends may be suggesting something else about the future for that business. When an industry is growing, and sales of a particular business seem relatively flat, what is the industry doing that the business might want to consider adding to bolster sales and profits? A dying industry does not necessarily mean that a particular business will die with their industry. An "edge" over competition can be instrumental to survival in a dying industry. Industries do not die out over night, and "niches" in a marketplace can be fundamental to long-term opportunities.

8. **Effect of population growth/restriction on the specific business.** United States census data are readily available through individual State Departments of Labor. Incredible amounts of information listed by age category, sex, race, home dwelling statistics, household income, head of household statistics, and population changes are collected by town, county, and state. State Departments of Transportation can provide results of traffic studies conducted at various times along selected roads, which reveal increases or decreases in movement of potential customers. Communities, through their voter registration, can indicate changes in population since the last U.S. census estimates. Community as-

sessors and local real estate brokers can verify trends taking place within given neighborhoods. When compared to the "makeup" of existing customers of a specific business, these data become particularly *telltale* in forecasting future sales.

9. **Effect of changes in product or service pricing strategy.** Experimentation through market research is critical to the establishment of appropriate pricing. Beware of the issue of *perception*. We each perceive value in different ways. If products or services are priced too high by the perceived *value system* of a wide-scale public, and the business owner's perception of their value system is on the blink, they will not sell according to any plan he or she may have developed. Balance of profit margin and volume must be maintained for expectations of reasonable demand and sales forecasts to be achieved. Unique products or services, when appropriately timed, can generate high profit/demand for awhile, but eventually competition or other influences creep in to stabilize pricing back to the perceived value system of a public at large.

10. **Relevant issues may play a part in the business's growth.** Rerouting of major roads and highways, along with other government legislative actions, have been notorious for impacting the growth of the smaller business. Not long ago, a client came to me in a very anxious state of mind. His son, a critically needed salesperson for 15 years in his business, decided to move on to another job. A smaller business can frequently be at risk to the strengths and beauties of its smallness. What internally generated risk is the business potentially exposed to? What are the chances of these events taking place? What has been done to reduce this risk?

Of course, additional factors will enter the picture for specific business or industry circumstances, but the preceding ten items cover a great deal of information available to assist a business owner in making reliable annual sales forecasts.

In the established business, historical sales trends must be closely examined to forecast future sales. What about past sales being consistent with *capability* of the existing business, and what can be done with internal or external forces to increase sales within this capability?

For the start-up enterprise, the process involves a much closer examination of industry and competitor data. Many industry associations can provide established criteria for locating the new business, product marketing experience, operating expense information, and expected levels of sales growth. Franchises, like McDonald's, for example, have become so expert in start-up requirements that their new operations rarely fail. Granted, this firm has valuable historical information, but each newly proposed location presents challenging requirements to be met.

If location is critical to a new business's sales, what does "siting" that business mean exactly? Is location a condition of traffic volume and impact of signs to attract sales? Is location based upon a certain population level, a certain earnings level, or a certain age bracket to assure sales? What role does *customer convenience* play in capturing sales?

Key indicators that predictably generate sales of products and services for the business should bear major influences on the overall sales forecast, for both established and start-up enterprises.

Forecasting Expenses

Cost of Goods Sold

When the picture of sales for each forecast period has been established, the next step is to assign an expense for the cost of goods sold. This task is made simpler when historical or industry experiences, or both, are translated into a percentage of sales. The sale of a product for ten dollars, which cost the business five dollars in material, labor, and freight, reveals the cost of goods sold expense to be 50%. It is important to bear in mind that cost of goods sold contains *only* materials, labor, and freight directly associated with manufacturing that product. For a retail store, cost of goods sold might involve only materials and freight, whereas in a restaurant, chef and kitchen wages might be included as product preparation labor—but not the wages of waiters and waitresses, which are included in "operating" expense categories. When forecasting the cost of goods sold, examine closely the prospect for purchasing materials, labor, and/or freight more attractively. Some smaller businesses join competitors, or associations, to form "pools," where purchases in bulk reduce material and freight costs. Associations of grocery merchants are one example that enable the small, independent store to stay reasonably competitive with large chains.

Operating Expenses

Not all operating expenses will change proportionately with different levels of sales. The next step is to determine which of your expenses are *fixed* and which are *variable* in nature. Expenses that businesses have very *little control over are interest paid, depreciation, insurance payments, most utilities, and rent.* More controllable expenses fall into categories of salaries paid, entertainment, advertising, or product/service promotion. Both the noncontrollable and controllable expenses are examples of fixed costs.

Variable expenses are those that track directly with or are caused by the movement of sales. Examples of variable expense could be direct manufacturing labor, raw materials purchased, cost of freight, direct sales labor, sales commissions paid, and the incurring of bad debts. Note that some variable expenses occur in a cost of goods sold category and some in operating expenses. When forecasting operating expenses for future years, figure the effect of controllable/noncontrollable fixed and variable expenses accurately into the picture.

ABC Company Example

In forecasting 1994 sales for ABC Company, we have considered all factors and estimate that sales equaling the 1993 level are most realistic. From analysis accomplished in several other chapters, we conclude that maintaining sales at current levels but reducing expenses associated with the cost of goods sold, as well as operating expenses, will be the primary task before trying to increase sales.

Changing the income statement to percentages both helps "flag" items needing attention and identifies items for which changes in practice might have the most impact on profits.

ABC COMPANY
Income and Loss Statement As of December 31
(Stated in Percentage Relationship)

	1991	1992	1993
Net Sales	100.0%	100.0%	100.0%
Cost of Sales	50.1	56.9	55.0
Gross Profit	49.9	43.1	45.0
Expenses*			
Salaries & Wages	4.9	5.7	7.7
Payroll Taxes	(a variable of payroll)		
Advertising & Promo	1.5	3.6	2.6

(continued)

ABC COMPANY
Income and Loss Statement As of December 31
(Stated in Percentage Relationship) *(continued)*

	1991	1992	1993
Auto & Travel	1.3	1.3	**2.0**
Bad Debt/Collection	0.7	0.4	**1.5**
Commissions	2.3	**3.7**	**2.8**
Contribution/Dues		(owner-controlled variable)	
Insurance	1.2	1.1	0.7
Office/Postage	1.8	2.0	1.5
Professional Fees	0.3	0.4	**1.0**
Rent—Equipment	—	—	**0.2**
Repairs/Maintenance	**0.5**	**0.4**	**0.5**
Show Expense	2.0	**3.6**	**2.9**
Taxes—Other	0.3	0.1	0.1
Telephone/Elec.	0.6	0.9	1.0
Utilities	0.1	0.2	0.2
Rent Expense	1.6	2.0	1.4
Misc. Expense	—	0.2	0.2
Owner Controlled			
Owner Salary	**23.2**	**8.9**	**11.5**
Payroll Tax		(a product of owner salary)	
Depreciation	1.0	0.7	0.9
Officer Life Ins.	0.1	1.0	0.9
Director Fees	—	0.7	—
Interest Expense	0.7	0.7	0.5
Total Expenses	45.4	39.0	42.8
Other Income	0.5	0.1	12.1
Income Taxes	1.3	1.2	1.0
Net Income (including all expenses)	**3.7**	**2.9**	**2.4**

*Expenses stated as a percent of sales or noted as a product of some other expense. *Important note:* The purpose of this statement is to compare numbers horizontally. Stated percentages have been rounded to fit individual categories—but not rounded to 100% from top to bottom.

In reviewing statements that are rendered to percentages, it is important to *understand the significance of what 1% may indicate.* For each year in the statement, 1% of sales equals the following dollar amount:

	1991	1992	1993
One Percent Equals	$14,823	$14,955	$17,527

As you can readily see, even a fraction of 1% carries weight to the overall bottom line.

Although cost of sales appears to be returning to 1991 levels, bad debt is up by 1.1% over 1992. In forecasting future expenses, what, if anything, can be done about collection experiences? Is the business making sales that are too risky for collection? Revenue increased in 1993 over 1992 by 17.2%, but commissions decreased by .9%. What caused this to occur? Is someone in direct sales contributing to increased bad debt? What can be changed in operations to improve current expense, and how does this translate into future or forecast performance?

Salaries and wages have increased at alarming rates. Is this a "luxury" choice or a real need in operations? What impact will a payroll reduction play in product delivery or service, price, and quality? How might changes translate into future years of operation?

Professional fees increased by .6% ($10,340). Can something be done to hold fees closer to 1991 and 1992 levels?

Repairs and maintenance, while stable in our example, can be a neglected area in forecast statements. Buildings, equipment, furniture, and fixtures wear out with time, and replacement must be planned in future years.

Show expense (trade shows), for this manufacturer, is perhaps more important to sales than that of advertising. What impact will the decrease of .7% have on future sales? Was the decrease a result of efficiency built in or a lack of planning or funds to complete necessary shows? What can be done to attend future shows in a timely and least-costly manner? How will implementation affect the forecast statements?

Salaries of owners in privately held companies frequently are the most significant variable found in the income statement. Regardless of how the income statement is constructed, whatever is left over after all expenses have been paid belongs to the owner in the form of salary, bonus, and working capital for the business. Viewing the income statement *without owner perquisites* can be more meaningful in developing forecast years. Owner salaries can be introduced to the statement after all other expense categories are forecast.

When percentages are developed from historical dollar performance for each expense item, it becomes relatively easy to *tie* expenses, in terms of estimated dollars, to each new year of projected sales. Each item stated in a dollar amount should then be reviewed in the context of questioning the probability of actual occurrence. Will I be able to achieve X with this dollar amount? Can I do the job for less? When I change *X*, what happens to other related expenses or sales?

Experience shows that all businesses hit plateaus of growth before increased profits are realized. New product or service introductions often carry heavy "front-end" costs, and profit from those introductions may take months or years to achieve. Major changes in the way of doing business can have the same effect. When, and with what impact, will proposed changes have an effect on existing and forecast years? For example, recovering from heavy debt has the tendency to take much more time than we realize. Have current and expected debt loads been addressed in the forecast statements? Has depreciation been recalculated to account for new equipment or other asset purchase?

In our sample, ABC Company, let's assume that we expect to complete the 1994 selling year at the same level of sales for 1993. Our plan is to *gradually* improve upon gross profit by reducing expense in cost of goods sold. The reason that cost of goods sold historically increased is that raw materials are purchased on another continent, and shipping time, lead-order time, freight, and import duty costs have all increased. Equal quality raw materials are not available in the United States, so we must work with what we have or decrease the quality of the end product. During the next 18 months, we will develop a long-range purchasing plan, based on expected sales, whereby we place a *guaranteed advance order* for one year of raw materials involving staged, quarterly shipments, each carrying penalties to the supplier when not received by a certain date. This arrangement is acceptable to the various suppliers and has the effect of slightly reducing the cost of bulk-ordered material; it also provides "windows" for the suppliers to produce and ship at slack times and for suppliers to coordinate ABC orders with other manufacturers or vendors, thereby reducing freight expense through use of bulk container shipment. This is a somewhat risky decision, however, because sales of ABC Company have been reasonably stable for the past three years, they appear promising for the future, and purchasing commitments are for one year at a time. When the purchasing plan is fully implemented, we expect to improve cost of goods by 3–4% and, more importantly, improve the delivery time to ABC customers. The sales for 1995 are expected to increase, only slightly, to $1,800,000; for 1996, to $1,900,000; for 1997, to $2,000,000. Six months completed into the 1994 year, ABC has achieved 65% of forecast year-end sales. ABC is meeting their sales expectation budget.

With this information in mind, we can begin the forecasting process. The first step involves development of a set of percentages to be used. Bear in mind that certain expenses do not relate proportionately to sales. Payroll taxes are a product of actual payroll. Insurance premiums for ABC have no relationship to sales made but are related more specifically to types and amounts of insurance coverage. A bit of old-fashioned "eyeballing" may be required.

ABC COMPANY
Income and Loss Statement
As of December 31
(Stated in Percentage Relationship)

	1991	1992	1993	Forecast 1994
Net Sales	100.0%	100.0%	100.0%	100.0%
Cost of Sales	50.1	56.9	55.0	55.0
Gross Profit	49.9	43.1	45.0	45.0
Expenses*				
Salaries & Wages	4.9	5.7	7.7	7.0
Payroll Taxes		(a variable of payroll)		—
Advertising & Promo	1.5	3.6	2.6	2.6
Auto & Travel	1.3	1.3	2.0	1.8
Bad Debt/Collection	0.7	0.4	1.5	1.4
Commissions	2.3	3.7	2.8	2.8
Contribution/Dues		(a variable)		—
Insurance	1.2	1.1	0.7	—
Office/Postage	1.8	2.0	1.5	1.5
Professional Fees	0.3	0.4	1.0	0.8
Rent—Equipment	—	—	0.2	0.2
Repairs/Maintenance	0.5	0.4	0.5	0.5
Show Expenses	2.0	3.6	2.9	3.0
Taxes—Other	0.3	0.1	0.1	0.1
Telephone/Elec.	0.6	0.9	1.0	0.9
Utilities	0.1	0.2	0.2	0.2
Rent Expense	1.6	2.0	1.4	—
Misc. Expense	—	0.2	0.2	0.2
Owner Controlled				
Owner Salary	**23.2**	**8.9**	**11.5**	**—**

(continued)

ABC COMPANY
Income and Loss Statement
As of December 31
(Stated in Percentage Relationship) *(continued)*

	1991	1992	1993	Forecast 1994
Payroll Tax		(a product of owner salary)		—
Depreciation	1.0	0.7	0.9	0.9
Officer Life Ins.	0.1	1.0	0.9	0.9
Director Fees	—	0.7	—	—
Interest Expense	0.7	0.7	0.5	0.5
Total Expenses	45.4	39.0	42.8	—
Other Income	0.5	0.1	12.1	10.0
Income Taxes	1.3	1.2	1.0	1.1
Net Income	**3.7**	**2.9**	**2.4**	—

*Expenses stated as a percent of sales or noted as a product of some other expense. *Important note:* The purpose of this statement is to compare numbers horizontally. Stated percentages have been rounded to fit individual categories—but not rounded to 100% top to bottom.

ABC COMPANY
Income and Loss Statement
As of December 31
(Translated from Percent to Dollars)

	Forecast 1994 (%)	Forecast 1994 ($)
Net Sales	100.0%	$1,760,000
Cost of Sales	55.0	968,000
Gross Profit	45.0	$ 792,000
Expenses*		
Salaries & Wages	7.0	$ 123,200
Payroll Taxes	(a variable of payroll)	7,343
Advertising & Promo	2.6	45,760
Auto & Travel	1.8	31,680
Bad Debt/Collection	1.4	24,640
Commissions	2.8	49,280

	Forecast 1994 (%)	Forecast 1994 ($)
Contribution/Dues	(owner controlled)	1,500
Insurance	(essentially fixed)	12,000
Office/Postage	1.5	26,400
Professional Fees	0.8	14,080
Rent—Equipment	0.2	3,520
Repairs/Maintenance	0.5	8,800
Show Expense	3.0	52,800
Taxes—Other	0.1	1,760
Telephone/Elec.	0.9	15,840
Utilities	0.2	3,520
Rent Expense	(essentially fixed)	24,000
Misc. Expense	0.2	3,520
Owner Salary	(predetermined—owner)	65,000*
Payroll Tax	(a variable of payroll)	6,175
Depreciation	0.9	15,840
Officer Life Ins.	0.9	15,840
Director Fees	N/A	0
Interest Expense	0.5	8,800
Total Expenses		$ 561,298
Other Income	10.0	17,600
Income Taxes	1.1	19,360
Net Income		$ 228,942*

*By establishing a market-based salary for the owner during forecasting, the bottom line can more realistically be viewed. How the owner actually chooses to remove available funds is unimportant to the forecasting process.

Once the forecast 1994 year has been estimated, forecasts for 1995, 1996, and future years can be made. Planned changes to cost of goods sold, reduction of payroll, reduction of bad debt, reduction of professional fees, etc., must be included in each year that they are planned to occur. For example, we planned to reduce cost of goods sold by 3–4% during the next several years and to reduce the cost of payroll by 6% by 1996. All expenses that are tied directly into levels of sales should track upward or downward as a percent of forecast sales. Forecasting is not a pure mechanical process. The owner needs to scrutinize each item. All must be realistic, based on historical results with a fair measure of future events.

ABC COMPANY
Income and Loss Statement
As of December 31

	Forecast 1994		Forecast 1995		Forecast 1996	
Net Sales		$1,760,000		$1,800,000		$1,900,000
Cost of Sales		968,000		972,000		1,007,000
Gross Profit		$ 792,000		$ 828,000		$ 893,000
% Gross Profit		**45.0%**		**46.0%**		**47.0%**
Expenses						
Salaries & Wages	(7.0)	123,200	(6.5)	117,000	(6.0)	114,000
Payroll Taxes		7,343		6,973		6,794
Advertising & Promotion		45,760		46,800		49,400
Auto & Travel		31,680		32,400		34,200
Bad Debt/Collection	(1.4)	24,640	(1.1)	19,800	(0.9)	17,100
Commissions		49,280		50,400		53,200
Contribution/Dues		1,500		1,500		1,500
Insurance		12,000		12,500		13,000
Office/Postage		26,400		27,000		28,500
Professional Fees	(0.8)	14,080	(0.6)	10,800	(0.5)	9,500
Rent—Equipment		3,520		3,600		3,800
Repairs/Maintenance		8,800		9,000		9,500
Show Expense		52,800		54,000		57,000
Taxes—Other		1,760		1,800		1,900
Telephone/Electric		15,840		16,200		17,100
Utilities		3,520		3,600		3,800
Rent Expense		24,000		24,000		24,000
Misc. Expense		3,520		3,600		3,800
Owner Salary		65,000		71,500		78,650
Payroll Tax		6,175		6,793		7,472
Depreciation	(0.9)	15,840	(0.8)	14,400	(0.7)	13,300
Officer Life Ins.		15,840		17,000		18,360
Director Fees		0		0		0
Interest Expense		8,800		7,200		5,700
Total Expenses		$ 561,298		$ 557,866		$ 571,576
Other Income		17,600		18,000		19,000
Income Taxes		19,360		19,800		20,900
Net Income		$ 228,942		$ 268,334		$ 319,524

In the previous example, I have assumed that no new debt has been added or that no new equipment has been purchased. Declining useful life accounts are for the decrease in depreciation, and loan amortization for the decrease in interest paid. Forecast income statements, to remain an effective management tool in planning, must be amended periodically to reflect actual performance.

Annual forecast statements can next be divided into monthly projections of sales, expenses, and cash requirements. In Chapter 5, there is an example of how this might be accomplished.

BALANCE SHEET STATEMENTS

Many items on the balance sheet have a direct relationship to sales. **Increased sales cause the need for increased assets.** Accounts receivables, cash, and inventory are good examples of *variable assets,* those that increase or decrease with sales.

Increased assets cause increased liabilities. For example, accounts receivable and inventory, as they rise, require funding through accumulated working capital, short-term loans, or accounts payables and, subsequently, become *variable liabilities.*

When the sales forecasts are completed, the next step is to determine what level of assets and liabilities will be required to support sales. This is accomplished through analysis of the *percentage relationship* that sales have to both variable assets and liabilities. Once again, we look to the past to predict the future need. The start-up company must look to industry and competitor standards as a reference guide in making actual cash outlays or incurring debt.

For the purpose of this example, we will return to the ABC Company balance sheet. However, before doing so, it is highly unlikely that the owner of ABC Company would permit the corporation tax consequences suggested by significant net incomes in the previous income statements. Let's assume that a bonus or salary increase to the owner will be paid in accordance with some degree of realism, similar to past practices of ABC. Therefore, the following restatement of income will be used during construction of forecast balance sheets.

ABC COMPANY
Income and Loss Statement
As of December 31

	Forecast 1994		Forecast 1995		Forecast 1996	
Net Sales		$1,760,000		$1,800,000		$1,900,000
Cost of Sales		968,000		972,000		1,007,000
Gross Profit		$ 792,000		$ 828,000		$ 893,000
% Gross Profit		**45.0%**		**46.0%**		**47.0%**
Expenses						
Salaries & Wages	(7.0)	123,200	(6.5)	117,000	(6.0)	114,000
Payroll Taxes		7,343		6,973		6,794
Advertising & Promotion		45,760		46,800		49,400
Auto & Travel		31,680		32,400		34,200
Bad Debt/Collection	(1.4)	24,640	(1.1)	19,800	(0.9)	17,100
Commissions		49,280		50,400		53,200
Contribution/Dues		1,500		1,500		1,500
Insurance		12,000		12,500		13,000
Office/Postage		26,400		27,000		28,500
Professional Fees	(0.8)	14,080	(0.6)	10,800	(0.5)	9,500
Rent—Equipment		3,520		3,600		3,800
Repairs/Maintenance		8,800		9,000		9,500
Show Expense		52,800		54,000		57,000
Taxes—Other		1,760		1,800		1,900
Telephone/Elec.		15,840		16,200		17,100
Utilities		3,520		3,600		3,800
Rent Expense		24,000		24,000		24,000
Misc. Expense		3,520		3,600		3,800
Owner Salary		65,000		71,500		78,650
Payroll Tax		6,175		6,793		7,472
Depreciation	(0.9)	15,840	(0.8)	14,400	(0.7)	13,300
Officer Life Ins.		15,840		17,000		18,360
Director Fees		0		0		0
Interest Expense		8,800		7,200		5,700
Total Expenses		$ 561,298		$ 557,866		$ 571,576
Other Income		17,600		18,000		19,000
Income Taxes		19,360		19,800		20,900
Net Income before Bonus		$ 228,942		$ 268,334		$ 319,524
Less: Bonus to Owner		172,942		210,334		259,524
Net Income		$ 56,000		$ 58,000		$ 60,000

ABC COMPANY
Balance Sheet
As of December 31

	1991	1992	1993
ASSETS			
Current Assets			
Cash in Banks	$ 69,726	$ 9,646	$ 48,744
Accounts Receivable	182,696	303,513	248,976
Allow Doubtful Accts	−5,500	−10,000	−6,000
Advances to Owner	2,619	16,289	—
Cash Investments	25,356	5,000	—
Inventory	185,958	197,668	171,128
Total Current Assets	$460,855	$522,116	$462,848
Property and Equipment			
Leasehold Improvements	$ 12,629	$ 12,629	$ 16,144
Furniture & Equipment	58,606	63,802	86,842
Vehicles	6,350	6,350	6,350
Subtotal	$ 77,585	$ 82,781	$109,336
Less: Accum/Deprec	52,466	63,628	80,001
Total Property & Equip	$ 25,119	$ 19,153	$ 29,335
Other Assets			
Cash Value—Life Ins.	$ 4,017	$ 8,477	$ 7,690
Total Other Assets	$ 4,017	$ 8,477	$ 7,690
TOTAL ASSETS	**$489,991**	**$549,746**	**$499,873**
LIABILITIES & EQUITY			
Current Liabilities			
Note—Bank	$ —	$138,000	$ —
Accounts Payable	183,897	211,610	176,943
Accrued Taxes	33,977	9,331	4,133
Accrued Retirement	—	—	18,136
Total Current Liability	$217,874	$358,941	$199,212
Noncurrent Liabilities			
Note—Owner	$124,965	—	$ 67,599
Total Noncurrent Liab.	$124,965	$ —	$ 67,599
TOTAL LIABILITIES	**$342,839**	**$358,941**	**$266,811**

(continued)

ABC COMPANY
Balance Sheet
As of December 31 *(continued)*

	1991	1992	1993
STOCKHOLDER EQUITY			
Capital Stock	$ 15,000	$ 15,000	$ 15,000
Retained Earnings	77,135	132,153	175,806
Net Income/Loss	55,017	43,652	42,256
Total Equity	$147,152	$190,805	$233,062
TOTAL LIABILITIES & EQUITY	$489,991	$549,746	$499,873

Sales for 1991 were $1,482,349; for 1992, $1,495,464; for 1993, $1,752,729. In this example let's assume that cash, accounts receivables, allowance for doubtful accounts, inventory, furniture and equipment, current debt, accounts payables, and accrued taxes are variable with sales accounts. These we will reduce to percentages of sales for each actual year. For clarity, all other numbers will be removed.

	1991	1992	1993	Estimate*
ASSETS				
Current Assets				
Cash in Banks	4.7%	.6%	2.8%	3.0%
Accounts Receivable	12.3	20.3	14.2	14.2
Allow Doubtful Accts.	−0.4	−0.7	−0.3	−0.2
Advances to Owner				
Cash Investments				
Inventory	12.5	13.2	9.8	12.0
Total Current Assets				
Property and Equipment				
Leasehold Improvements				
Furniture & Equipment	4.0	4.3	5.0	5.0
Vehicles				
Subtotal				
Less: Accum./Depreciation				
Total Property & Equip.				
Other Assets				
Cash Value—Life Ins.				
Total Other Assets				

	1991	1992	1993	Estimate*
TOTAL ASSETS				
LIABILITIES & EQUITY				
Current Liabilities				
Curr./Por. L.T.D.	0.0	9.2	0.0	3.0
Accounts Payable	12.4	14.2	10.1	11.0
Accrued Taxes	2.3	0.6	0.2	0.4
Accrued Retirement				
Total Current Liability				
Noncurrent Liabilities				
Note—Owner				
Total Noncurrent Liab.				
TOTAL LIABILITIES				
STOCKHOLDER EQUITY				
Capital Stock				
Retained Earnings				
Net Income/Loss				
Total Equity				
TOTAL LIABILITIES & EQUITY				

*As mentioned several times in the text, estimating is not a precise science. This is a judgment call on the part of the owners, their knowledge of what is occurring, and the opinion of their accountant.

	Estimate	1994	1995	1996
ASSETS				
Current Assets				
Cash in Banks	3.0%	3.0%	3.0%	3.0%
Accounts Receivable	14.2	14.2	14.2	14.2
Allow Doubtful Accts.	−0.2	−0.2	−0.2	−0.2
Advances to Owner				
Cash Investments				
Inventory	12.0	12.0	11.0	10.0
Total Current Assets				
Property and Equipment				
Leasehold Improvements				
Furniture & Equipment	5.0	5.0	5.0	5.0
Vehicles				
Subtotal				
Less: Accum./Deprec.				
Total Property & Equip.				

(continued)

	Estimate	1994	1995	1996
Other Assets				
Cash Value—Life Ins.				
Total Other Assets				
TOTAL ASSETS				
LIABILITIES & EQUITY				
Current Liabilities				
Curr./Por. L.T.D. (notes)	3.0	3.0	3.0	3.0
Accounts Payable	11.0	9.4	7.2	6.3
Accrued Taxes	0.4	0.4	0.4	0.4
Accrued Retirement				
Total Current Liability				
Noncurrent Liabilities				
Note—Owner				
Total Noncurrent Liab.				
TOTAL LIABILITIES				
STOCKHOLDER EQUITY				
Capital Stock				
Retained Earnings				
Net Income/Loss				
Total Equity				
TOTAL LIABILITIES & EQUITY				

This, once again, is a judgment call on the part of an owner. Just as the estimate is formed in historical performance, so should the forecast be tempered by history and, additionally, by what the owner is attempting to achieve through operations.

Bear in mind that our objective is not only to increase sales but also to stabilize raw materials and inventory, manage collection in accounts receivable, and decrease payables—preferably to a 1:2 ratio with receivables.

Applying each forecast year percentage to each forecast year sales, this statement can now be translated into a *forecast balance sheet*. For easy reference, sales are $1,760,000 in 1994, $1,800,000 in 1995, and $1,900,000 in 1996.

	1994	1995	1996
ASSETS			
Current Assets			
Cash in Banks	$ 52,800	$ 54,000	$ 57,000
Accounts Receivable	249,920	255,600	269,800
Allow Doubtful Accts.	− 3,520	− 3,600	− 3,800
Advances to Owner	0	0	0
Cash Investments	0	0	0
Inventory	211,200	198,000	190,000
Total Current Assets	$510,400	$504,000	$513,000
Property and Equipment			
Leasehold Improvements	$ 16,144	$ 16,144	$ 16,144
Furniture & Equipment	88,000	90,000	95,000
Vehicles	6,350	6,350	6,350
Subtotal	$110,494	$112,494	$117,494
Less: Accum./Deprec.	83,485	84,770	86,055
Total Property & Equip.	$ 27,009	$ 27,724	$ 31,439
Other Assets			
Cash Value—Life Ins.	$ 7,690	$ 8,477	$ 9,691
Total Other Assets	$ 7,690	$ 8,477	$ 9,691
TOTAL ASSETS	$545,099	$540,201	$554,130
LIABILITIES & EQUITY			
Current Liabilities			
Note—Bank	$ 52,800	$ 54,000	$ 57,000
Accounts Payable	165,440	129,660	119,700
Accrued Taxes	7,040	7,200	7,600
Accrued Retirement	N/A	N/A	N/A
Total Current Liability	$225,280	$190,800	$184,300
Noncurrent Liabilities			
Note—Owner	$ 67,599	$ 67,599	$67,599
Total Noncurrent Liab.	$ 67,599	$ 67,599	$ 67,599
TOTAL LIABILITIES	$292,879	$258,399	$251,899
STOCKHOLDER EQUITY			
Capital Stock	$ 15,000	$ 15,000	$ 15,000
Retained Earnings	218,062	274,062	332,062
Net Income/Loss	56,000	58,000	60,000
Total Equity	$289,062	$347,062	$407,062

(continued)

	1994	1995	1996
TOTAL LIABILITIES & EQUITY	$581,941	$605,461	$658,961
Asset/Liability Variance	$ 36,842	$ 65,260	$104,831

As it turns out, we will have to reduce note-bank and/or note-owner to reconcile the balance sheet. We could pay down accounts payables; however, interest associated with notes make them the ideal first target.

Adjusting note-bank and note-owner, the forecast balance sheet is as follows:

	1994	1995	1996
ASSETS			
Current Assets			
Cash in Banks	$ 52,800	$ 54,000	$ 57,000
Accounts Receivable	249,920	255,600	269,800
Allow Doubtful Accts.	− 3,520	− 3,600	− 3,800
Advances to Owner	0	0	0
Cash Investments	0	0	0
Inventory	211,200	198,000	190,000
Total Current Assets	$510,400	$504,000	$513,000
Property and Equipment			
Leasehold Improvements	$ 16,144	$ 16,144	$ 16,144
Furniture & Equipment	88,000	90,000	95,000
Vehicles	6,350	6,350	6,350
Subtotal	$110,494	$112,494	$117,494
Less: Accum./Deprec.	83,485	84,770	86,055
Total Property & Equip.	$ 27,009	$ 27,724	$ 31,439
Other Assets			
Cash Value—Life Ins	$ 7,690	$ 8,477	$ 9,691
Total Other Assets	$ 7,690	$ 8,477	$ 9,691
TOTAL ASSETS	$545,099	$540,201	$554,130
LIABILITIES & EQUITY			
Current Liabilities			
Notes—Bank	$ 15,958	$ 0	$ 0
Accounts Payable	165,440	129,660	119,700
Accrued Taxes	7,040	7,200	7,600
Accrued Retirement	N/A	N/A	N/A
Total Current Liability	$188,438	$136,800	$127,300

	1994	1995	1996
Noncurrent Liabilities			
Note—Owner	$ 67,599	$ 56,399	$19,768
Total Noncurrent Liab.	$ 67,599	$ 56,399	$ 19,768
TOTAL LIABILITIES	$256,037	$193,139	$147,068
STOCKHOLDER EQUITY			
Capital Stock	$ 15,000	$ 15,000	$ 15,000
Retained Earnings	218,062	274,062	332,062
Net Income/Loss	56,000	58,000	60,000
Total Equity	$289,062	$347,062	$407,062
TOTAL LIABILITIES & EQUITY	$545,099	$540,201	$554,130

Forecasting can provide "windows" in which to view the future health of a business. ABC Company, assuming that sales and other target goals are met, should be able to fund growth internally and should not be required to incur outside debt—a luxury that not many smaller companies enjoy. But, cash abundance must be managed, as well as cash shortages.

Particular mention is directed to accumulating retained earnings. Without compelling justification, and to the extent that ABC Company's retained earnings exceed $250,000 after 1995, substantially higher taxable dividends to the stockholder may have to be declared. Stockholder (owner) personal earnings appear marginally high in the context of IRS rules and assessment when these earnings are compared with comparable wages paid in other jobs of similar worth. While environmental and unusual business requirements can provide justification for nontaxable excess over the $250,000 level of accumulated earnings, nothing presented in the known elements of the ABC case suggests an avoidance of dividend payment. Note that IRS regulations impose an additional tax on nonjustifiable accumulated earnings greater than $850,000.

Corporate investment in new equipment, real estate, retirement plans, or acquisition of another company may be in order. Any number of possibilities exist when an abundance of cash is present.

Cash-short conditions can be estimated through application of the following formula. Examples of variable assets are accounts receivable, cash, and inventory, and for variable liabilities good examples are working capital, short-term loans, and accounts payables. Side-stepping ABC Company for a moment, and to clarify use of the formula, let's use actual sales of $250,000 and a sales forecast of $400,000 in an example. Let's further assume variable assets of $124,000 and variable liabilities of $56,000 in the forecast balance sheet; $16,000 will represent net income.

$$\frac{\text{Variable Assets}}{\text{Sales}} \times \frac{\text{Sales}}{\text{Increase}} - \frac{\text{Variable Liabilities}}{\text{Sales}} \times \frac{\text{Sales}}{\text{Increase}} - \frac{\text{Net}}{\text{Income}} = \frac{\text{New}}{\text{Debt}}$$

$$\frac{\$124,000}{\$400,000} \times \$150,000 - \frac{\$56,000}{\$400,000} \times \$150,000 - \$16,000 = \frac{\text{New}}{\text{Debt}}$$

$$[(31.0\%)(\$150,000)] - [(14.0\%)(\$150,000)] - \$16,000 = \frac{\text{New}}{\text{Debt}}$$

$$\$46,500 - \$21,000 - \$16,000 = \$9,500 \; \frac{\text{New}}{\text{Debt}}$$

If in this example the sales forecast of $400,000 is to be met, the company will need $46,000 of new assets, incur liabilities of $21,000, and require $9,500 of new debt. Forecasting debt requirements in advance of need reduces last minute or crisis borrowing situations. Carrying the forecast three to five years into the future helps determine whether short- or long-term borrowing will be required.

Without doubt, planning and forecasting take considerable time and are a lot of work. The smaller-business owner will always be pressed for time to make sales, order materials, collect receivables, pay bills, and work through customer and employee concerns. Time must be allocated for family and play to balance out life. While it is a matter of choice, the alternative to not finding time for understanding the business seems clear. Would you prefer that the business run you, or would you prefer to run the business? Good financial management cannot be replaced with intuition and hope-I-can-do attitudes. Successful entrepreneurs must know where they stand in the present and in the future, or personal goals will certainly not be achieved with any regularity. The process of applying financial tools becomes easier with practice and time.

5

The Cash Budget

For development of the cash budget, *annual* forecast statements must be divided into **monthly** forecasts of sales and expenses. Spread forecast sales over 12 periods, as you expect them to occur. Cost of goods sold and expenses are spread across each period in their relationships to sales or known requirement for payment. Insurance, for example, is customarily paid annually or quarterly. Isolate expenses that traditionally are paid one, two, three, or four times per year, and insert the full amount when regularly due. In thus doing, a truer picture of cash requirements can be estimated. Month-to-month estimates subsequently can be made for each future and forecast year.

In our sample ABC Company, sales are experienced in "bursts" from a major and minor peak customer delivery season. For example, we have examined monthly past sales and found that ABC experiences peak seasons culminating by April 15th and a lesser peak by October 15th. Sales build up to these key dates starting in February and in late August each year. The balance of sales remain fairly constant month to month.

THE CASH BUDGETING PROCESS

The monthly sales history exhibits the following pattern in occurrence:

	Historical Experience	Forecast 1994	Forecast 1995	Forecast 1996
Jan	4.01%	$ 70,576	$ 72,180	$ 76,190
Feb	9.08	159,808	163,440	172,520
Mar	15.08	265,408	271,440	286,520
Apr	19.58	344,608	352,440	372,020
May	5.26	92,576	94,680	99,940
June	4.41	77,616	79,380	83,790
July	4.69	82,544	84,420	89,110
Aug	6.83	120,208	122,940	129,770
Sept	9.83	173,008	176,940	186,770
Oct	12.08	212,608	217,440	229,520
Nov	4.80	84,480	86,400	91,200
Dec	4.35	76,560	78,300	82,650
Totals	100.00%	$1,760,000	$1,800,000	$1,900,000

For easy reference, the three-year-forecast income statements are repeated in the following:

ABC COMPANY
Income and Loss Statement
As of December 31

	Forecast 1994	Forecast 1995	Forecast 1996
Net Sales	$1,760,000	$1,800,000	$1,900,000
Cost of Sales	968,000	972,000	1,007,000
Gross Profit	$ 792,000	$ 828,000	$ 893,000
% Gross Profit	**45.0%**	**46.0%**	**47.0%**

	Forecast 1994	Forecast 1995	Forecast 1996
Expenses			
Salaries & Wages	123,200	117,000	114,000
Payroll Taxes	7,343	6,973	6,794
Advertising & Promo	45,760	46,800	49,400
Auto & Travel	31,680	32,400	34,200
Bad Debt/Collection	24,640	19,800	17,100
Commissions	49,280	50,400	53,200
Contribution/Dues	1,500	1,500	1,500
Insurance	12,000	12,500	13,000
Office/Postage	26,400	27,000	28,500
Professional Fees	14,080	10,800	9,500
Rent—Equipment	3,520	3,600	3,800
Repairs/Maintenance	8,800	9,000	9,500
Show Expense	52,800	54,000	57,000
Taxes—Other	1,760	1,800	1,900
Telephone/Elec.	15,840	16,200	17,100
Utilities	3,520	3,600	3,800
Rent Expense	24,000	24,000	24,000
Misc. Expense	3,520	3,600	3,800
Owner Salary	65,000	71,500	78,650
Payroll Tax	6,175	6,793	7,472
Depreciation	15,840	14,400	13,300
Officer Life Ins.	15,840	17,000	18,360
Director Fees	0	0	0
Interest Expense	8,800	7,200	5,700
Total Expenses	$ 561,298	$ 557,866	$ 571,576
Other Income	17,600	18,000	19,000
Income Taxes	19,360	19,800	20,900
Net Income before Bonus	$ 228,942	$ 268,334	$ 319,524
Less: Bonus to Owner	**172,942**	**210,334**	**259,524**
Net Income	$ **56,000**	$ **58,000**	$ **60,000**

ABC COMPANY
Monthly Income and Loss Statement—1994 (Adjusted)

	Jan	Feb	Mar	Apr	May
Net Sales	$70,576	$159,808	$265,408	$344,608	$ 92,576
Cost of Sales	42,108	38,807	87,884	145,974	189,534
Gross Profit	$28,468	$121,001	$177,524	$198,634	$ −96,958
Expenses					
Salaries/Wages	$10,266	$ 10,267	$ 10,267	$ 10,267	$ 10,266
Payroll Taxes	611	612	612	612	612
Adver./Promo.*	1,835	4,155	6,901	8,960	2,407
Auto/Travel*	1,270	2,877	4,777	6,203	1,666
Bad Debt/Coll.*	988	2,237	3,716	4,825	1,296
Commissions*	1,976	4,475	7,431	9,649	2,592
Contrib./Dues	125	125	125	125	125
Insurance			3,000		
Office/Postage*	1,059	2,397	3,981	5,169	1,387
Prof. Fees	1,000	1,000	1,000	3,080	1,000
Rent–Equip.	293	294	293	294	293
Repair/Maint.	700	800	900	700	600
Show Expense	2,112	21,120	2,112	2,112	2,112
Taxes–Other	146	147	146	147	146
Tele./Elec.*	635	1,438	2,389	3,101	833
Utilities	504	504	504	380	200
Rent Expense	2,000	2,000	2,000	2,000	2,000
Misc. Expense	200	300	500	700	300
Owner Salary/Tax	6,015	7,190	26,015	106,015	6,675
Depreciation	1,320	1,320	1,320	1,320	1,320
Office Life Ins.			3,960		
Interest Expense	733	733	733	733	733
Total Expenses	$33,788	$ 63,991	$ 82,682	$166,392	$ 36,563
Other Income	1,466	1,466	1,466	1,466	1,467
Net Income before Tax	$−3,854	$ 58,476	$ 96,308	$ 33,708	$−132,054
Income Taxes	1,613	1,613	1,613	1,613	1,613
Net Income	$−5,467	$ 56,863	$ 94,695	$ 32,095	$−133,667

June	July	Aug	Sept	Oct	Nov	Dec	Total
$ 77,616	$82,544	$120,208	$173,008	$212,608	$ 84,480	$76,560	$1,760,000
50,917	42,689	45,391	66,144	95,154	116,934	46,464	968,000
$ 26,699	$39,855	$ 74,817	$106,864	$117,454	$-32,454	$30,096	$ 792,000
$ 10,267	$10,266	$ 10,267	$ 10,267	$ 10,267	$ 10,266	$10,267	$ 123,200
612	612	612	612	612	612	612	7,343
2,018	2,146	3,125	4,498	5,528	2,196	1,991	45,760
1,397	1,486	2,164	3,114	3,827	1,521	1,378	31,680
1,086	1,157	1,683	2,422	2,977	1,183	1,070	24,640
2,173	2,311	3,366	4,844	5,954	2,365	2,144	49,280
125	125	125	125	125	125	125	1,500
3,000			3,000			3,000	12,000
1,164	1,239	1,803	2,596	3,190	1,267	1,148	26,400
1,000	1,000	1,000	1,000	1,000	1,000	1,000	14,080
294	293	293	293	293	293	294	3,520
600	700	800	900	900	600	600	8,800
2,112	2,112	10,560	2,112	2,112	2,112	2,112	52,800
147	147	147	147	147	146	147	1,760
699	743	1,082	1,557	1,914	760	689	15,840
80	40	40	80	180	504	504	3,520
2,000	2,000	2,000	2,000	2,000	2,000	2,000	24,000
100	100	200	320	400	200	200	3,520
7,015	7,015	7,015	26,015	36,015	7,015	2,117	244,117
1,320	1,320	1,320	1,320	1,320	1,320	1,320	15,840
3,960			3,960			3,960	15,840
734	733	734	733	734	733	734	8,800
$ 41,903	$35,545	$ 48,336	$ 71,915	$ 79,495	$ 36,218	$37,412	$ 734,240
1,467	1,467	1,467	1,467	1,467	1,467	1,467	17,600
$-13,737	$ 5,777	$ 27,948	$ 36,416	$ 39,426	$-67,205	$-5,849	$ 75,360
1,613	1,613	1,613	1,614	1,614	1,614	1,614	19,360
$-15,350	$ 4,164	$ 26,335	$ 34,802	$ 37,812	$-68,819	$-7,463	$ 56,000

*Expenses that vary with sales.

Business plans or forecast financial analysis reports should **include completion of monthly forecasts for at least the first projected year.** Monthly or quarterly forecasts should be completed for each additional future year. However, in our example, we will work with just the 1994 monthly forecast (see the Monthly Income and Loss Statement on pages 68 and 69).

In a month-to-month forecast, several factors must be considered. For example, cash receipts from individual sales may not be received until 30 or more days after the sale is completed. Sale-to-receipt lag times can be analyzed and adjusted, if necessary, through accounts receivable turnover. From the forecast balance sheet in Chapter 4, we see that accounts receivables are $249,920. Forecast sales for this same period are $1,760,000.

$$\begin{array}{l}\text{Accounts} \\ \text{Receivable} = \\ \text{Turnover}\end{array} \quad \frac{\text{Sales}}{\text{A/R}} = \frac{1,760,000}{249,920} = 7.04 \text{ Turns}$$

$$\begin{array}{l}\text{A/R} \\ \text{Collection} = \\ \text{Period}\end{array} \quad \frac{365}{\text{A/R Turns}} = \frac{365}{7.04} = 51.8 \text{ Days}$$

We can see in this example that it takes 51.8 days, on average, to collect cash from a sale. Next it is necessary to determine *when* materials are paid for. To keep the analysis on a cost basis, accounts payables are examined in relationship to cost of goods sold rather than to sales. The forecast balance sheet reveals accounts payable to be $165,440. Cost of goods sold are $968,000.

$$\begin{array}{l}\text{Accounts} \\ \text{Payable} = \\ \text{Turnover}\end{array} \quad \frac{\text{Cost of Goods Sold}}{\text{Accounts Payable}} = \frac{968,000}{165,440} = 5.89 \text{ Turns}$$

$$\begin{array}{l}\text{A/P} \\ \text{Payment} = \\ \text{Period}\end{array} \quad \frac{365}{\text{A/P Turns}} = \frac{365}{5.89} = 62.0 \text{ Days}$$

At this point, we can readily see that it takes an average of 51.8 days to receive payment for sales made and that ABC Company delays payment of their own bills on an average of 62 days.

We could dig into past sales, receivables, and payables accounts; determine precise individual receipt or payment history by month; and then develop more exacting percentages to be used in projected income statements. This would be an incredible chore for most businesses. A more practical approach, and one that may already be done, is to compile monthly profit and loss (P & L) statements. If this is not being done, monthly sales receipts, payment for cost of goods sold, and expenses can be obtained directly from business checkbook stubs. Arraying monthly over a preceding two- or three-year period and averaging to smooth out irregularities in experience will do wonders to refine percentage relationships for future projections. Much less work is involved when sales are made with an immediate or 30-day cash payment plan and when materials are paid for within 30 days.

Let's assume that income from forecast monthly sales represent an accurate picture of when they are actually received. Also, bear in mind that expenses incurred are essentially a variable of sales, a fixed monthly cost, or an optional expense for the owner and that these expenses reflect accurately when they are paid. To emphasize the effect that 60-day payment practices might have on the bottom line, we can shift January cost of goods sold into February, February into March, and so on down the line. December's cost of $42,108 will be put into January for this example of the ABC Company's Monthly Income and Loss Statement, as shown on pages 72 and 73.

Due to a computer formula used in calculating the first example for cost of goods sold, slight changes were necessary in the second example so that the annual 55% for cost of goods sold could be maintained. Note the significant change in monthly cash requirements between the first and second statement examples. While the annual forecast remains the same, monthly cash requirements can shift dramatically, depending upon how receivables and payables are handled by an owner. In the second example for ABC Company, the timing of owner bonuses could do much toward eliminating the negative monthly cash flow. This may not, however, always be possible, and short-term loans may be required to fund slack months.

Capital budgeting is discussed in Chapter 6; however, capital equipment purchases must be tied into the cash budgeting process. Cash disbursement for equipment purchase must be allocated to the month(s) in which they occur in the monthly forecasts. If purchases are partially paid through loans, then monthly forecasts for continuing interest payments must be included in the appropriate number of future months until paid in full.

ABC COMPANY
Monthly Income and Loss Statement—1994

	Jan	Feb	Mar	Apr	May
Net Sales	$70,576	$159,808	$265,408	$344,608	$92,576
Cost of Sales	38,817	87,894	145,974	189,534	50,917
Gross Profit	$31,759	$ 71,914	$119,434	$155,074	$41,659
Expenses					
Salaries/Wages	$10,266	$ 10,267	$ 10,267	$ 10,267	$10,266
Payroll Taxes	611	612	612	612	612
Adver./Promo.*	1,835	4,155	6,901	8,960	2,407
Auto/Travel*	1,270	2,877	4,777	6,203	1,666
Bad Debt/Coll.*	988	2,237	3,716	4,825	1,296
Commissions*	1,976	4,475	7,431	9,649	2,592
Contrib./Dues	125	125	125	125	125
Insurance			3,000		
Office/Postage*	1,059	2,397	3,981	5,169	1,387
Prof. Fees	1,000	1,000	1,000	3,080	1,000
Rent—Equip.	293	294	293	294	293
Repair/Maint.	700	800	900	700	600
Show Expense	2,112	21,120	2,112	2,112	2,112
Taxes—Other	146	147	146	147	146
Tele./Elec.*	635	1,438	2,389	3,101	833
Utilities	504	504	504	380	200
Rent Expense	2,000	2,000	2,000	2,000	2,000
Misc. Expense	200	300	500	700	300
Owner Salary/Tax	6,015	7,190	26,015	106,015	6,675
Depreciation	1,320	1,320	1,320	1,320	1,320
Office Life Ins.			3,960		
Interest Expense	733	733	733	733	733
Total Expenses	$33,788	$ 63,991	$ 82,682	$166,392	$36,563
Other Income	1,466	1,466	1,466	1,466	1,467
Net Income before Tax	$ −563	$9,389	$ 38,218	$ −9,852	$6,563
Income Taxes	1,613	1,613	1,613	1,613	1,613
Net Income	$−2,176	$ 7,776	$ 36,605	$−11,465	$ 4,950

June	July	Aug	Sept	Oct	Nov	Dec	Total
$77,616	$82,544	$120,208	$173,008	$212,608	$84,480	$76,560	$1,760,000
42,689	45,399	66,114	95,154	116,934	46,464	42,108	968,000
$34,927	$37,145	$ 54,094	$ 77,854	$ 95,674	$38,016	$34,452	$ 792,000
$10,267	$10,266	$ 10,267	$ 10,267	$ 10,267	$10,266	$10,267	$ 123,200
612	612	612	612	612	612	612	7,343
2,018	2,146	3,125	4,498	5,528	2,196	1,991	45,760
1,397	1,486	2,164	3,114	3,827	1,521	1,378	31,680
1,086	1,157	1,683	2,422	2,977	1,183	1,070	24,640
2,173	2,311	3,366	4,844	5,954	2,365	2,144	49,280
125	125	125	125	125	125	125	1,500
3,000			3,000			3,000	12,000
1,164	1,239	1,803	2,596	3,190	1,267	1,148	26,400
1,000	1,000	1,000	1,000	1,000	1,000	1,000	14,080
294	293	293	293	293	293	294	3,520
600	700	800	900	900	600	600	8,800
2,112	2,112	10,560	2,112	2,112	2,112	2,112	52,800
147	147	147	147	147	146	147	1,760
699	743	1,082	1,557	1,914	760	689	15,840
80	40	40	80	180	504	504	3,520
2,000	2,000	2,000	2,000	2,000	2,000	2,000	24,000
100	100	200	320	400	200	200	3,520
7,015	7,015	7,015	26,015	36,015	7,015	2,117	244,117
1,320	1,320	1,320	1,320	1,320	1,320	1,320	15,840
3,960			3,960			3,960	15,840
734	733	734	733	734	733	734	8,800
$41,903	$35,545	$ 48,336	$ 71,915	$ 79,495	$36,218	$37,412	$ 734,240
1,467	1,467	1,467	1,467	1,467	1,467	1,467	17,600
$-5,509	$ 3,067	$ 7,225	$ 7,406	$ 17,646	$ 3,265	$-1,493	$75,360
1,613	1,613	1,613	1,614	1,614	1,614	1,614	19,360
$-7,122	$ 1,454	$ 5,612	$ 5,792	$ 16,032	$ 1,651	$-3,107	$ 56,000

*Expenses that vary with sales.

All known extraordinary and/or one-time expenses must also be included in monthly forecasts.

SUMMARY

Cash budgeting predicts **short-term borrowing needs,** identifies **when** it will be **required,** and provides **lead time to secure** appropriate financing. Cash budgeting can provide convincing evidence to a bank of how and when the loan will be paid back. Cash budgeting puts order to cash needs and substantially reduces the hassle from involuntarily being driven from one cash crisis to another. The cash budget may actually be one of the most important tools used in managing the smaller business, particularly when a hand-to-mouth business environment exists. When the monthly plan for forecast income and expenses has been developed, it is important to review the plan in light of actual monthly performance. When substantial differences occur, review operating performance, make appropriate changes to operations, or change the forecast plan to include the differences.

6

Capital Budgeting

My experience with people in general leads me to wonder if we mostly, as many do, too quickly develop love affairs with the *what* or *things* versus the *who* in our lives. Sometimes we buy for the sake of buying, and equipment and other small-business asset purchases are frequently made based on whimsical desire rather than from any longer-term plan. Extra cash? So, buy a new widget, particularly if it is shiny. It is okay to fall in love with homes and personal autos, if we can afford this ownership. Not so for the business itself nor for its assets. A cardinal rule of business is that to become and remain profitable, the business must pay for itself out of cash flow, within a reasonable amount of time. If used equipment fits the overall bill, then purchase used equipment. Bells and whistles have no useful place in the business environment without capital investment justification. Bells and whistles that do not help to attain personal and small-business goals are no more than emotional wish lists and may lead to the business's ultimate downfall.

CAPITAL BUDGETING

Capital budgeting is simply the long-term planning for replacement of old or inefficient equipment and/or additional equipment or physical plant when growing business conditions warrant. Through financial forecasting covered in other chapters of this handbook, we can reasonably well determine when we might be able to *afford* these purchases. Thorough examination of repair records and production schedules often forecast replacement needs. Market exploration reveals what brand or model of equipment is most appropriate to fit specific needs. Equipment suppliers can provide cost, useful life, and estimated salvage value.

A decision to purchase a particular machine, or to purchase at all, must be based in fact and provide satisfactory business-related answers to two fundamental questions. How much will be *saved* in terms of production costs, or what additional *income* can be generated through this purchase?

Vacationing to a particular place is usually a question of want/afford versus personal enjoyment, and it is a personal goal. To reach that personal vacation goal, the small-business owner must often count on the profits from his or her business. Profits hinge partially on asset investment rates of return. Equipment or facility purchase decisions require the balancing of a need for profit against cost to attain. There are a number of sophisticated record keeping schemes and formulas to predict equipment replacement. However, many small-business owners require nothing more than a simple approach.

For example, consider an old and inefficient piece of production equipment. Repair costs during the past year amounted to $2,000. In downtime, four production days were lost, which idled $800 in labor. A replacement model will save one man-day of labor or $400 in each quarter of a year. Total annual savings of $3,200 through purchase could, theoretically, be attained. Since depreciation is a noncash expense, it is not customarily figured into the analysis. Cost of the replacement model is discovered to be $10,000, with a useful life expectancy of six years. Salvage value is estimated by the manufacturer to be 10%, or $1,000.

Does it make business sense to pay $10,000 to receive $3,200 for a period of six years? A quick answer is found by calculating the **payback period.**

$$\text{Payback} = \frac{\text{Equipment Cost}}{\text{Est. Annual Saving}} = \frac{\$10,000}{\$3,200} = 3.13 \text{ years}$$

In just over three of the six useful life years, the equipment will be paid off and will provide an estimated $1,000 salvage value toward the equipment's sixth-year replacement. The approximate rate of return in this instance is 25%, which was estimated through use of a *present value table*, which can be obtained from the business section of almost any bookstore.

These tables are not reproduced in this handbook. Most of the small businesses to whom this handbook is directed replace major items only occasionally, and rates of return are not the primary reason. If a business owns just one production machine and it's on the blink, it must be replaced! When simultaneous replacement problems surface and funds are in short supply, rates of return take on significance and help prioritize which items are most beneficial to replace or add first. For the most part, the determination of payback time is all that is required of the small-business owner to forecast capital equipment replacements into his or her business or financial plan.

In this example, a replacement statement might read: When the age of this machine reaches six years or when repairs approach $2,000 per year, the company must allocate $10,000 for replacement. With a six-year useful life, a replacement reserve of $10,000 − $1,000 = $9,000 divided by six years, i.e., $1,500 per year, must be established. If not from reserve, a loan must be secured during the sixth year of useful life. Assuming that a bank would be unlikely to finance much longer than one-half the life expectancy of equipment—or in this case three years—and that prevailing economies might suggest a 10% interest rate, the added cost for interest on $9,000 over the loan term would be $1,455, a 14.5% premium. This seems like a pretty stiff penalty to pay when a $1,500 replacement reserve deposited each year in a bank could earn 3–4% or $735 in interest. Thus viewed, the premium for borrowing is not only the $1,455 in interest but also the loss of the possible earned interest of $735. Taken together, the actual premium is $1,455 + $735 = $2,190 divided by $10,000, or 21.9%. Calculated for each major capital item, replacement can be planned in advance and timed with periods of increased business cash flow. Leaving replacement planning to chance is particularly risky for the smaller business that depends upon single equipment or machines for production or sales.

I understand how simple this chapter on capital budgeting may seem. For a moment, put yourself in a banker's seat. Cash is short with a customer who applies for an equipment purchase loan and who provides you with his or her business plan. The forecast numbers look fairly tight, so what justifies the purchase, and how will the loan be paid back? The customer responds that they can save approximately $3,200 per year on the $10,000 purchase, and those savings pay for the purchase in just over three years of the equipment's six-year useful life. Interest paid is recovered during the first half of the fourth year, and there will be two and one-half useful-life years remaining of debt-free use. This provides enough time to establish a reserve for at least reducing the borrowed amount necessary to replace this machine in two and one-half years. The equipment has an estimated $1,000 salvage value at the end of the sixth year, for trade on its future replacement. Annual savings pay all or much of the cost associated with the loan.

Beyond the assistance that capital budgeting provides in developing replacement reserves, the exercise can also provide a deciding factor in obtaining loans.

7
Long-Range Planning

Perhaps the foremost compelling reason for long-range planning can be found in the body of compiled statistics on why 80% of all businesses fail during their first ten years of operation. I dislike the underlying connotation implied in the word "bad" for its guilt-producing element, but when termed at least as a weakness of management, it explains precisely why businesses fail. The greatest advantage as well as the greatest weakness of the smaller business is its simplicity. Often, the manager is also the owner. It seems clear to me that regardless of outward symptoms, many problems leading to failure should have and could have been recognized and solved by the manager or owner. Harry S. Truman, when at his peak in the presidency of the United States, is still quoted today from his four-word style of management, "The buck stops here!"

The part of me formally educated in psychology clearly underscores why many of us are adverse to the process of long-range planning.

1. As individuals, to stay reasonably comfortable in our life surroundings we are traditionally cautioned to stay focused on the present time—the here and now. Feelings trapped in the past or exacerbated by thoughts involving future events that may or may not occur become those principal feelings that make us especially uncomfortable. Long-range planning requires us to concentrate not only on the past and future but also on the present state of our business affairs, and the process cuts deeply into a territory of personal feel-

ings. We learn to *feel* better off not knowing what the future holds when in reality, consciously or unconsciously, formally or informally, everyone makes choices that influence long-term outcomes. The successful entrepreneur overrides **fears of the unknown** and plans for the future so that he or she can appropriately handle future events through *anticipation*. It is simply better to be somewhat prepared than not prepared at all.

2. As individuals, we are filled with **suspicions,** which are frequently confirmed through experience, that even the best made plans rarely take place as expected. This occurrence in planning is often true for companies as well. However, to become and remain profitable in business requires endless effort. Too often, a business without planning does not perceive the need for change until it is upon them and possibly too late for adequate response.

3. Rarely does anyone have **enough time** to do all that they want to do. Only when we *schedule* what we *need* to do will tasks get accomplished. When people get anything done effectively, it is because they have succeeded at planning, preparing, and implementing what they wanted to do. When they fail, it is usually because they have tripped over self-imposed obstacles of optimism, pessimism, procrastination, excuses for lack of time, job too big or too small, failure to prepare, and not being focused.

4. Perhaps the primary reason for not planning is **inexperience** with the concept and other elements of the planning process. From infancy we learn that through crying we get attention for our hunger or relief from being wet, and through cooing and smiling we get affection when we require nurturing; however, these are unplanned reactions to fill immediate needs. It is through education and experience that we learn to *plan* actions that foster the achievement of some future event. An old saying tells us that *"where there is a will, there is a way."* When we have the will to get things done, we can learn the way to do them right. The business planning process need not be complicated and can be easily learned.

Do Long-Range Plans Really Help Prevent Failures?

The following list answers this question:

1. Yes, say the experts—if you know how to and do use them.

2. Studies show that companies that set goals, determine priorities, and develop plans to attain them consistently outperform companies that make decisions informally.

3. Most firms with a sales volume of five million dollars and above cannot now avoid establishing the direction of company growth for many years ahead.

4. Studies further indicate that businesses are more apt to fail where there was the following:

   a. Failure to provide sufficient time to thinking ahead on management problems.

   b. Failure to organize properly.

   c. Failure to plan adequately.

   d. Failure to understand fundamental operating and financial relationships.

OVERVIEW OF THE PLANNING PROCESS

Long-range planning in larger companies begins with a **Mission Statement**. What is the *purpose* for the business's existence, and where does the business expect to be in three, five, or ten years? This too must be defined for the smaller business.

However, there is an elementary difference for the smaller business, particularly where ownership is held solely by the entrepreneur. That difference is in *where* the planning process should begin. From the impersonal setting of the large corporation, the planning process rarely gets down to include individual, personal goals. Personal goals, however, may be *equal* to or greater than business goals in a private ownership scenario. For example, if the entrepreneur wants a bigger home, a fancy car, and substantially improved overall lifestyle, he or she will look to business earnings to make this possible, whereas the corporate planner may be limited to obtaining personal goals through customary pay increases alone. The fundamental difference in how people view achieving personal goals forms the primary reason why people enter the private business ownership sector.

Therefore, long-range planning in the closely held enterprise begins with detailing an **owner's personal goals.** What do *you personally* want from the future? How long before you expect to reach these goals? What skills must be learned, and what must be done to achieve these goals? Are your personal goals achievable through this business or at all? If not this business, then what business? How does your family participate in these goals? Can dominating elements of your personality and character along with those of your family withstand the inevitable trials, and is the necessary motivation present to achieve your goals? How much effort are you willing to expend to reach these goals? Will business ownership provide adequate private time for you and your family?

When personal objectives are well defined and well understood, the framework for a "mission statement" for the business itself will become more clear.

It must be recognized, however, that a majority of small businesses simply cannot provide achievement of all personal goals. This fact can be considered during the business planning process. For example, the plan can specifically indicate that when this business reaches a certain level of sales and earnings, it will be sold. Perhaps it will be replaced with a larger or step-up concern. Acquisition or merger consideration might also be a prospect outlined in the plan. Changes to personal goals must be translated into changes to business plans and vice versa.

REDUCING GOALS AND PLANS TO WRITING

When establishing goals, be specific in terms of performance toward achieving each goal. Each goal should be stated such that it can be *measured*. Major goals must be broken into segments, establishing dates when each is expected to be achieved. *Plan* the *action* you must take to attain each goal. *Exercise care not to plan for too much action for reaching too many goals.* Establish *priorities,* and act upon them one at a time. It is okay that goals and plans contain some lofty objectives, but they must be within reach of your *reasonable* capability. When extemporaneously formulated, an unrealistic plan can impact negatively on financing considerations and, more importantly, on personal motivation. *Goals and plans that excite personal motivation to act are goals and plans that produce results.* All others tend to be dreams and wishful thinking that produce vague results. It is better to have a few achievable targets than a difficult-to-achieve, grandiose plan.

OBSTACLES TO PLANNING

I planned to attend the event this evening, but frankly, I'm just too *tired*. I really would like to participate in that seminar *someday*. I'll make that sales call *tomorrow*. I'm sorry that I didn't get that job done *yesterday*. I *hope* that I'm able to do that job. I *should* have asked for the order. I *can't* muster the energy to make that call. Why don't *you* do that for me.

Obstacles of optimism, pessimism, procrastination, lack-of-time excuses, job too big or too small, failure to prepare, and not being focused can forestall any planning or action effort. We encounter obstacles every day of our lives. Some obstacles can be momentarily real, because of existing skills or size of the business. Many times, however, obstacles can present future opportunities to grow. The Chinese character for crisis is also the character for opportunity. Confucian belief states that in all crises, there exists an equal amount of opportunity.

Viewing tasks by their worldly whole creates anxiety and encourages procrastination. Broken down into segments, these same tasks can take on the appearance of reasonable achievement. Prioritize the most important goals, and *act* upon them immediately. The rest will usually fall into line.

During the goal setting and planning process, unanticipated events may occur, or new opportunities may develop. You must then do what is needed to bring both personal and business goals up to date. I caution myself about change by recalling this ancient Chinese proverb, "No man can step in the same spot in the river twice . . . because the river is flowing and ever changing, just as we are always changing."

SUMMARY—LONG-RANGE PLANNING

The long-range plan is a broad and general picture of forecast events over the next few years, usually three to five years, including an overview of factors that might impact functions of your business. The following summarizes the process:

1. Establish personal goals.
   a. Assess goals within realm of personal capability.
   b. Examine goals in relationship to family life.
   c. Prioritize goals and establish time frames for achievement.

2. Establish business goals.

   a. Examine external influence of local competition and technology and of social, economic, political, and regulatory trends.

   b. Examine overall industry trends, innovations, and accomplishments.

   c. Detail threats to your business; explore and spell out alternatives to combat these threats.

   d. Detail strengths of your business, and establish avenues for most predictable growth.

   e. Examine internal physical and staff capabilities, and establish the realistic picture of financial strength.

3. Develop mission statement.

   a. Keep statement brief, but include the basic purpose of your business—what you want the business to be, markets served, and products to be developed.

4. Establish target objectives and rationale for product mix.

   a. Set desired growth in terms of sales and profit. Establish time frames for achieving target goals.

   b. Define how and when you will increase your market share.

   c. Divide products or services into levels of sales and profitability. Decide which products or services you plan to concentrate on growing—why and by when.

Without the formulation of long-range plans, it may not become clear how short-term objectives play into the achievement of overall personal goals. For example, if I presently earn $30,000 per year and want to earn $80,000 per year by the end of three years, what must I do with my company to meet this objective? A difference of $50,000 is what I must accomplish in just three years, which is a 267% increase! Stated another way, I must increase my personal earnings by $16,667 in each of the three years. Examination of my company's historical and future variables, when compared with my own capability, will confirm or negate the likelihood for achieving the personal goal with this specific company.

A long-range plan for the business to accommodate my personal goal of earning $80,000 helps establish staged segments (short-term plans), which I must accomplish to meet this ultimate goal. When the "reality" painted by a long-range plan falls short of meeting personal expectation, then alternative options, such as sale, acquisition, or merger, must also be planned.

Long-range plans for the business are customarily included and form justifying dialogue for the business plan. Personal goals are usually not spelled out but are subtly implied by the financial objectives forecast in the business plan.

8

Financing Growth

It can be wonderful to reflect upon the prospect of owning a company that may be experiencing phenomenal growth. Exceptional growth, however, can present its own set of difficult challenges. Financing rapid growth might be a major problem. Reaching higher levels of sales may necessitate additional and continuing investment in both current and fixed assets. Sales may be available for the asking, but existing production capability may not be able to fill the larger numbers of orders. Growth, without management control, can force the company into a cash-starved position. Cash is required to purchase new equipment and personnel. Increased bank debt may dilute balance sheet strengths and create higher risk to the banker considering the granting of a loan. Borrowing ability may become strangled and, eventually, customers may become angry or lost due to untimely delivery of their orders. Developing growth within limitation or boundaries can allow the business to grow profitably and avoid spiraling pitfalls often present during unchecked growth.

Beyond financial realities, psychological factors must also be considered. People naturally resist change, and growth means change in the way jobs are performed and in the way that employees relate to each other. *Layers* of supervision creep in, and separation from the owner begins to occur. Informal atmospheres give way to structured rules. Once-existing cooperation may turn into either healthy or unhealthy competition in the work force. Segregation of the old employee from the new one may accompany the addition of new machines and new employees. Some individuals may not be able to adjust to the expanding conditions and may require replacement. New employees may be more costly to attract. Growth may require implementing new wage scales or bonus systems to successfully integrate the change into a fast-growing company. When understood and managed, personnel idiosyncrasies can be turned into powerful aids to assist in growth. Specific needs of current and additional personnel cannot be ignored in the growth-oriented company. There is no formula to calculate the "people cost" in growth, but these *hidden costs* can rise to exacerbate even the best designed plan.

It is normal, expected, and required that owners also change with growth. Frequently, an owner will not fully recognize his or her own strengths and limitations until trouble brews in the more conspicuous ways. A search for expansion capital can become overwhelming not only in terms of demands on an owner's time but also in terms of his or her waning attention to business. To remain effective, the owner/manager must critically analyze personal strengths and weaknesses as early as possible during the expansion process, concentrating on his or her own strengths, and then learn or enlist help to supplement areas of weakness. By far, the most common area of weakness found in the small, privately held business owner is his or her own lack of knowledge about the use of financial management tools. This lack of knowledge, according to U.S. government statistics, is the primary reason that so many small businesses fail. Controlled growth affords time for both owners and employees to learn, to adjust, and to gradually integrate with new methods and technology. Controlled growth affords time for essential planning.

In the end, the motivation to grow successfully comes back to rest on the *personal goals* of owners. If achieving wealth is a personal goal, then working "smart" will be much more productive than working hard; however, it takes hard work to attain the constant level of intuitiveness necessary to stay in control of the fast-paced, high-growth-oriented business. Nietzsche said, "Everyone has a path, although most of us don't listen to ourselves long enough to find out what it is." Dag Hammarskjold made famous the saying, "The longest journey is the journey inwards." And from a simpler life of the Chippewa medicine man, Sun Bear, "If your philosophy doesn't produce corn, I don't want to hear about it." Listen to yourself. Examine your shortcomings; learn what must be learned to achieve business and personal goals.

FINANCING GROWTH

Rapid sales growth has the tendency to weaken the debt-to-worth picture in the balance sheet, which, in turn, creates a financing dilemma for the bank that might otherwise provide a loan. Expansion capital must come from some source, and unless the owner is very well endowed, that capital will come from financial institutions. Therefore, the **name of the game** becomes, **"How fast can I grow sales without weakening my balance sheet picture?"** **"Should new debt be short term, long term, or infusions of investment capital, and how can I repay the new debt?"** There are sophisticated formulas for targeting sales growth to maintain, increase, or decrease current debt-to-worth ratios. These are important and useful formulas, primarily used to target necessary sales growth when compared with expected financing requirements. This growth will not dilute current balance sheet ratios or future levels of risk in borrowing. Larger, fast-growing companies will want to routinely apply these concepts in their long-range planning process. Bear in mind that while a formula may provide future sales targets, it may not fully evaluate a particular company's *capacity* for achieving those targets. Capacity is highly judgmental and calls upon the owner's thorough understanding of all that his or her equipment, facilities, and employees may be realistically capable of accomplishing, within the framework of existing means. For example, capacity may not be entirely filled, and formulas may not recognize this critical fact. Existing and new capacity must always be in the forefront while planning for growth. Example formulas are shown for reference; however, no actual calculations will be made. For readers with above average interest, more information on these formulas can be obtained from almost any accounting text found in local bookstores.

The following is an example formula to maintain the same debt-to-worth ratio:

$$\frac{(\text{Net Profit \%}) \left(1 + \dfrac{\text{Existing Debt}}{\text{Worth}}\right)}{\dfrac{\text{Variable Assets}}{\text{Sales}} - \left[(\text{Net Profit \%}) \left(1 + \dfrac{\text{Existing Debt}}{\text{Worth}}\right)\right]} = \frac{\text{Sales}}{\text{Growth \%}}$$

The following formula indicates sales growth necessary where no additional financing will be required:

$$\frac{\text{Net Profit \%}}{\dfrac{\text{Variable Assets}}{\text{Sales}} - \dfrac{\text{Variable Liabilities}}{\text{Sales}} - \text{Net Profit \%}} = \frac{\text{Projected Sales Growth \%}}{}$$

It has been my experience that the average small-business owner will be more interested in a *simpler* way of revealing to a bank that improving conditions are possible through sales growth.

Let's again examine the XYZ Company, where balance sheets and income statements can be found in the first few pages of Chapter 2. XYZ is a start-up firm involving *excess capacity* in both machines and manpower. The challenge is to fill capacity and to show evidence that the debt-to-worth ratio can be improved. We know from the dialogue provided that XYZ is suffering from a cash shortage and is under a heavy and poorly structured existing debt. We know that the safety ratio of 7.8 (debt to worth) already points to high risk for any bank who may be considering a loan request. If we meet our 12-month sales projections and secure new financing, we learn that we might reduce the debt-to-worth ratio to 2.6. Old debt comprising $79,944 of 90-day notes and $497,398 of three-year/12% long-term debt is proposed to be refinanced in a new long-term debt of $606,355 over five years at 9.5% interest. This new debt includes $28,993 of cash for working capital. XYZ has operated for 5 out of 12 months of their first year in business. The following is how a financial institution might review their proposal.

Equity Ratio

	12/31/94	5/31/94
Total Owner Equity	$243,404	$79,230
Total Assets	$878,239	$700,505
Equity Ratio	27.7%	11.3%

XYZ professes to gain a higher equity ratio and to reduce leverage by year end, *suggesting an increased rate of return on assets over the rate of interest paid to creditors.*

Number of Times Interest Earned

Banks, understandably, want to know that their investment is safe during the terms of a loan. Quite frequently, they expect *wide margins* of safety and above average assurance that a company will remain stable and solvent. Debt safety can be identified through the following ratio:

	12/31/94		5/31/94
Operating Income (before interest & income taxes)	$299,228	(divide by)	$ 1,774
Total Interest Expense	$ 71,208		$ 29,670
Times Interest Earned	4.2		0.06

The changing ratio shows progress toward safety. A ratio of 4.5 to 5.5 would be considered quite strong in many industries.

Debt Ratio

Banks want to see high levels of personal investments by owners.

	12/31/94	5/31/94
Total Liabilities	$634,835	$621,275
Total Assets	$878,239	$700,505
Debt Ratio	72.3%	88.7%

The lower the ratio, the more comfortable a bank is with an owner's level of personally contributed funds. Ratios of 35–45% are often expected. In the case of XYZ, the ratio, while decreasing, is still quite high. A condition for loan approval might require an owner to leave earnings in his or her company, as further protection against shrinkage of assets. It is likely that personal endorsements (pledge of all personally owned property) would also be required for securing the loan.

SUMMARY

A balance between assets, liabilities, and net worth are key to the successful financing of growth. Calculating the equity ratio, number of times interest earned, and debt ratio on a year-to-year basis will substantiate the historical experience in borrowing. What has been borrowed to date is fact. Now, how much more, if any, can be borrowed to fund growth? Wherever new assets must be purchased to increase sales, how much profit can be expected from increased sales to pay for these asset purchases? Will new sales and profits take two, three, or more years to pay for the new assets? What is the level of new sales and profits required to pay for the added debt? Difficult-to-grasp formulas forecast answers to several of these questions; however, these three simple ratios can provide nearly the same information. An upward trend in the debt ratio may indicate a decreasing prospect for future borrowing. Managing the business to allow amounts of after tax earnings to accumulate in retained earnings will increase the equity ratio.

A practical resolution to *any* question about adding business debt must be found in some future ability to pay debt back over a reasonable period of time. Growth of sales may not always be the best answer to growing or maintaining profits. Many lifestyle-type businesses will discover that increased efficiency through operations can produce better results. For example, a gradual lowering of debt load (payments) may have as much impact as more debt and greater sales. Occasionally, the blending of statements and elimination of duplication through acquisition of a competitor can accomplish greater growth than that of increased sales. No growth is worthwhile when the amount paid for that growth requires too long to pay back.

Financed growth makes predictable sense only when a balance between income and outflow and a balance between assets and debt can be maintained. Although bankers expect to see sales growing, they are much more concerned over safety of their loan. Increasing profit on essentially flat sales can be made acceptable to a bank when these three ratios indicate progress toward safety and ability to repay loans.

9

How to Deal with Banks

It's a fact! For significant loans to be granted by financial institutions, your business must show **how** these loans can be *paid back out of business cash flow*. Unless your business can provide reasonable *collateral* as safety for the bank's money, it is most likely that you will not get the loan! Bankers customarily seek **three sources** of repayment. They expect repayment of loans from cash flow of the business but usually require security for the unpaid principal in the form of pledged collateral. Most commercial bankers today also require *personal guarantees* from business owners. In the banker's eyes, the personal endorsement represents a psychological commitment by the owner to make a success of his or her business. If a loan fails, the bank will seek to recover their money through disposal of pledged collateral. When sale of collateral is inadequate to cover unpaid principal, the bank will seek restitution for the excess out of the owner's personal resources.

It is not the bank's initial intent or desire to go through foreclosure as a means of recovering their investment. Not only is the foreclosure proceeding costly, but unusual levels of failed loans trigger questions raised by stockholders and regulators in terms of the bank's ability to make safe decisions.

Banks, in reviewing loan applications, make lending decisions based on the **5 Cs of credit: character, capacity, capital, collateral, and conditions.** If an applicant's *character* and trust are in question, the bank will not work with them, no matter how good the deal might appear. *Capacity*

92

relates to a business's financial strength and track record. How much of your own personal *capital* is invested in the business plays into the evaluation as well. Banks are more apt to welcome you as a customer when there is a 70% loan to appraised *collateral* ratio. How the local and national economy affects business *conditions* will also be considered. Securing a commercial or business loan requires salesmanship and educating the bank.

Financial institutions are businesses first, before they are lending institutions. Think of their money as you would your product or service. Will you sell your products and services to someone who cannot or will not pay you? When you do accept business that seems a bit *risky,* what are the prevailing *features* and *benefits* that caused you to take that risk with a customer? Surely, it wasn't because of the customer being a *nice person.* More than likely, some factual, explainable feature or benefit was the reason for this decision. Financial institutions require logical, explainable, and tangible evidence that their product, money, can be returned at a profit, interest. It is the **responsibility** of the **business owner** or manager, not the bank, **to prove within reason** that such can be **achieved.** This proof is traditionally spelled out in a *business plan.*

The bottom-line decision *always* comes down to the business's *financials* and the collateral pledged. But do not neglect the dialogue portion of business plans. Educate by describing, explaining, or otherwise rationalizing historical and precipitous past and future actions. Be as convincing in your dialogue as you can be in person. Bear in mind, however, unless you find justifiable ways in the numbers to pay back a loan, then all the dialogue in the world will still be useless.

DISCOVERY! DISCOVERY! DISCOVERY!

In financial and accounting circles, the *process* of review is called DISCOVERY. For you, the businessperson, it is discovery of your own strengths and weaknesses. For the bank, it is discovery of reasonable proof that you are or are not correct in your assumptions. Both you and the bank have the *same tools* available for use in this process.

Discover what makes your specific business worth lending sums of money. Do you serve a unique or niche marketplace? What products or services are most profitable and why? What are you doing to increase sales of these more profitable items? Is growth sustainable for these items, and why do you believe this is true? What influences will competition have on future sales? What influence has competition played in past sales or profit? What industry or legislative changes do you foresee? Which of these changes will affect you the most and/or least? Why and how will your business survive into the future? Where in your financials can you support this belief? Each business will have strengths and weaknesses. **Concentrate on your strengths while writing the business plan!**

For existing businesses, the search and discovery process begins with historical financial statements. A review of case #2 in Chapter 2 will provide a beginning guide for analysis of your business. Do not stop with suggestions contained in this guide! Discovery is an endless process, and each business possesses its own character, capacity, and conditions. More often, the *real* character in small business is the *owner influence* over that particular business. Discover and explain the role that you have personally played in causing certain events to occur. What is it about you that will influence the business's future? What have you done in the past?

Discover what has been done poorly, less profitably, or not at all. What is your plan to correct the problem? When will the plan be implemented? What impact on business operations will the implemented plan make? All businesses have weaknesses as well as strengths. The prudent businessperson researches both. A wise man said, "Concentrate on your weaknesses—strengths will take care of themselves. Concentrate on your strengths, and strengths will join your weaknesses." I believe that businesspeople need to concentrate on both. *Improve* upon *weaknesses* and *capitalize* on *strengths.* Do not sidestep a full explanation of business weakness. More than likely, correcting a perceived weakness is the purpose for securing a loan. Outline the weakness, but capitalize on your plan to correct it. Translate into financial forecasts how the corrective plan will *positively impact* business operation. Educate! Educate! Educate!

A financial institution is at a disadvantage concerning information on your business. You are the chief supplier of information. When your information "hangs together" reliably, chances improve at getting the loan. Discovery through *research* and documentation supported by fact substantially increase information *believability.* The English philosopher Thomas Hobbes wrote in his *Leviathan:* "The best prophet naturally is the best guesser, and the best guesser (is) he that is most versed and studied in the matters he guesses at, for (it) is he (that) has the most signs to guess by."

Dialogue in the business plan must be about you and your business.

Dialogue must include assessment of you, the business, its customers, its suppliers, its creditors, its competition or industry, and its future. Dialogue must be convincingly supported by fact and/or *educated guesses* into the future, called **forecasts.** Significant loans are rarely granted without convincing financial forecasts that are explained in the dialogue and supported by convictions of owners.

For the newly formed business or *start-up,* the task of discovery lies in *research of what has been done by others.* A review of case #1 in Chapter 2 will provide beginning reference. A new venture or start-up business is often the more difficult project to finance. Financial institutions simply are more comfortable when historical performance exists to support any lending decision they make. The challenge of discovery lies in researching industry and prospective competitor experiences. Industry information may be more easily obtained; however, competitor data is conspicuously unavailable. If you have not already selected an accountant or consultant to represent you, it may be wise to telephone several firms, asking if they represent clients within your field. Industry associations occasionally provide lists of accounting professionals who specialize in their industry. Some consulting and accounting firms maintain data banks on selected industries or represent clients in similar firms. While actual financial information is confidential and not available for public use, when translated into percentages or ratios, the range of experiences can greatly enhance the reliability in any projections you propose.

If an idea or product has significant inventive or technical merit or serves a specialized niche marketplace, venture capital may be the best source to approach. These venture groups, however, very seldom provide capital to more traditional or customary small business. When extended, venture capital is generally infused through some form of ownership in the firm. Often, the venture group expects to withdraw their ownership, principal, and earnings by the end of the third, fourth, or fifth year. Venture capital firms provide both cash and management expertise and can play a major role in the growth of a company. Mr. Kenneth Olsen and Digital Equipment Corporation represent a large and classic example of a successful union between inventor and venture capitalist.

For the most part, the average start-up entrepreneur will be left confronted with the extraordinary task of providing evidence to banks that he or she can succeed with the new idea or product. If a concept has merit, evidence can be found to support its inception. Research and documentation represent much of the key to securing a loan. Conviction on the parts of entrepreneurs represent the remainder of the key. *Focus on re-searching reliable sources, document findings, forecast conclusions, and mea-sure against existing skills.*

SUMMARY

Always, when working with bankers, keep focused on the fact that they are businesspeople *before* they are lenders. Their product or service is money on which they expect to make their profit. Like you, they also expect to get paid, on time, for their business work. Frequently, banks are publicly owned, with *stockholders* who expect returns on investments. Banks operate under *regulations* from state and federal governments. Managements and employees of banks have obligations to stockholders for returning profits, and they must follow regulations to stay in business. When a loan request is denied, it is usually not a personal matter. It is, however, often about ability. Ability to repay the loan. Ability to provide a return to stockholders. It is also about responsibility. Responsibility to follow regulations, to other customers, to employees, and to stay in business. These elements take precedence in every loan decision. The connotation implied in the term "friendly banker" is a myth! The banker may actually be and usually is friendly; however, his or her obligation and responsibility is to the bank, **not** to the borrower. Lose sight of this fact and chances are good that you will lose control of your application and not secure the loan.

Contrary to some negative belief, *bankers are actually looking for reasons to grant a loan.* Money is their *inventory,* and just as with your business, the bank cannot make a profit if this inventory is not sold in the form of loans. Good bankers are *major assets* to most businesses.

Most businesses relish debt to some degree and for several reasons. The first reason is that it is difficult, if not impossible, to accumulate sufficient capital to pay for all assets in one fell swoop. The second reason is found in an investment principle: "If you can make a profitable dollar off someone else's money, irrespective of cost, then why use your own money?" Banks survive and profit off this concept of "*leverage*." Businesses more often cannot survive without reasonable levels of leverage.

The obligation and responsibility of businesspeople is to **prove** the **need** and to **prove** the **payback**. Bankers, by their nature and responsibility, are acutely focused in on financial data. Don't waste time on business plan dialogue until your financial statements, past and forecast, justify what you want to accomplish. Then add dialogue to the business plan to explain what you have done, are doing, and will do to achieve expected performance, and pay back the loan.

For a business loan to be secured, chances are at least, to coin an old phrase of magnitude, 90:1 that the only significant communication with the **bank,** the **decisive** communication, will be a detailed, **written business plan.** *Count on it! Plan for it!* Formulate and execute a business plan when working with bankers and other financial institutions. This is how to work effectively with banks: first as educator through the business plan, then as salesperson, displaying your verbal convictions.

10

Valuation of a Going Concern

PREAMBLE

Around 1771, French writer Francois-Marie Arouet Voltaire wrote that in order to effectively communicate, man must "define thy terms." In business valuation, which is partly art and partly science, Voltaire's reference to defining terms is particularly important to bear in mind.

Business valuation, in reference to its art form, demands awareness of people's cognitive nature. Among other psychological factors that must be examined, **purpose** becomes the point of beginning. What is the purpose of the business valuation assignment? What is the *primary* purpose of the party or parties who initiate business valuation? I dwell on this element of purpose for good reasons. While the science form of mathematics is precise, the manipulative science form of statistics is not. Irrespective of the precision found in the science of mathematics to solve for unknowns, man created from a disciplined imperium a vaguer new science called statistics, to solve for *variables and unknowns.* We have, perhaps, all heard of similar stories about the statistician's ability to "lie" with numbers. Mind you, however, I am not suggesting that statisticians do intentionally lie. I am simply referring to a well-known fact that when humans can organize material for personal or for another's advantage, they sometimes do lie. Little, if any, manipulation can occur in mathematics, where formulas are well established for precisely solving an unknown. Therefore, we can safely conclude that there is **vagueness** in the *artistic* portion, **preciseness** in the *math* portion, and **variableness** in the *statistics* portion of business valuation. These human frailty and more scientific aspects must all be considered for a successful conclusion to the valuation assignment.

Webster's New World Dictionary of the American Language defines valuation as "The determining of the value of anything, **determined** or **estimated** value." The distinction between determined and estimated is particularly important to bear in mind when seeking the value of a business. A value is **precisely** determined when parties actually complete a transaction. Up to this point, value can only be estimated and remains essentially vague. Most business valuation assignments, regardless of who produces them, are estimations of value. Little need continues for the business valuation exercise when a value has been determined by market transaction.

From our daily lives, we all have had the experience of possibly wanting some object but not buying it because we felt that it was too expensive in our individual judgment. Too expensive might have been a reflection from our own pocketbook. The price may have been fair . . . but simply beyond our own financial reach. However, if a large number of prospective buyers have this same problem or just feel that the object is too highly priced or not desirable at that price, the object may not sell over a long period of time or not at all. In a free economy, estimated value, therefore, equals **perceived** value in the eyes of the beholder. How each of us perceives this value will always be different. Too high, too low, or just right are all individual perceptions of value, until a marketplace determines just which perception is accurate.

In product or service marketing, accuracy of perceptions or estimates are *refined* through techniques of **market research.** If we produce and expose product A to the market at X dollars, what is the probability (a statistical tool) that A will sell? Will we sell enough of A? Will we be able to sell A profitably? Market research can be incredibly reliable in refining the accuracy of forecast events.

Accuracy in estimating *value for a smaller business* can be substantially improved through market research. This holds true to a lesser degree for the large giants, such as General Motors. General Motors enjoys sales in excess of $12 million per hour. The company is likely to exist for many years into the future. It is unlikely that anyone possesses sufficient cash or buying power to purchase this company individually. Many individuals in corporate unison, on both the buying and selling sides, might participate in a value decision. Market research might be hard pressed to measure unison or composite thinking quite as accurately as in measuring the reactions of the individual as primary decision maker.

Whether value is being estimated for eventual sale or not, knowledge about both *buyer and seller mentality* is critical to the valuation of smaller businesses. Smaller business is defined herein as any business where all principal decisions are made exclusively by owners who control all or the vast majority of the ownership. Carried further, this definition also includes businesses where major decision making is essentially an individual process, and checks and balances rest also within that same individual.

Let's look at an example of how mentality might affect the smaller-business valuation. A few years ago, I was approached by the owner of a *garbage removal business,* who was considering retirement. The business was comprised of 15 large, ten-wheeler dumpster trucks. Well-maintained assets exceeded one million dollars in value. The owner personally earned in excess of $200,000 per year in each of the past eight years. The business was 35 years old and enjoyed a captive market. Reflecting a capital-intense business, few new businesses might competitively enter the field. It was obvious that this business had earned more than a token value and that it would require several hundred thousand dollars as cash deposit to purchase this business. Consider several *mentality issues:* First, it's a fact that the personal accumulation of several hundred thousand dollars usually requires above average ingenuity. Second, persons with these amounts of funds traditionally seek a more "appealing" business. Third, people from higher levels of wealth often enjoy the cocktail circuit and *need* the self-esteem generated by what they do for a living. Finally, while this business's income-generating value appeals to affluent buyers, the *nature* of the business itself does not. What then is this business's value?

In this scenario, the *asset/income value* of the business has not changed, but the *market value* is clearly an unknown. When valuing the smaller business, the *degree of desirability,* determined by the nature of the business itself, must be a realistic consideration in establishing value. Pure accounting approaches can produce ineffective and unreliable estimates of value, especially with regards to purchase/sale scenarios involving unrelated parties.

To summarize, when an owner of a smaller business wants to know what the market value of his or her business might be, the purpose or use of the ultimate answer must be determined first. If a sale to an unrelated party is contemplated, then the answer given might be twofold: asset/income value is estimated at *A*, and market value is estimated at *Y*. If a

sale is contemplated to a related party, the ultimate answer might be somewhere between A and Υ, recognizing some related involvement. If the
purpose is for insurance, inheritance, or partnership reasons, the value may
not resemble either A or Υ but become $A - / +$ or $\Upsilon - / +$. Answers to
the estimated value of any business are **variable** but can be refined by
purpose and **knowledge of the marketplace** involving the specific business. **Actual value** can only be **determined** by completed **arms-length
transactions.**

DILEMMA PRESENTED BY METHODS OR FORMULAS

In mathematics, formulas are established, and practitioners routinely apply
the same formula rule. The variable rule of statistics offers the dilemma
presented in business valuation. I wonder if anyone really knows just how
many methods of business valuation actually exist. Perhaps as many different methods as there are practicing business valuators: rules-of-thumb
methods, discounted cash flow methods, book value methods, adjusted
book value methods, excess earnings methods, comparison methods, and
on and on. To these, practitioners have modified, amended, abridged, or
otherwise changed methods to *fit* their own rationale. The **actual method
of valuation** may not be as important as the **tracking system** employed
to **refine accuracies** in the estimate of the value being rendered.

It is not my intent to provide opinions on various methods employed,
because *how* one arrives at value is unimportant. What is important is that
estimated value itself be accurately reflected in and by the realism of purpose as well as the marketplace in which a particular business exists. I will,
however, mention something about the method called *discounted cash
flow*. This method is often considered the "best" by many astute practitioners. When parameters are fully understood, this method can be among
the best and more often is the method of choice when valuing a large
business. Without going into finite description, the method calls for valuing *future* years of *earnings*. All well and good for companies such as
General Motors, where future earnings are more than reasonably assured.
Recalling the statistical fact that 80% of all small businesses fail within their
first ten years should be reason enough to question the product of any
method that evaluates value in the context of earnings five, six, or ten
years out. Perhaps it is only in my perception of the value of the smaller

business, but I personally have great difficulty conceptualizing a future earnings value in businesses that traditionally struggle from year to year. I believe that a value, when established on future and questionable earnings, becomes difficult, if not impossible, to sell to the average small-business person. Granted, people buy because they expect to earn from future value, but in the smaller business, that future value belongs to the future owner. The method of estimating value is not important if the end result can predict reasonably close to that value estimate. A primary approach employed by my firm is through a **modified hybrid excess earnings method.** This method is neither better nor worse than any other method; it is simply our method of choice for valuation of the smaller business.

A BUSINESS VALUATION EXERCISE

Our sample valuation case, ABC Company, is a manufacturing concern, established for some years, and both product and business rank fairly high on the scale of desirability in terms of buyer acceptance. The purpose of the valuation is to estimate market value for prospective sale of the business. The process of valuation begins with financial analysis of balance sheets and income statements, as presented in Chapter 2. For reference in this exercise, statements are again reproduced, but the previous analysis is not.

ABC COMPANY
Balance Sheet
As of December 31

	1991	1992	1993
ASSETS			
Current Assets			
Cash in Banks	$ 69,726	$ 9,646	$ 48,744
Accounts Receivable	182,696	303,513	248,976
Allow Doubtful Accts	− 5,500	− 10,000	− 6,000
Advances to Owner	2,619	16,289	—
Cash Investments	25,356	5,000	—

	1991	1992	1993
Inventory	185,958	197,668	171,128
Total Current Assets	$460,855	$522,116	$462,848
Property and Equipment			
Leasehold Improvements	$ 12,629	$ 12,629	$ 16,144
Furniture & Equipment	58,606	63,802	86,842
Vehicles	6,350	6,350	6,350
Subtotal	$ 77,585	$ 82,781	$109,336
Less: Accum./Deprec.	52,466	63,628	80,001
Total Property & Equip.	$ 25,119	$ 19,153	$ 29,335
Other Assets			
Cash Value—Life Ins.	$ 4,017	$ 8,477	$ 7,690
Total Other Assets	$ 4,017	$ 8,477	$ 7,690
TOTAL ASSETS	**$489,991**	**$549,746**	**$499,873**

LIABILITIES & EQUITY

	1991	1992	1993
Current Liabilities			
Note—Bank	$ —	$138,000	$ —
Accounts Payable	183,897	211,610	176,943
Accrued Taxes	33,977	9,331	4,133
Accrued Retirement	—	—	18,136
Total Current Liability	$217,874	$358,941	$199,212
Noncurrent Liabilities			
Note—Owner	$124,965	—	$ 67,599
Total Noncurrent Liab.	$124,965	$ —	$ 67,599
TOTAL LIABILITIES	**$342,839**	**$358,941**	**$266,811**

STOCKHOLDER EQUITY

	1991	1992	1993
Capital Stock	$ 15,000	$ 15,000	$ 15,000
Retained Earnings	77,135	132,153	175,806
Net Income/Loss	55,017	43,652	42,256
Total Equity	$147,152	$190,805	$233,062
TOTAL LIABILITIES & EQUITY	**$489,991**	**$549,746**	**$499,873**

ABC Company
Income and Loss Statement
As of December 31

	1991	1992	1993
Net Sales	$1,482,349	$1,495,464	$1,752,729
Cost of Sales	742,664	851,227	964,080
Gross Profit	$ 739,685	$ 644,237	$ 788,649
% Gross Profit	**49.9%**	**43.1%**	**45.0%**
Expenses			
Salaries & Wages	$ 72,067	$ 85,168	$ 134,660
Payroll Taxes	2,349	6,217	8,843
Advertising & Promo	21,616	53,220	46,096
Auto & Travel	19,899	19,169	35,490
Bad Debt & Collection	10,460	6,711	**27,165**
Commissions	34,507	55,940	49,241
Contributions/Dues	2,908	2,192	1,719
Insurance	17,394	16,860	11,681
Office/Postage	27,190	30,172	25,429
Professional Fees	5,125	6,392	**16,732**
Rent—Equipment	—	—	4,086
Repairs/Maintenance	7,629	5,780	8,977
Show Expense	29,412	53,247	50,495
Taxes—Other	4,977	2,099	1,202
Telephone/Electric	9,214	13,388	17,281
Utilities	1,957	3,196	3,654
Misc. Expense	218	2,878	3,742
Subtotal Expense	$ 266,922	$ 362,629	$ 446,493
Owner's Salary	**344,060**	**133,700**	**201,628**
Payroll Tax	11,246	9,737	13,105
Depreciation	16,127	11,162	16,373
Office Life Ins.	1,096	14,540	16,251
Director Fees	—	**10,000**	—
Interest Expense	9,813	10,028	8,386
Rent Expense	**24,000**	30,000	**24,000**
Property Tax	—	1,954	4,025
Retirement Plan	—	—	**19,324**
Total Expenses	$ 673,264	$ 583,750	$ 749,585
Add: Other Income	7,596	1,665	21,192
Net Income before Tax	$ 74,017	$ 62,152	$ 60,256
Less: Income Taxes	19,000	18,500	18,000
Net Income/Loss	$ 55,017	$ 43,652	$ 42,256
As Percent of Sales	3.7%	2.9%	2.4%

What Is Being Sold?

When a thorough review of the financial statements has been completed, the next step is to determine what assets and liabilities of the business are actually being sold.

We learn through discussions with the owner that he would like to retain the real estate. The owner will lease the facilities at $24,000 per year over the next five years. Two options to extend the lease for five more years will also be provided. Each year of the options will be adjusted for inflation by changes in the consumer price index. The lease will require all expenses, including real estate taxes and internal maintenance, to be paid by the tenant.

The owner will liquidate debt, with the exception of accounts payables, as well as remove stockholder equity.

The balance sheet provides a starting point for review of other assets being proposed for sale. Although the most current balance sheet is stated as December, 1993, during this exercise we will assume that this statement accurately reflects account balances as of the time of our valuation report.

Careful observation of the assets of ABC Company reveals an important consideration. Hard assets of leasehold improvements, furniture, fixtures, and vehicles total $109,336; inventory totals $171,128, for an overall total of $280,464. General review of cash flow statements suggests the possibility that business value might be much higher than the hard asset value and will create a bank financing dilemma. It must be recognized that the concept of leverage is well understood by both buyers and sellers and that buyers are rarely willing to pay more than 20–30% of the purchase in cash. Few buyers, if any, are willing to make up the entire spread between bank financing and purchase price in cash. With this precept in mind, it appears likely that the seller may have to hold some part of the sale price in a second mortgage position. *What can be done to reduce the seller's amount of secondary financing?*

Although many small-business owners will sell only inventory and hard assets, it is important to remember that the purchase of cash, accounts receivables, and accounts payables provides both business continuity and working capital to the new owner, as well as additional assets toward financing. Thorough study of accounts to determine whether an asset or liability will be incurred is always indicated. For the purpose of this exercise, the accounts are deemed current and reliable.

To potentially reduce the amount of seller financing, the owner has agreed on the following assets and liability to be offered for sale:

ABC Company
For Sale Balance Sheet
As of December 31, 1993
(Assumed as at time of valuation)

ASSETS

Current Assets

Cash in Banks	$ 48,744
Accounts Receivables	248,987
Allowance for Doubtful Accounts	(6,000)
Inventory	171,128
Total Current Assets	$ 462,848

Property & Equipment

Leasehold Improvements	$ 16,144
Furniture & Equipment	86,842
Vehicle	6,350
Total Property & Equipment	$ 109,336
TOTAL ASSETS FOR SALE	$ 572,184

LIABILITIES

Accounts Payable	$ 176,943
TOTAL LIABILITIES FOR SALE	$ 176,943
UNDEPRECIATED EQUITY	**$ 395,241**
TOTAL LIABILITIES & EQUITY FOR SALE	$ 572,184

Financing conditions, through an increase in assets being sold, have been improved by $114,777, from $280,464 to $395,241. Important to note is that working capital is now being provided for within the transaction and on a long-term financing basis. Granted, a purchaser could secure a line-of-credit loan; however, these lines traditionally afford use of capital during 11 months out of 12-month periods. When structured as provided in this example, longer-term use of working capital provides another positive edge for the new entrepreneur. Purchasing both receivables and payables provides psychological continuity for vendors and customers.

Once what is being sold has been established, we can next proceed with analysis of cash flow and the valuation exercise. For purpose of this exercise, balance sheet items are stated at their *fair market value.*

INCOME ANALYSIS

The following text will explain the rather unusual layout for the income and loss statement. You may recall several references to the role of managements in business. The *financial management* of the privately owned business is often to minimize the tax implications of the bottom line, whereas the financial management of public companies is to provide profit for stockholders. Therefore, it is important to the valuation assignment to fully understand **what** is being done by the private owner with his or her tax consequent numbers of the business. These, when determined, must be **reconstructed** to **conform** with what is *usual and customary* or conform with a new set of parameters.

ITEMS FOR RECONSTRUCTION

This part of the exercise is for identification and removal. The second part will be to determine what is usual and customary and to insert a possible new buyer scenario. Note the following items:

1. An owner's personal consumption of business products or services offered can affect cost of goods sold, sales, and gross profits. The owner of ABC Company made no personal use of business profits, and therefore, no reconstruction was deemed necessary.

2. Auto and travel expense might be of trivial amounts or may contain significant expenditures for personal enjoyment. This expense item in our case study was all made for company benefit. No reconstruction was considered.

3. Commission expense contained approximately 50% paid to a related party. Further examination revealed that the *job was necessary* to business sales and that the amount paid was *usual and customary* for work of this type being performed. Therefore, no reconstruction was necessary in our case study. Care must be exercised to exclude situations of "make work," where children or spouses of owners are paid but do not necessarily perform equivalent work related to an essential job in the company's business.

4. Insurance expense contained an item for $350 per month of health care insurance for the owner. Since this amount might be consid-

ered usual and customary for *any* person performing the management task, the expense was not excluded or considered necessary to reconstruct.

5. Professional fees, repairs, maintenance, telephone, utility, and miscellaneous expenses are notorious for containing personally used items. Thorough examination of expense *significance* must be made and a reconstruction included wherever indicated. ABC Company is operated without personal expense inclusion in these items. Professional fees in 1993, however, included an extraordinary and onetime charge of $10,000 for consulting, which must be removed.

6. Owner's salary and payroll tax are often the most significant variable to the bottom line in private companies. Frequently, salary is based upon profit versus any comparable market worth for the job of managing the company. These must be removed from the equation for the time being.

7. Depreciation is a product of *original prices* paid by an owner. In a purchase/sale scenario, a new value for assets most likely will be clarified by the details of transaction, and new schedules for depreciation will be established. Depreciation must be removed for reconstruction at a later point in the valuation exercise. The valuation of a business for reasons other than sale might suggest that depreciation allotment remains as incurred.

8. Officer life insurance carried on an owner by a privately owned company can frequently be extraordinary in its face value amount. Subsequently, premiums can be higher than those traditionally provided for management of the publicly owned counterpart. The ABC Company carries a $400,000 face value life insurance policy on the owner, and the cost of this must be initially removed from the equation.

9. Director fees paid are more apt to be found in the larger-sized company, but they are uncommonly paid in companies the size of ABC. When exhibited, they frequently turn out to be another form of compensation to a party who is related to the owner. Such was the case in our sample study and therefore must be removed entirely for the business valuation exercise.

10. Interest expense is a product of the present company's debt structure. In the purchase/sale scenario, mortgage and equipment fi-

nancing will most likely change, and the new interest expense will be reflected in the final judgment of value. The valuation of a business for reasons other than sale might suggest that this expense remain as incurred. Since ABC is being held out for sale, interest expense must be initially removed.

11. Rent expense must be thoroughly examined for conditions of business owner involvement. If the real property has been "arm's-length" leased from an unrelated party, then the expense may require full inclusion. However, if the real property is owned by the specific business, or through ownership separate from the business but by the same owner, an assessment must be undertaken of comparable rental rates for the community where the business is operating, and these comparable findings must be used in lieu of "booked" rent expense. The owner of ABC Company personally owned the real estate, but comparable rates indicated a fair payment of rent at $24,000 per year.

12. Property taxes will occasionally include personal property taxes of owner's residences. This was not the case for ABC Company, and therefore, property taxes were left in as reported.

13. Retirement plan expenses of $19,324 during 1993 were found to be substantially available only to the owner and members of the family. To avoid lengthy tax and legal implication, according to ABC's accountant and lawyer, the method employed would meet IRS scrutiny. The amount was treated as personal salary and removed from the valuation exercise.

These items comprise the subsequent adjustments used in the recasting of income statements for the ABC Company, which follows. Other income related to interest received from cash deposits and sale of equipment. Other income in the case of ABC Company was not considered germane to the business valuation assignment and therefore was removed from reconstructed cash flow.

ABC Company
Income and Loss Statement (Reconstructed)
As of December 31

	1991	1992	1993
Net Sales	$1,482,349	$1,495,464	$1,752,729
Cost of Sales	742,664	851,227	964,080
Gross Profit	$ 739,685	$ 644,237	$ 788,649
% Gross Profit	49.9%	43.1%	45.0%
Expenses			
Salaries & Wages	$ 72,067	$ 85,168	$ 134,660
Payroll Taxes	2,349	6,217	8,843
Advertising & Promo	21,616	53,220	46,096
Auto & Travel	19,899	19,169	35,490
Bad Debt & Collection	10,460	6,711	27,165
Commissions	34,507	55,940	49,241
Contributions/Dues	2,908	2,192	1,719
Insurance	17,394	16,860	11,681
Office/Postage	27,190	30,172	25,429
Professional Fees	5,125	6,392	10,732
Rent—Equipment	—	—	4,086
Repairs/Maintenance	7,629	5,780	8,977
Show Expense	29,412	53,247	50,495
Taxes—Other	4,977	2,099	1,202
Telephone/Electric	9,214	13,388	17,281
Utilities	1,957	3,196	3,654
Misc. Expense	218	2,878	3,742
Rent Expense	24,000	30,000	24,000
Property Tax	—	1,954	4,025
Total Expenses	$ 290,922	$ 394,583	$ 468,518
Net Income/Loss before taxes, depreciation, interest, and owner salary**	$ 448,763	$ 249,654	$ 320,131
As Percent of Sales	30.3%	16.7%	18.3%

**Reconstructed income or cash flow.

The valuation process involves adding back comparable (market rate) amounts of salaries, insurance, interest, and depreciation as soon as they are estimated. Interest and depreciation elements are estimated during the method's process; however, salary and insurance can be reasonably estimated through calls to employment or insurance agencies. The following were indicated for the ABC Company:

Net Income (loss) before taxes, depreciation, interest, and owner salary**	$ 448,763	$ 249,654	$ 320,131
Less: Comp./Salary	54,000	58,000	60,000
Less: Life Insurance	3,500	3,700	3,900
Net Income (loss) before taxes, depreciation, and interest, **but after salaries**	$ 391,263	$ 187,954	$ 256,231

**Reconstructed income or cash flow.

At this point, consideration can be given for a current and incomplete year. Often, this is accomplished by *forecasting* for the remaining balance of a year, reflecting a *most likely* statement of earnings. Without going through the numbers, let's assume that the forecast 1994 year for the ABC Company reveals $269,118 of net income before taxes, depreciation, and interest, but after insertion of comparable salaries.

Attempting to value each year's individual stream of cash is cumbersome and may not produce the desired end result. A formula that takes average earnings into consideration is usually more productive in reaching a single indication of value from the average stream of cash. All weighting processes are arbitrary to some extent, but then this is where seasoned judgment comes into play.

In this exercise, I will use a weight of 1 to represent the oldest year, suggesting that this year has the least impact on value. A weighting of 2 will represent the next oldest, 3 for the next, and 4 for the current and pro forma year—in essence, weighting the most current periods the heaviest.

$$
\begin{array}{rlrl}
1991 & = \$391{,}263 & (1) & = \$\ \ 391{,}263 \\
1992 & = \$187{,}954 & (2) & = \$\ \ 375{,}908 \\
1993 & = \$256{,}231 & (3) & = \$\ \ 768{,}693 \\
\text{Pro Forma } 1994 & = \$269{,}118 & \underline{(4)} & = \underline{\$1{,}076{,}472} \\
\end{array}
$$

The product of weights and dollars are   10 & $2,612,336

The total of weighted cash streams equals $2,612,336, which is then divided by 10, producing a weighted average earnings of $261,234. In this example, $261,234 equals a cash stream below the 1991 level but slightly greater than the stream actually produced in the last completed year of 1993. Compelling arguments can be made at this point for any initiatives being taken that will improve cash flow, but from our financial analysis of ABC Company, we see that ABC Company is laboring under moderate degrees of difficulty. The amount of $261,234 of weighted average earnings appears to be a reasonable place for departure into the valuation process.

THE VALUATION EXERCISE

Business Valuation Worksheet

Name of Business: ABC Company
Owner: Mr. ABC
Analysis by: W. M. Yegge
Date: July 5, 1994
Reason for Analysis: Possible Sale

Cash flow reconstructed net operating income before taxes, interest, and depreciation, but after comparable salaries (weighted)	$ 261,234
Less: asset replacement reserve	5,000
Less: contingency reserve	10,000
Net cash stream to be valued	**$ 246,234**
Cost of Money	
Market value of real estate	$ N/A
Market value of other tangible assets (not including inventory or WC)	$ 152,080
Book value of inventory	171,128
Working capital requirements (usually A/R less A/P)	72,033
Total Tangible Asset Value	$ 395,241

Times: Applied lending rate	× 9.5%
Annual cost of money	$ 37,548
Excess of Cost of Earnings	
Return net operating income	$ 246,234
Less: Annual cost of money	37,548
Excess of cost of earnings	$ 208,686

Intangible Business Value

Intangible business value is a highly judgmental aspect of business valuation and requires conscientious attention. The IRS roughly defines intangible value, or goodwill, as that amount paid for a business in excess of the market value of hard assets. Numerous rating schemes have been developed through the years to determine intangible value. Many provide logic to the rationale and assist in developing more *defendable* values for the parties involved. In the final analysis, however, technical competence and experienced financial judgment must win out. We use the following simply as a guide. The final value judgment must meet tests of cash flow analysis, but at this point in the valuation exercise, we do not know what that value number is to be.

Professional service organizations, such as physicians, lawyers, accountants, consultants, etc., are among the more difficult types of businesses for which to establish an intangible value. Practitioner characteristics, personalities, and *reputation* play heavily into the generation of cash streams. Take the specific practitioner out of the business, and the cash stream will quite often suffer considerably. A fundamental question, therefore: How much business value is directly attributable to a "person," and how much of that value will remain if he or she leaves? To the unwary, this can present the classic dilemma of "getting lost in the numbers." Subsequently, the purchase of a "sole practitioner" business can be much more risky than the purchase of a business with multiple practitioners who remain after the purchase. These "people" or owner-restrictive element can be present in all types of businesses and, with safety in mind, cannot be overlooked. A "business continuation" risk tends to decrease with increasing size of staff and, when the present owner is more separated from *practice work,* by the demands of administrative duty.

Service businesses in general, unless cash flow is quite substantial, tend rarely to command a net multiplier greater than 3.0. Many will fall below 2.5.

On the far side of the spectrum, we might find "asset-intense" businesses, such as motels and other operations, where significant investments in machinery, equipment, and physical plants are present. These type of businesses frequently sell their "wares" to customers who tend to be less "attached" to owners. Bear in mind also that hard assets will comprise most of the financing collateral for loans and that "market value" is substantially influenced by *prevailing economies.* **An existing bank "climate" will affect market value.** Additional cash and/or attractive seller financing will generally be required to make up the difference when purchase prices above market values are contemplated.

Businesses of this type can often be assigned net multipliers of 5.0 to 8.0. But, as I say in my firm, "only God gets 8.0."

Most small businesses will fall in the net multiplier range between 2.0 and 5.0. These are the mainstay small operations in America—restaurants, grocery stores, retail operations, small wholesalers, small manufacturers, and also many service businesses.

From this discussion, it could be concluded that a higher hard asset value might translate into a lower intangible value (net multiplier range). In the reverse, a low asset value might then bring a higher net multiplier range. Quite often this assumption turns out to be true. However, the element of cash flow, frequently a reason for purchase, would then be ignored. In choosing an intangible net multiplier, one must clearly decide what part of value is tangible (hard assets) and what part of value is intangible (goodwill, as defined by the IRS).

The physical or "touchable" portion of intangible value is partially revealed in the cash stream. Some part of the stream pays for human and physical assets in the form of outflow to cover expenses, including debt service and a return to an owner. What's remaining as "excess" or flows over and above these costs might therefore be viewed as cash flow, leading to assignment of intangible values. Applying this logic, little or no excess subsequently equals little or no intangible value and vice versa. Every business with an operating history has some intangible or goodwill value. Sometimes this intangible value is equal to the value of hard assets, and sometimes it is greater than the value of hard assets. Discerning a difference is key in establishing intangible value—one that can be "sold" at arm's length and outside of the definition laid down by the IRS.

The charts on pages 116 and 117 (Figures 1 and 2) may provoke insight and provide guidance.

I apologize for this interruptive dialogue during the valuation exercise; however, it is at this precise point where some people tend to lose sight of the overall process of business valuation. For nearly 30 years I have wrestled with the question, What is business value?, and to this day, assignment of intangible value in small business remains the more perplexing task. There simply is no "pat" answer or formula. My way is neither right nor wrong, and the task is not really made easier with experience. If I have learned one common essential, it would be "exercise *caution*" in assigning intangible value and throughout the whole process.

In this case of our example, ABC Company, we have selected a net multiplier of 3.0. Hard assets are relatively low, but cash flow is essentially strong.

a. Intangible net multiplier assigned	3.0
b. Multiple excess of cost of earnings	$ 208,686
Intangible business value (a × b)	**$ 626,058**
Add: Tangible asset value	$ 395,241
Less: Working capital requirement	$ N/A*
TOTAL BUSINESS VALUE	$1,021,299

*To be included when working capital must be provided from outside sources. In the case of ABC, working capital is being purchased with other assets.

FINANCING RATIONAL

Total investment	$1,021,299
Less: Downpayment	200,000
Balance to be financed	**$ 821,299***

(Assumed terms of 9.5% interest, financed over 20 years)

Amount:	$821,299
Monthly payment:	$ 7,656
Annual payment:	**$ 91,872**

*Some portion, perhaps as much as $580,000, may be necessarily provided in owner financing.

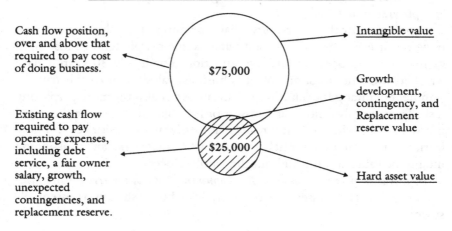

EXAMPLE A: *Assumed Total Business Value $100,000*

Cash flow position, over and above that required to pay cost of doing business.

$75,000

Intangible value

Growth development, contingency, and Replacement reserve value

Existing cash flow required to pay operating expenses, including debt service, a fair owner salary, growth, unexpected contingencies, and replacement reserve.

$25,000

Hard asset value

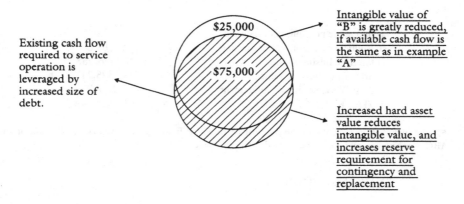

EXAMPLE B: *Assumed Total Business Value $100,000*

$25,000

Intangible value of "B" is greatly reduced, if available cash flow is the same as in example "A"

Existing cash flow required to service operation is leveraged by increased size of debt.

$75,000

Increased hard asset value reduces intangible value, and increases reserve requirement for contingency and replacement

If the profits in example B were substantially increased, the "rings" might more resemble those presented in example A and total business value might increase proportionately. A lessor cash flow in example B, might present little or no room for intangible value, and might in fact, present inadequate returns for more than a "net asset sale." In other terms, insufficient cash flow provided to appropriately cover the cost/value of hard assets.

Figure 1. High/low hard asset effect on intangible business value when the cash stream is equal.

Typical Businesses	*Net Multiplier*	One Or More Considerations
<u>Professional services</u>, i.e., physician, dentist, attorney, accountant, optometrist, architect, engineer, chiropractor, veterinarian, real estate, insurance, etc.	1.0–1.9	• Earnings relatively flat • Dependent upon skill of owner • Fierce competition • Labor versus capital intense • Low hard assets • Start-up requires minimum capital outlay
<u>Other services</u>, i.e., advertising, funeral, entertainment, laundry, transportation hauling, printing, restaurant, janitorial, beauty salon, travel, employment agency, leasing services, etc. <u>Contractors</u>, i.e., general, electrical, plumbing and A/C, painting, masonry, etc. <u>Retail</u>, i.e., computer, equipment, fuel oil, gift, video, stereo and TV, apparel, office supply, drug, general merchandise, food/beverage, liquor, florists, jewelry, sporting goods, floor covering, hardware, auto, etc. <u>Wholesale</u>, i.e., building materials and supplies, food/beverage, auto supplies, electrical and plumbing supplies, etc. <u>Manufacturing</u>, leased facilities and modest equipment investment.	2.0–3.5	• Average growth of earnings • Skill of owner important but replaceable with short-term training • Expected amount of competition • Labor/capital intenseness mixed • Modest investment in hard assets in relationship to cash stream • Start-up requires larger cash position and larger amounts of working capital
	3.6–5.0	• Significant growth of earnings • Skill factor more removed in administrative versus "hands-on," high degree of transferability • Virtually no competition • Asset base high, requiring large initial cash outlay • Start-up costly in terms of up-front costs
<u>Services</u>, i.e., motel, nursing home, parent bank, parent insurance, hospital, etc. <u>Retail and manufacturing</u> owned real estate and large inventory and/or equipment investment.	5.1–8.0	• Predictable growth or stability of earnings • Operating skills transferable with education and/or minimal training • Expected degree of competition • Real estate and capital equipment intense • Start-up almost cost prohibitive

(Majority of Small Businesses)

Figure 2. Guide to selecting net multipliers.

Testing Estimated Business Value

Return: Net cash stream to be valued	$246,234
Less: Annual debt service (P + I)	$ 91,872*
Pretax cash flow	$154,362
Add: Principal reduction	$ 14,463*
Pretax equity income	**$168,825**
Less: Estimated depreciation	$ 19,057
Less: Estimated income taxes	$ 41,661
Net operating income (NOI)	**$108,107**

*Annual debt service includes $14,463 of principal payment. The $14,463 principal payment is traditionally recorded on the *balance sheet* as a reduction in debt owed. However, it is a part of pretax equity income for the purpose of calculating return on equity and return on total investment in the privately owned company. This amount is returned to an owner out of cash flow from the business. Bear in mind that this is a snapshot in time, and we are not adjusting to a balance sheet at this point.

Return on Equity:

$$\frac{\text{Pretax Equity Income}}{\text{Down payment}} = \frac{\$168,825}{\$200,000} = 84.4\%$$

Return on Total Investment:

$$\frac{\text{Net Operating Income}}{\text{Total Investment}} = \frac{\$ 108,107}{\$1,021,299} = 10.6\%$$

In the privately owned business, there is significant flexibility in whether taxes are mostly paid by the company or by the individual. Various tax shelters might also be built into operations. Therefore, pretax return on total investment may be more useful than the traditional return on total investment calculation.

Pretax Return on Total Investment:

$$\frac{\text{NOI + Tax}}{\text{Total Investment}} = \frac{\$108,107 + \$41,661}{\$1,021,299} = \frac{\$149,768}{\$1,021,299} = 14.7\%$$

PROSPECTIVE BUYER CASH FLOW

Buyer salary	$ 60,000
Pretax cash flow	154,362
Add: Principal reduction	14,463
Effective pretax cash flow	$228,825

SELLER'S POTENTIAL CASH BENEFIT

Cash down payment	$200,000
Est. bank financing (60%)	240,000
Cash receipts	$440,000
Less: Liabilities	
Accrued taxes	4,133
Accrued retirement	18,136
Note—Owner	Recovered
Tax on retained earnings	51,814
Net cash	$365,917*

*Plus seller financing for $580,000 at 9.5% over 20 years, but perhaps ballooning at the end of the seventh year. Monthly payments of $5,406 and annual receipts of $64,872 anticipated.

PROJECTED CASH TO SELLER AT END OF SEVENTH YEAR

Pretax cash from transaction	$365,917
Less: Capital gains/personal tax	122,585
Add: 7 years interest payment	360,595
Less: Estimated taxes	100,967
Add: Principal repayment	580,000
Less: Estimated taxes	174,000
Approximate after-tax proceeds	$908,960

Perhaps worth noting is that interest receipts of $360,595 pay 90.7% of the $397,552 of tax implication. Also worth noting is that the owner financing generates $64,872 of annual earnings over seven years, at which time $545,816 in balloon principal is further provided.

The myth that sellers can receive all of their deal in cash is, in fact, just a myth! In today's banking climate, as a seller, you can count on financing some portion of your sale. The net result of not doing so more or less translates into a reduced selling price. For additional reference, refer to Chapter 9. Banks do not finance the "fluff," and if a seller wants his or her price, then be prepared to offer financing. Buyers and their advisors want to see a portion of owner financing in the deal. Owner financing exhibits confidence that the owner's price is fair and reflects honesty by the owner that information is truthfully provided. Yes, there is risk, but it has been said that the greatest hazard in life is to risk nothing—only a person who risks is free. The secret to wealth building is to risk intelligently and to apply common sense.

What Does This Valuation Assignment Tell Us about the Buyer? Can We Build the "Profile of a *Likely* Buyer?"

The answer to the second question is yes. First, we know that the prospective buyer will need $200,000 in cash, plus a good credit history. Derived from the owner's experience in running his or her business, we can arrive at a reliable definition of technical knowledge that will be minimally required in a buyer. During the financial analysis of ABC, we learned that the business may have grown beyond the financial skills of the present owner. ABC might be getting out of control, and financial management capability in a new owner can be a definite asset.

Although few details are supplied, let's assume, for the sake of this exercise, that technical product knowledge is easily learned and that management ability is the principal attribute for continued success of ABC.

Unfolding, therefore, is a "résumé" of background and an *allusion* to financial wherewithal to search for in purchase candidates. He or she must be a good all around manager, possess selling skills, and be particularly adept in financial management. In addition, the candidate must have $200,000 in cash for a down payment and a good credit rating to secure bank and owner financing. These are the knowns.

Knowns can lead to hints of the unknown about purchase candidates. For someone to accumulate $200,000 in cash, outside of inheritance or lottery winnings, is not an easy task. Bear in mind that our job is to profile **likely** and more numerous buyers, not those who are unique by special conditions of their lives.

It is quite probable that the prospective buyer we wish to attract will own a home, furniture, an automobile, and other personal assets. Although it is impossible to precisely view the unknown lifestyle being lived, we can, however, draw some fundamental conclusions. A likely candidate enjoys a relatively high degree of affluence. The home will be reasonably well maintained and well furnished, and the autos will perhaps be new. Home mortgages may represent no more than 50% of fair market value. Automobiles, along with most other assets owned, might traditionally be paid for in cash. It is possible that the candidate holds considerable equity in stocks, bonds, or other liquid investments. Investment concepts are understood. Wealth accumulation to this extent customarily requires time, which suggests that the individual sought may be over age 40 and will have a college degree or exceptional work experiences. This guesswork suggests that the likely candidate will have a minimum net worth of between $300,000 and $500,000. If not, then it does not seem possible for the individual to purchase and finance the deal.

Armed with specific information obtained in the valuation process, one can project the **profile** of prospective purchase candidates. Many owners express concern that employees, suppliers, and customers can develop unnecessary anxiety from the unknowns during the business marketing period. Realistically developed profiles can be used to **screen applicants** and, through their use, **minimize** the prospect of a **premature disclosure** of a plan to sell.

Through experience, coursework, publications, and the plethora of available information, buyers come armed with expectations to the negotiating table. A summary of typical buyer expectations is listed as follows:

Business Is Priced Fairly If:	Results of ABC Company:
1. Average reconstructed profits from several years is used to establish value.	1. Three years used.
2. There is at least 10% sales growth per year.	2. Essentially flat until 1993.
3. Asking price is not greater than 150% of net worth (except where reconstructed profits are 40% of asking price).	3. Asking price is 258% of net worth. Reconstructed profits are 25.6% of asking price.
4. Annual reconstructed profits are at least 25% of asking price.	4. 25.6%.
5. Down payment is approximately the amount of one year's reconstructed profit.	5. Reconstructed profit equals $261,234, and downpayment, $200,000.
6. Terms of payment of balance of purchase price (including interest) should not exceed 40% of annual reconstructed profit.	6. Reconstructed profit equals $261,234, and P&I payments equal $91,872, or 35.2%.
7. Cash flow analysis provides for debt coverage, comparable worth owner/manager salary, and return on investment.	7. At average or slightly above.
8. Return on investment of at least 25%.	8. 10.6%.
9. Return on equity of at least 20%.	9. 84.4%.

Not all buyers follow these benchmarks; however, a financially inclined individual is almost certain to develop criteria along these lines plus add more of their own.

Item number three provides food for defense of a major argument against the estimated price. However, leverage, as indicated in item numbers 5, 6, and 9, tends to soften the impact of this argument. Through experiences in sales transactions involving over 300 small businesses, I have found increasing willingness of buyers to pay higher prices wherever the down payment is kept low. A return on equity of 84.4%, under the proposed value/purchase structure for ABC Company, becomes a key focal point for asking and selling the high price estimated for the company. Close examination reveals that if a new owner can operate ABC Company equally as well as the current owner, then that new owner can quite possibly return his or her down payment by the end of the first operating year. Not an elementary fact relating to accounting principles, but a fact of reality that many would-be buyers of the smaller business observe more closely than rates of returns. If one can recover down-payment money during a first year, the deal can't be all that bad.

VALUE IN THE EYES OF A PROSPECTIVE BUYER

When buyers offer prices different than those being asked, I routinely ask how they arrived at their number. Answers run the full gambit, and "rules-of-thumb" are not considered all that "dumb" in the eyes of buyers. However, generally some method appears to evolve in their process. In a generic sense, their opinion seems partly founded in accounting and valuation principles and partly founded in emotion and personal rationale. I cannot begin to fully describe the multiplicity of response; however, the scenario goes something like this:

(Net worth) (150%) =	
($395,241) (150%) =	$592,862
Adjusted by Weighted Cash Flow (C/F)	
(Weighted C/F) (160%) =	
($261,234) (160%) =	$417,974
Difference equals =	$174,888
Add: Net worth at 150% =	592,862
Total Business Value =	**$767,750**

Even though it's not very sophisticated in approach, it amazes me how closely this simple formula matches buyer perception of value.

The asking price by the owner of ABC Company is $1,021,299, or $253,549 apart from what a qualified prospective buyer might initially wish to pay. The variation in perception now becomes issues that both owner and buyer must *sell* to each other. If both want the deal, they will be willing to negotiate.

ABC's low asset base, but strong cash flow, supports the prospect for a higher selling price. Modest leverage being offered also assists in maintaining the higher price. Nevertheless, there are limits to which a buyer may want or is able to go. To secure a sale to a selected buyer, trade-offs may be required, as well as a possible settlement in the vicinity of $895,000 to $900,000.

My report to the owner of ABC Company might therefore read as follows:

High of Value:	$1,021,299
Most Likely Selling Price:	$ 900,000

The choice now rests with the owner in the offering strategy he or she wishes to pursue.

CONDITIONS OF "IF"

If the owner is willing to wait out the long dollar and finance a substantial portion of the sale, then a value estimate of $1,000,000 is not out of order.

If the owner wants a more predictable, timed sale, yet still finance a substantial portion, then a value estimate of $900,000 is more in line.

If the owner is unwilling or unable to finance a portion of the sale of ABC, the value might be depressed as low as net worth plus $200,000 plus whatever additional equity in assets a prospective buyer may be able to pledge to a bank.

$395,241 + $200,000 + ? = ?

$595,241 + ? = ?

or possibly,

$600,000 to $700,000

As you can now see, business valuation is **not** a precise science. Decisions being made about value in the small, private sector of business are deeply steeped in emotion. It follows, therefore, that negotiation on both sides must consider all psychological and factual elements in a deal (see Appendix A for tips). Value simply is *perceived* differently by each person who views *events* differently.

We started this exercise with an emphasis on *purpose* of the report, and the purpose remains very essential. There is one more element that must be considered: *who we as valuators are doing the work for.* In the case of ABC Company, our assignment is in working for the owner/seller. Therefore, the *loyalty* element in our task is to reveal the highest possible value obtainable and to outline salient features to *defend* or justify why a prospective buyer may be willing to pay that price. Feedback must be honest and include qualifying remarks as to the market probability of obtaining that price.

Conversely, a valuator working for a buyer might want to reveal the lowest predictable price that an owner may accept, along with salient features to be used in negotiating toward that lower price.

In other words, the *valuator* must assume the **perception** of the person for whom he or she works and, in addition, be frank, honest, fair, and realistic in all feedback.

For an assignment to effectively include the perception of both buyers and sellers, employment must come through a disinterested third party. Although the purpose has not changed, the value rendered may be neither high nor low, but more in the middle and as fair as possible to both. *It is important to remember, however, that this midline value must always be reported regardless of for whom the valuator is working.*

SUMMARY

The value of any enterprise, large or small, is influenced by many factors. Terms of the financing package frequently exert the most pressure on values rendered. Emotions of the participants can significantly influence decisions in the smaller, private company, whereas facts tend to control decision making in the larger, public companies.

It is the American way to sell for as much as we can get but to try and buy for as little as possible. This principle is a much greater influence in the valuation of smaller, privately owned companies. Thus, the valuator must consider psychological and socioeconomic conditions prevailing in the "bulk" of the middle buying power American and be influenced by practices through *emotions* of these individuals. For example, very few of the hundreds of sellers and buyers that I have worked for spend much time with ratio analysis and rates of return. They should, but they factually don't.

The principle of perception creates a most difficult obstacle to objectivity for individual sellers or buyers who conduct their own valuation assignment. It can be and is done successfully. Henry M. Boettinger, author of *Moving Mountains,* wrote, "People seldom buy an idea without buying its author in the process. When they sense that they are treated as equals, all working together in the search for the right course of action, they eagerly join in discussion with good will, even if your idea is repellent." Many times we must dive way beneath the surface of events to get to the treasure. Examining thought pathology of our predisposition or factors about ourselves that prepare us to react can be very beneficial to buyers and sellers attempting to conclude a transaction.

Successful valuation lies somewhere between understanding the thought processes of humans, and in being mindful of an old saying, "When we get lost in numbers, things just don't always add up." Estimation of value, however, sets the stage and becomes a benchmark for negotiation.

11

Basic Operating Controls

COST ACCOUNTING SYSTEMS

From my experience in working with hundreds of small businesses, I suspect that many more readers will be interested in *job cost* systems rather than *process cost* techniques. I hope that I am not wrong in my assumptions, as I will not cover process cost accounting.

While the words "cost accounting" suggest that cost work may be a distinct and separate form of accountability, cost accounting is actually no more than an extension of regular accounting. For example, the profit and loss statement is actually cost accounting for a period of time involving the whole company. It is when consolidated statements fail to tell us all that we need to know about elements of the company that cost accounting performed on divisions, product lines, or single products can be particularly useful. Therefore, cost accounting objectives are to break down the summarized profit and loss activity into *units* to which cost can be assigned.

In the generic sense, cost accounting systems are more frequently used by the manufacturing firm. However, there is absolutely no reason why they cannot be applied in any form of business. Cost accounting systems have been used by restaurants, motels, retailers, wholesalers, the government, hospitals, banks, utility companies, professional practices, and by more.

Let's first dispel a *common misconception*, which is that there can be *precision in* cost accounting *measurement.* Frankly, it is nearly impossible to precisely measure the cost of anything. Even the most detailed record keeping will not reveal the precise relationship between cost incurred and the output produced. The problem in measurement is well reflected in an old Chinese proverb: "The search for fact is never lost, or never won—only fought for." Subsequently, cost work can be the most complex task in accounting or financial control. Bear in mind, however, that most of the data required in cost work is available from either *formal* or *informal* business records. Informal records are those that many businesspeople keep in their desk drawer and use to *really run* the business. You more than likely do the same.

Most accounting texts will at this point go into great detail to explain *period costs,* which are essentially fixed noncontrollable expenses, such as rent, real estate taxes, building insurance, etc., and other expenses that are stationary with time intervals and do not vary with sales, goods, or services. They detail *product costs* or expenses that cannot always be accurately matched to periods in which they occur. I'd like to forget accounting terms for the purpose of this chapter and go straight to the heart of job cost accounting. However, we may have to take a cue from Voltaire and further define some elements as they present themselves in the exercise.

A JOB ORDER COST PROCESS

The job order cost exercise is highly useful whenever each product or job might be unique. For example, building contractors often employ job order costing, because each project is often quite different. For our sample company, we will return to data supplied in Chapter 2 for the XYZ Company. XYZ owns heavy equipment, which is moved from job to job and the projects are priced individually. XYZ Company is an ideal candidate for job order costing. For just a moment we will get complicated and explain the effect of cost transformation. For example, fuel is purchased, which becomes *potential* energy to run the equipment, and is booked into the fuel ledger, which in turn is an *asset account.* When consumed it becomes *active* energy booked to a specific machine, also an *asset account.* Eventually, when the job is finished, *consumed fuel* is transferred to the *cost of goods sold* account, but booking is now charged to an *expense account.* The accountant must understand the transformation in costs, but operating managers can function quite well without this detailed accounting knowledge. However, it is important to realistically assign costs to each actual job. If we purchased 100 gallons of fuel but used 50 gallons on job *A*, we must be clear to book just 50 gallons to that job. If total payroll is *Y* and we used *X* labor on a specific job, then we must book only that amount. **Individual job order cost sheets** should be developed to be used for **each job** or product. With a clear understanding of job costs, these data can be transferred into developing more accurate *job estimating worksheets* to create *standards* of price or cost. XYZ charges the standard price for daily machine use of $1,300.

From a description of XYZ in Chapter 2, we recall that this company has been operating for only five months. Information taken from beginning months is unlikely to be as reflective of evolving stability in operations as those data taken from the month of May, the last full month of operation. Due to the new status of XYZ, we simply may not be able to obtain more accurate information and must go with what we do have. It will be very important for XYZ to revise and update job costing data on a monthly basis, until some stability in the company is reached. The owner provides us with the following schedule of cost/estimating information being currently used, along with his or her operating statement for the month of May.

One Day of Equipment Operation

Equipment billing per day	$1,300
Expense	
Principal + Interest Payment	$ 296
Loader Cost	5
Trucking Cost	17
Equipment Parts	117
Wages	167
Insurance	83
Fuel	42
Telephone	17
Rent	17
Tolls	17
Trailer Cost	25
Day's Contingency Provision	72
Expense Total	$ 875
Cash Flow Per Day	$ 425

Income and Loss Statement—Month of May Only

Sales	$76,592
Expenses	
Wages & Taxes	$ 9,917
Insurance	3,500
Rent	1,000
Fuel	3,408
Equipment Repairs	2,366
Parts	4,358
Equipment Rental	3,799
Telephone	588
Misc. Expense	162
Principal + Interest Payments	17,743
Owner Salary	none
Total Expenses	$46,841
Cash Flow for Month of May	$29,751

This is the only information provided and available at this time. We can note immediately, however, that there seems to be no allocation for owner salary in the job cost/estimating format. Although no degree of precision appears likely, what can be minimally done to improve on cost/estimating? One thing for certain is that no owner plans to work very long for nothing. We could assume that he might want to earn at a rate of $36,000 per year and add 1/12th, $3,000, to the month of May expenses. We could discuss reliability of costs for each account with the owner, adjusting those that still contain start-up expenses or those where expenses may be low in terms of future operation. The checkbook may reveal other information as well. But at this stage of development, XYZ maintains no further records. XYZ operates two pieces of equipment, which represent the "backbone" or express purpose for the business. All operation revolves around these two machines. Equipment is moved from job to job, and projects extend from one to thirty days each. With these given, we can minimally construct the following cost information.

Income and Loss Statement—Month of May Only

		30 Per Day	2 Per Machine
Sales	$76,592	$2,553	$1,277
Expenses			
Wages & Taxes	$ 9,917	$ 331	$ 166
Insurance	3,500	117	58
Rent	1,000	33	17
Fuel	3,408	114	57
Equipment Repairs	2,366	78	39
Parts	4,358	145	72
Equipment Rental	3,799	127	63
Telephone	588	20	10
Misc. Expense	162	5	3
Principal + Interest	17,743	591	296
Owner Salary	3,000	100	50
Total Expenses	$49,841	$1,661	$ 831
Cash Flow Month of May	$26,751	$ 892	$ 446

At first glance, some degree of sales efficiency appears present in the business. We note that estimating attempts to derive $1,300 per day, and the month of May reflects an average of $1,277 per day, per machine. Therefore, at least one month operated at near full capacity, 98.2%. This is a good sign, as long as sales continue at the May level and expenses do not get out of control.

Due to lack of additional information, we are limited to simple line-item/category comparison. This can be accomplished on a percent or on an actual dollar basis. When dollar amounts get large, percentage comparisons can be especially helpful. In this case, we will go with comparative dollars.

	May Average	Est. Sheet	Variance	Adjusted Estimate
Sales	$1,277	$1,300	$ −23	$1,325
Expenses				
Wages & Taxes	$ 166	$ 167	− 1	$ 166
Insurance	58	83	−25	58
Rent	17	17		17
Fuel	57	42	+15	57
Equipment Repairs	39	0	+39	39
Parts	72	117	−45	72
Equipment Rental	63	0	+63	63
Telephone	10	17	− 7	10
Misc. Expense	3	17	−14	3
Principal + Interest	296	296		296
Owner Salary	50	0	+50	50
Load/Truck/Trailer	0	47	−47	47
Day's Contingency	0	72	−72	0
Total Expenses	$ 831	$ 875	−44	$ 878
Cash Flow Month of May	$ 446	$ 425	$ +21	$ 447

Paper changes to job estimating worksheets cannot be made from these experience relationships alone. For example, a major problem might exist with raising the daily price charged for equipment to $1,325. Perhaps the $1,300 daily rate may already be at the high end of what the market will bear. If not, it may be possible to gradually increase quotes for new work.

Note that the existing worksheet has a provision for contingency expense but neglects line-item detail for equipment repairs and equipment rental, which account for 12.3% of total expenses. Also, $446 pretax profit represents a 34.9% free cash flow during the month of May. Perhaps an owner salary can be added.

While the original job estimating worksheet projects a reasonable overall picture of actual operating outcome during May, comparative job order cost analysis provides a test against performance and affords the inclusion of other important expenses from developing cost experience. In the sample case of XYZ, equipment repairs and rental equipment appear to be "creeping" expenses that bear close watch, particularly as equipment grows older.

During the formative months of XYZ Company, it is quite obvious that the owner has a better-than-average understanding of his or her early stage costs. It would be particularly important that this company follow monthly revenue and expenses until they reach more stable levels in operation. The worksheet on page 133 might be one possible format to implement for tracking costs and providing guidelines for estimating standards.

The past two-month average could be changed to quarterly or even biannual formats, as operations begin to stabilize over time. This simple costing format, once developed, can be *easily maintained, directly from monthly company checkbook entries*. Costs on a category-by-category basis can be observed, and pricing strategies can be established. When a sales estimate needs to be quoted for less to attract a certain job, the marginal effect on profit can be intelligently surveyed. This fundamental worksheet may well suffice as all the cost accounting needed, for several years into XYZ's future. Tracking costs are always imperative to a business's survival; however, cost accounting in the newly formed enterprise can make the difference in surviving even a first year. Cost examination habits developed by owners during formative years have a tendency to carry over into future growth years.

The job/standard cost example herein could just as easily be completed for a product, a product line, or a service being offered. Most lifestyle businesses are not so complex that major cost accounting systems need be considered. Where such complexity exists, it may well be most advisable to engage the company's accountant to work with owners in developing specific criteria.

For example, many companies produce a product where costs cannot be identified by the job or by the product batch. Subsequently, the focus of cost measurement becomes the cost center, such as a manufacturing unit, department, or the process itself. These costing systems are referred to as *process cost accounting*. These systems customarily require more in-depth knowledge of bookkeeping and accounting procedures. Because of the much smaller numbers of lifestyle businesses where process cost accounting might be *practically* used, this handbook will not deal with that subject.

As a minimum, however, keeping track of individual product sales and their direct cost of goods sold, by product, can be particularly helpful in present and future studies of costs.

XYZ Company — Job Order Cost Estimating Worksheet

	2nd Oldest Month Act.	Past Month Actual	Current Estimate Schedule	Adjustment	Estimating Used	Actual Cost Experience
Sales		$ 1,277	$ 1,300	$ -23	$ 1,325	
Cost Sales		0	0	0	0	
Gross Profit		$ 1,277	$ 1,300	$ -23	$ 1,325	
Expenses						
Wage/Tax		166	167	$ -1	$ 166	
Insurance		58	83	-25	58	
Rent		17	17	0	17	
Fuel		57	42	15	57	
Equip./Repair		39		39	39	
Parts		72	117	-45	72	
Equip./Rental		63		63	63	
Telephone		10	17	-7	10	
Misc. Exp.		3	17	-14	3	
Prin./Int./Pay		296	296	0	296	
Owner Salary		50		50	50	
Load/Tr./Tral.			47	-47	47	
Other			72	-72		
Total Expenses		$ 831	$ 875	$ -44	$ 878	
Cash Flow		$ 446	$ 425	$ 21	$ 447	

JOB NAME: _____ Date: _____

Estimator: _____

No. Work Days Estimated: _____ Days Actually Worked: _____

Simple Checkbook to Income Statement Accounting

The cost for detailed accounting services can be out of reach for many smaller businesses. Many use their accountant principally to complete year-end statements and for tax purposes.

The company checkbook, when adequately maintained, is the primary source of year-end financial information. When items are properly identified by entry, the checkbook contains sales, operating, and capital expense data, and therefore, daily, weekly, or monthly income and loss statements can be constructed from these entries. For the purpose of internal records, items such as depreciation and interest expense might not be important on a daily, weekly, or monthly basis. But full principal and interest payments on debt may be required. The internally generated income and loss statement may actually become a "watchguard" for cash uses or needs. Highly simplified statements such as these can be particularly useful even when cost of goods sold is not periodically adjusted by changes in inventory. For those who wish to adjust cost of goods sold, the following formula can be applied:

Last Period *Beginning* Inventory	
Add:	Purchases
Less:	Returns, Allowances, Discounts
Add:	New Freight Charges
Add:	New Direct Labor Cost
Less:	Present Period *Ending* Inventory
Equals:	Cost of Goods Sold

Frequent actual inventory taking is just not possible for many small businesses; however, inventory costs associated with sales made from preexisting inventory can be estimated with a fair degree of accuracy. If we sell one Y from an inventory of ten Ys, then the present period ending inventory is the value of nine Ys. If we purchase two Xs, but one X does not get sold until some future period, then ending inventory is the value of one X, etc.

Many small businesses can derive sufficient sale/cost information without adjusting for inventory changes. Inadvertent inventory accumulation must, however, be carefully guarded against. For example,

Total Sales	
Cost of Actual Sales	
Add:	Direct Freight for Actual Products Sold
Add:	Direct Labor in Actual Products Sold
Equals:	Gross Profit on Actual Sales Made

The reconstruction of expenses from a checkbook may or may not recognize fully all of the real period costs. Insurance and other expenses may be paid once or twice per year. Payables may not get paid when they are due. A review of cash budgeting in Chapter 5 may be helpful to any exercise contemplated for the construction of internal statements. Reoccurring, fixed costs, such as rent, and known expenses, such as principal and interest payments, can be prenoted on the format used. The best model for your own internal document format would be taken from your company's last annual *formal* income statement. Bear in mind that the *accrual method* of accounting records sales and attendant expenses when the sale is completed, regardless of when actual cash is received. *Cash methods of accounting* record sales and expenses at the precise time that cash is received. Attendant to informal income statements should always be a detailed list, including dates due, of all accounts receivables and payables, as such accounts exist. These records should be revised each time to coincide with the same period covered by the informal income statement.

An example format for internally generated income statements could be as follows:

Monthly Sales
Less: Monthly Cost of Goods
Equals: Monthly Gross Profit

Expenses
    Wages & Employment Taxes
    Owner Salary & Taxes
    Advertising
    Auto/Travel/Entertainment
    Known Uncollectable Debt for the Month
    Commissions Paid
    Contributions/Dues
    Insurance
    Office/Postage
    Occasional Labor
    Principal & Interest
    Payments
    Professional Fees
    Rent—Facilities
    Rent—Equipment
    Repairs/Maintenance
    Rubbish/Snow Removal
    Taxes—Sales

Taxes—Real Estate
Taxes—Other
Telephone
Electric
Water/Sewer
Heat
Miscellaneous
Minus: Total Expenses

Equals: Monthly Net Cash Flow Before Depreciation and Tax

In summary, simple internal controls can go beyond the accounting area and should be developed as overall plans to coordinate and safeguard the company's assets, promote operational efficiency, and/or check accuracy and reliability of expected levels of profitability. Internal controls for smaller businesses should be *usable by management* on a daily, weekly, or longer-term basis. An imbalance of time spent on record keeping may affect sales, but sales and expenses without record keeping are likely to get out of hand. The small-business owner must strike a time-oriented balance in the use of his or her time. A job or product costing system, coupled with simple internally generated statements, may be all that is required for control improvement in the smaller, privately owned business. A word of caution, however, static thinking about control measures will not help the business grow. As the business changes, so must thinking and measurement change. The prudent small-business owner is one who is ever watchful in the never-ending challenge to maximize *profitable sales* and to *contain costs*.

12

Finding the Business and Preparation for Purchase of a Going Concern

AN AID TO THE SEARCH AND DISCOVERY PROCESS

In an attempt to find an appropriate small business to acquire, the obvious first step is to determine what to search for and find out which companies are available. Along with this process is the need to inform the marketplace that you have become a prospective buyer. This can partially be achieved by informing business acquaintances, your bank, and other banks; your accountant, attorney, and stock broker; and those fraternities of individuals who are known as "finders" or business brokers. The last group will, on the whole, be more receptive to your needs.

The business opportunities section of newspapers is another source of leads for available businesses as well as providing a method for stating your quest. Some buyers meet with success through a direct advertisement outlining their wish. Occasionally buyers turn creative, produce a brochure, and direct mail their query to companies with products or services of interest. This method is frequently employed by venture capital and significant investment groups. It can be an expensive process and generally is awkward for the average small-business buyer. Contacting industry associations and/or visiting industry conventions can be worthwhile, when a specific industry is the target.

Any or all of these quite simple things can very quickly shake out what the marketplace initially has to offer.

WHY BUSINESSES ARE FOR SALE—AND WHO PLAYS WHAT ROLE

Often foremost in generic recommendations for selling a business is the owner who wishes to retire or has no succession of management in place. These can be ideal, and in some lofty place they do exist; unfortunately, they exist far too seldom for a large number of would-be buyers. Buyers for these kinds of ideal purchases are likely to materialize from within the ranks of the business itself, from members of family or their relatives, and sometimes, from staff members of advisor firms. Only infrequently will this type of opportunity become available to most of us.

It is sad, but common indeed, that the average business for sale becomes available due to a current owner's inability to secure adequate returns. The sorting process is endless and will involve significant time. Some prospective buyers search for years before locating a choice. A consideration of some brokers is to label a buyer as serious only after the buyer has experienced the search process for at least a year. This is more often prompted by unrealistic expectations set up during the early stages of their search. Called "seasoning," these brokers, from their experience, feel that it takes time for the buyer to adjust to actual market conditions and to understand that the purchase of a small business simply does not follow the text of college courses or large company wisdom.

Some owners are anxious to sell, some are willing but noncommittal, and some have given little, if any, thought to the process of selling. Few are willing to negotiate their harbored expectations away. While this less-than-committed group may comprise some of the best candidates, they are indeed difficult to contact and explore. Such firms receive inquiries on a regular basis, most of which end without response in the proverbial circular file. It requires a persistent and plausible approach to tap this particular market. Experienced finders have developed through years of hit or miss experiment the what, why, when, and where of making contact. Only a few work the process on a regular basis, and these few, due to expense involved, limit their practice to the larger deal.

When considered against a backdrop of the "great wave" in the merger movement that took place during the early 1960s and continuing into the 1980s, one becomes immediately aware of the inversion of conventional buyer/seller practices found in the marketing of one's products or services. Contrary to conventional product buying efforts, it is the business purchaser who must organize those intensive programs to advertise and to attract their customer, the potential seller. Their campaign must reach far and wide in search of the motivated candidate. In short, the seller assumes a passive role, whereas the buyer must take the active initiative to effectuate a purchase.

For this reason, the following is structured as a "buyer-oriented" presentation. The buyer must eventually recognize that he or she faces intense and, quite often, more qualified competition from other buyers in their process of successfully locating and completing a transaction—often, conditioned on the fact that there are just "too many dollars chasing too few deals."

Without drawing too fine a line, sellers generally fall into two categories:

1. Investment ownership: Ownership is purely financial in nature, i.e., individuals, venture capital, institutional, etc.
2. Management ownership: Ownership is both financial and operational.

The motivation of the first is quite simple: a distinct preference for cash returns, without being tied directly to the business operation. This form of investment can be most beneficial to a cash-starved but growing business and/or where new product development is critical to future success. However, this type of investor can be merciless in his/her drive for rates of returns and may restrictively involve himself/herself in controls specifically designed to protect his/her interests. They often remain indifferent to all but the cash consideration, and negotiations with them can become incredibly frustrating. The second is made more complex by the psychological investment of each owner but may, in fact, present more opportunity for eventual purchase by a qualified buyer. The following is, therefore, directed more toward the second type of seller.

OWNERS AS SELLERS

There are perhaps as many reasons for selling a business as there are owners waiting to sell . . . and money is not always the final consideration in selecting a buyer. General factors prompting a sale can be divided into two essential categories: **business necessity** and **psychological requirement,** which are difficult but necessary to identify.

Business necessity is typically satisfied at the moment of sale, and regardless of the explanation, it almost always involves a need for cash to displace the problematic situation that is occurring. Following are some examples:

1. *Dissension among owners:* While an early business formation period often strengthens a partnership, it is not uncommon for irreconcilable squabbles to develop in later, more established years. This may be divided into two classes:

   a. Partners who start the business together frequently develop "community" and a sense of rowing the same boat together. This forms an adhesive that binds them together at the outset. As the business prospers, individuals tend to revert to their initial self: old habits and styles reappear, skill levels may not develop equally, and differences complicate a united or uniform direction for the company. This is a classic problem that occurred in many computer software development companies during the past 10–15 years. It should be noted, however, that partnerships formed at the inception of a business stand a better chance of longer-term, successful relationships. When they are good, they are really good! When they are bad . . . well, we all have heard the stories.

   b. New partnerships that later develop with one or more of the remaining partners make it incredibly difficult for the new kid on the block to catch up. Even in situations where the "old-timer" may become junior by his total investment, much power and informal leadership continues to be exerted by him. These latter-stage arrangements frequently end in controversy and form the subject matter for often-heard stories about the "risks in partnership." Dissension does not occur overnight; therefore, a thorough understanding of the differences need to be explored. It is in these groups that an acquisition candidate may develop, where price may exhibit itself as a lesser consideration.

2. *Personal diversification:* Owners occasionally find themselves at risk with all of their eggs in one basket, operating a business that no longer provides the challenge once enjoyed. Complacency can stymie both the growth of a business and that of employees as well. These situations create opportunity for a new owner who might find them as challenging to his or her personal skills. A conflict may

develop, however, with a seller who seeks maximum cash at closing to be used in a larger purchase.

3. *Narrow product line:* A sale or merger may be the wise choice when the scope of a small enterprise involves too narrow a product line and where product development is hampered by limited funds. Bringing a new product on-line is an expensive process, and subsequently, these types of businesses may represent a least-cost scenario to the larger, integrated corporate buyer. Due to the costs associated with developing new lines or products, these types may not provide the financially sound purchase for an individual buyer. Unless, however, that buyer has product expansion ideas that can be merged effectively into operations without materially affecting the existing cash flow. These frequently represent a more troublesome form of acquisition for novice buyers who fail to economically rationalize their sources and uses of both operating and development cash.

4. *Death in family:* The death of an owner-manager or partner may create a sudden need for cash and/or management expertise. The more technical or complex the business, the more likely this may occur. Members of surviving families often have not gained the necessary skills and can find themselves strapped by estate settlement expenses that drain their present means. There exists a select group of venture investors who target companies where age or health of principals might soon put a company at risk. They become very scientific in their exploration and wait for an obituary to signal their next move. To some this may seem vulturine, but acquisition is the name of their game. To the family, this venture capitalist's preparedness may divert a crisis that time required in traditional selling might otherwise evoke. These may well represent viable candidates for both the individual buyer and the corporate buyer alike. Caution must be exercised during the discovery process when much operating wherewithal may have been lost with the death of the owner.

5. *Automation:* The 1970s through the 1990s have witnessed decreases in equipment expense; however, automation may still represent a major investment in tooling costs and technical skill necessary to operate. Automation, including computer and robotic application, has become necessary to remain competitive in many industries and companies. Some owners are unable or unwilling to make the transition. Where the investment in modern equipment

and technology is within reach of an individual buyer, these candidates can present exciting prospects for their acquisition. When the investment becomes too large, they are best passed up the ladder to the large corporate buyer. Do not underestimate the training, setup, debugging, parallel run, and lost production expenses of new technology. Stories abound where these costs can exceed prices paid for equipment.

6. *Complexity of business:* The nature of doing business is increasingly more complex, and some owners are forced to engage costly outside professional help. According to the New England Association of Manufacturers, prevailing market and production technology in today's society changes rapidly in spans of less than ten years. The outlook is set in change, involving even less time in the future. Some owners will not functionally bridge this gap. A detailed assessment of education and skills might be indicated for the individual buyer before proceeding with this type of prospect.

7. *Vertical integration:* Integration or merger with a larger and more evolved corporation may eliminate variables of small-business owner dependence on sources of supply or methods of sale and distribution. Production technology can also be merged to reduce both fixed and variable overhead costs. Opportunity may also exist for two marginal companies to merge into one profitable venture. Rarely does this situation present viable acquisition for the individual buyer, unless he or she can effectively purchase and merge two or more entities.

8. *Squeeze on working capital:* A fast-tracked and growth-oriented company creates its own unique financial and human relations problems. Even with adequate capital, people need time to adjust for change. Survival-oriented businesses plan for their growth within the framework of available cash and provide the necessary time for acclimation of the human element. As sales increase, so do inventories, accounts receivables, personnel, and cash requirements—those principal elements of "working capital." Cash requirements to operate an expanding business become the *leads,* and cash from sales become the *lags.* The funding of expansion must come from profits, from borrowing, or from personal "tills," and the collection of receivables involving terms just never seems to be enough to cover all of the needs during significant growth. Profits tend to be small during the formation years, and bankers restrict loans to the

level of earnings. Owners are inclined to tap personal resources to the limit prior to seeking outside assistance. These can present significant opportunity for the experienced buyer who has both cash and operating knowledge.

Occurring too frequently are situations where novice buyers have financially extended themselves beyond their means in the original purchase. They start off in cash-starved positions and find themselves out on a limb within the first year or two of operation. These scenarios are difficult to fully assess. Discovery is complicated by embarrassment of owners to admit a shortcoming that probably took place during their initial purchase or that occurred through intervals of mismanagement. They tend to blame others for mistakes in their own judgment. Participating banks may be somewhat to blame when they approve loans without provisions for operating lines of credit. Existing institutional debt may be frightfully large, cash flow decreasing or excessively strained, creditors knocking hard on the door, and the owner in emotional turmoil. An onset of depression usually accompanies the lingering financial duress and will often foster a "why bother" attitude over keeping records for the operation. Both employees and customers will eventually discover the problem. Caught while still in an early stage of deterioration, these businesses may represent a worthwhile consideration for the experienced buyer. However, often is the case when embarrassment of an owner or an ill-founded belief in miracles will frequently lead the business to a point of no recovery before the prospect of sale is considered.

9. *Lack of management succession:* Owners of the smaller firm often do not plan for their eventual retirement. Habit often drives them to remain with their business beyond levels of enthusiastic support, and the business may experience serious contraction along with their own faltering desire. It is where the owner makes early identification of retirement that some of the most viable acquisition candidates are presented. Requirements for significant cash at closing are less evident, and an attractively financed purchase can often be negotiated. Some owners actually enjoy the status of maintaining an office and continued involvement in activities of the company. Trade-offs might be achieved in purchase price and terms, through some definitive role for the previous owner. Roles must be well defined and adhered to, or these arrangements can turn sour with time.

Most sale prospects will fall into one or more of these business need categories, and their identification is found in the process of evaluating not only the business but also the buyer's own level of capability. More subtle and less determinable are issues of the **psychological requirements** of sellers. Subjects of price and how they wish to be paid usually surface early during discussions. However, the personal state of mind of a seller is not always easily discerned.

1. Explicit though not always expressed is the concern about how his or her future can be improved through a sale. Personal goals are often the reason for sale, not the least of which is money.

2. Perhaps a seller will have concerns he or she wishes to be respected after the sale is consummated.

3. There are times that a seller may want assurance that selected employees or customers are treated in certain ways.

4. A need for more security in terms of retirement, health, life, vacation, and various other employee group plans.

5. A need to stabilize earnings.

6. A desire to earn more than the smaller business provides.

7. A regret for leaving the corporate environment and need for group acceptance.

8. A change in education or career direction. A desire to return to school.

9. A divorce or marriage.

10. Loss of family members, and wane in interest.

There generally prevails an atmosphere of wanting his or her cake and being able to eat it as well.

There will always be underlying psychological reasons for the sale, which tend to be unique with each individual seller. Development of questioning techniques to elicit appropriate response will help bring these issues to the surface. Some will require careful handling.

No matter how valid are the business or personal considerations, the act of selling is a momentous decision for an owner. It is filled with agonizing uncertainties and personal stress. Success in the competitive buying arena demands that a purchaser be quick to grasp both financial and psychological motivations. A show of willingness and cooperation will go a long way toward convincing a seller that a buyer's eventual purchase will give him peace of mind. Meeting this challenge often calls upon all of the ingenuity and creativity that can be mustered.

Third-party intermediaries can assist in the identification and formation of the basic plan and to assess and implement a successful purchase. Be certain, however, that all understand who the broker or finder is *really* working for. Most will be agents of sellers and *do not* represent any interest of buyers. The concept of "buyer broker" has evolved in contemporary society and can be employed to represent buyers. In some situations, it may be advisable for both seller and buyer to engage and jointly employ an independent facilitator or broker to work out alternatives for consideration.

PRELIMINARY SCREENING PROCESS

The need for pre-established acquisition criteria is key to the successful elimination of undesirable candidates. Costs associated with investigations can be excessive where no plan exists or is followed. Criteria need be practical and within the reach of an individual buyer. To search on an "empty stomach" is an invitation to disaster, and "sugar daddy" financing often disappears when needed the most. For example, think of the times when perhaps your own children or a relative "returned to the well" time after time for your assistance. It eventually becomes frustrating to the giver, and these sources of funds tend to dry up or become unavailable and/or undependable. Draw up a plan with predictable reality for funding in mind.

Self-image plays a major role in the screening process. Most successful people feel good about themselves and what they do for a living. Much screening can occur by imagining ownership of a particular business and then considering what it will be like when describing this form of work to friends or relatives. Unless a buyer can comfortably feel a sense of pride in the business, they may be best advised to pass on to the next, regardless of how good the numbers might appear.

Obtain and generally review a current balance sheet and at least three to five years of historical earnings performance. Hopefully these will include a recasting to exclude the current owner's legitimate perquisites. From these preliminary and unverified data, consider the asking price in its relationship to total "hard" assets offered and in the context of existing cash flow. This process should eliminate 80–90% of available prospects and point to a few, where a thorough investigation will be required.

First-time buyers may want to establish fairly tight evaluation criteria and limit their search to smaller and fairly priced candidates. Gain confidence and success, and then possibly, trade up. Experienced buyer/operators may wish to add risk to their search and consider the larger, complex, distressed, or leveraged situations.

In any event, some or all of the following should be a part of sound evaluation criteria:

1. Assessment of personal skills and independent financial capability, and establishment of goals that are consistent with this assessment.

2. Measure against established purchase criteria.

3. Analysis and reconstruction of operating statements involving a minimum of the past three years. Consider no more than one forecast in weighing the price requested. Future earnings belong to the particular owner-of-record at the time they might occur.

4. Business under consideration should show at least 10% sales growth per year.

5. Asking price is not greater than one and one-half times net worth (hard assets), except where reconstructed profits are 40% or more of the asking price. Understand financing conditions where assets do not support conventional bank financing.

6. Down payment requested does not exceed approximately the amount of one year's reconstructed profit.

7. Terms of payment of balance of the purchase price (including interest) does not exceed 40% of the most current year of reconstructed profit.

8. Most current year's reconstructed cash flow provides latitude for debt coverage and fair market owner/manager salary.

9. Return on total investment in the range of 20–30%.

10. Return on equity (cash down payment) of not lower than 20%, except in situations involving valuable real estate where future values can be clearly determined.

About Value in Business

The processes of valuing business worth are endless, and there is just no safe rule of thumb to consider. Consider an old saying, "rules-of-thumb are dumb." Do the necessary homework, and compare these data to personal situations. Any price paid for a business is fair as long as the business pays for itself in a reasonable period of time. Minimally, the business should provide for the following:

1. Interest on down payment equal to or greater than what is currently received or available from capital when placed in other, perhaps safer investments.

2. Salary for operating the business that is at least equal to the cost of hiring an outside manager to do the specific job required.

3. Business must pay for itself out of earnings over a reasonable period of time. Depending upon the circumstance, reasonable can be as short as three to five years or as much as ten or more years. Terms of purchase dictate much in the establishment of time required.

4. Prospect for growth.

5. Prospect for continued and growing profit.

If these conditions cannot be clearly determined or obtained, any price that a buyer pays is TOO MUCH!

What Is Being Purchased

While the indicated value of a business is more often found in the relationship of the stream of cash to the purchase price, hard or "bankable" assets are the key to financing the deal. A buyer who pays significantly more than a fair market value of that business's tangible net worth can get in serious trouble before turning the key in the lock for the first time. It is critical during an early period of the discovery process to determine what exactly is being purchased with the price. Somewhere in the decision-making process should be provision for independent appraisal of not only real estate but furniture, fixture, and equipment as well.

Elements of sale can include some or all of the following:

1. Facilities:
   a. Real estate to be purchased will often require appraisal if it is to be pledged as collateral. Regardless of how taxes are allocated, the fair market value should be completely understood.
   b. Leased facilities can present a series of problems through their immediate transferability and in their long-term use. Seeking legal advice prior to contract is always advisable for any type of buyer. The purchased lease must minimally provide 5–7 years or more of uninterrupted use.

2. Furniture, fixture, and equipment: These items present various degrees of difficulty in establishing their value, particularly due to the "stand-alone" value versus the theoretical "in-service" value sometimes applied. Institutional banking will seldom recognize more than a part of their stand-alone value. Qualified appraisers can often shed light on condition and remaining useful life. Occasionally, they can provide insight to available parts and service as well. There are instruments for a fairly wide array of production equipment that can predict wear-related failure, and these tests may be a worthwhile consideration for evaluation of critical assets.

3. Vehicles: Blue book values can easily be obtained. It is advisable to consider buying a mechanical assessment, especially where this asset is sizable in the purchase price or where vehicles are significant to operating the business.

4. Inventory: Special care needs to be exercised when evaluating the condition and value of inventory. Rare is the business that maintains only saleable stock. Human errors in orders or misjudgments in markets do occur. Inappropriate inventory at high levels not only can indicate opportunities for improving profits but also may signal that the business is out of control. It is inadvisable to purchase the mistakes of another and compound those we may make of our own.

5. Work in progress: An item combining inventory, labor, manufacturing, and administrative overhead costs. Without their purchase, a business might fail to meet promised delivery schedules. Their value is found in examining an accounting process and where a buyer may find it extremely useful to engage professional assistance to review.

6. Customer deposits: Tied to some stage of work-in-progress, these need to be transferred along with new ownership. Inventory,

work-in-progress, and customer deposits require integrated analysis that often is best performed in conjunction with the buyer's financial advisor.

7. Customer lists: These are a necessary item to the continuing success of a business. However, their value is difficult to establish with any degree of certainty. Institutional financing can rarely be obtained.

8. Covenant not to compete: This element is an important feature in all sales. While a retiring owner may indicate no continuing interest in the business of the company, he or she nevertheless possess proprietary information that could ultimately put the newly acquired company at risk. Ask for and expect noncompetitive agreements, but recognize that they must be reasonable in order to be enforced. An attorney can provide the appropriately structured agreement.

9. Patents, copyrights, and trademarks: These might represent the essence of business continuity and, where existing, should be examined by appropriate legal professionals.

10. Office and shop supplies: Rarely more than a small part of the overall deal, they can represent annoyance and distraction when concentration on more important matters is required.

11. Transferable franchise agreements or territorial licenses: When existing, these form an integral part of authority to conduct business. Appropriate legal advice is always indicated.

12. Service contracts: Examine closely for expected costs to maintain these contractual agreements. In certain companies, these can represent significant "future" obligations that may not have been factored into the purchase price. When service contract obligations are significant, their estimated cost to uphold must be considered in pricing a business.

13. Employment contracts: Examine the cost and consequences of these agreements. Check for "golden parachute" clauses that a previous owner may have included to reward past service of an employee or to gain a cooperation during the sale process. Unless you can find future benefit for these promises, then you may be buying a pig in a poke.

14. Accounts receivables: The best for last is advised to be first on the list. Accounts receivables often represent a major element of work-

ing capital. Strongly consider purchasing the "deemed collectible" portion of this *liquid* asset. Negotiate the remainder with a seller, including his warranty of those that may be in question. Although institutional financing is available for at least some part of receivables, it is usually beneficial long term to keep this out of pledged collateral for the basic loan. Receivables can sometimes be "factored" for quicker returns of operating cash. The penalty for this action can include significant discounts from amounts due, thereby impacting the quantity of profit.

The determination of fair market value of each element being purchased is often complex, costly, and time consuming. It is, however, vital to any purchase price being paid, financing of the deal, and often, to the continued success of the business. Prior to signing a purchase agreement, it is advisable to consult with accountants and attorneys, as their advice may save countless headaches and financial duress. Far too often, a squeeze on working capital was predictable on the day of purchase. Even knowledgeable, wise, and prudent physicians do not treat themselves, though they more than likely control the overall process.

History in Prologue

It has been said that if potential buyers knew in advance what earnings might be over the ensuing ten years, then they would never make a bad purchase. There will always be risk associated in buying businesses, but organized study of the industry and each particular company will reduce this risk.

The only absolute suggestion offered is that after determining fairness of price, look to the future of the industry and specific enterprise under consideration. With eyes straight ahead, the past will help interpret and forecast the future . . . and the buyer's skills and money will determine the appropriate action to take. The here and now is how to buy, but the future for the business must hold appropriate promise for a steadily increasing value. Never lose sight of the fact that hard assets have *stand-alone* values. Cash flows from the business utilizing those assets may or may not support their acquisition. When cash flows are inadequate to reasonably amortize hard assets purchase, the business portion may have marginal or no value beyond the value of those hard assets. Business cash flows supporting *less* than the estimated market value of hard assets create a *negative* business value and should be of serious concern to prospective buyers. Paying more for the enterprise than the value estimated through its earning stream predicts cash starvation on the day of purchase. Sellers financing part of this type of transaction are at risk collecting the balance of their sale. Figure 1 generally demonstrates this point.

TROUBLESOME MISTAKES BUYERS OFTEN MAKE IN PURCHASING BUSINESSES

The remainder of this chapter addresses mistakes buyers tend to make while purchasing a business. Note the following:

1. Fails to establish "personal need criteria." Establish a list of personal and family requirements. Consider available work/family time constraints as well as basic income needed *immediately*. While few buyers get all that they hope for, well thought out criteria helps screen in, or out, the available acquisition candidates. Following these basic-need criteria will save time, energy, and money and will provide a framework through which appropriate businesses can be analyzed. Acquisition criteria serves another useful purpose: that of forcing the buyer to review his or her own personal qualities such that purchase of an inappropriate business is minimized. Enthusiasm leads people into trouble as well as moves them ahead. Purchase criteria enhances the thinking process necessary to formulating the business plan.

2. Becomes overanxious with a specific business or in purchasing a business. Generally, if we move too quickly, we invariably walk into the proverbial bear's den without weapons for defense. Like shopping for food on an empty stomach, we tend to "bite off more than we can chew." In attempting to acquire a business, we fortuitously develop a belief that we are stronger, more qualified, wiser, and better managers than the previous owner, and therefore, we will do what he or she was unable to do. We will produce wealth, where he or she failed. At times, we actually blind ourselves by bolstering our innate abilities to that point of a superhuman quality. Somewhere along the line in most previous owners' his-

tories is a saga of monstrous proportion to them and their families—they are likely to have fought dearly for survival in their business. The "wild" creature in us all will step forward when boxed in a corner or caged. Keep in mind that a *previous experience* with operations, employees, and customers formed a distinct "edge" when the door to their business world was closed.

Do not overestimate your own skills. Do not be so anxious to overlook "red flags" pointing to danger. Do not allow yourself to be put in a compromising position. Take the necessary time to work the discovery process—or stay gainfully employed through the ownership process of others. Mistakes made during discovery put not only you at risk but your family in jeopardy as well. Stay calm, and the obvious will appear. Search, and the hidden will be found. Ask, then question all things, and your answer will be presented.

Any price paid for a business can be fair as long as that price will be paid back out of cash flow during a reasonable period of time. The term "reasonable length of time" is best defined by the buyer's own value system. Being too anxious will certainly complicate a person's own definition and belief. In most situations, a business should return the investment in 5–7 years.

Always bear in mind that sale and purchase of a business is a matter of *survival,* for **both** sellers and buyers. There are no "deals," except possibly in foreclosure, and those should be approached with extreme caution.

3. Fails to allocate time for "discovery" and information verification. Gathering the necessary data takes inordinate amounts of time. Sometimes this effort alone gets in the way of arraying and examining, and the important qualifying features are overlooked. Pressure to make a decision is being exerted by the seller and his or her staff. Haste makes waste, and acceptance on face value may lead to bankruptcy. Review, check, recheck, question, recheck, and verify; the seller's records are *guilty* until proven innocent! To approach the process in any other way is surely an invitation to disaster.

When a seller fails to produce the complete financial history or becomes secretive, watch out for your chips! Be assured that surprises will still be plentiful, in spite of a thorough search.

Reject what you cannot support from the records. Where a "paper trail" fails to support claims, there is likely no "pot of gold." Use of an accountant during the discovery process can be of great value, to even the most experienced buyer.

Avoid hunches. Get the facts straight!

4. Inadequate assessment of business needs. Unrealistic expectations, for a quick turnaround of a sick and dying business, have empowered a substantial number of would-be entrepreneurs. Run-down businesses take years to succumb to their depleted state and often take inordinate amounts of smart work, capital infusions, and years to re-establish their success. Chapter 11 bankruptcy filings (those where prospect for business continuation exists) suggest that only a few that are sold will actually make it back to prosperity. Many of these were being operated by experienced turnaround specialists, and yet they failed.

    A privately owned, well-operated business will rarely be on the block at an attractive price. It seems not in the cards for owners in general to price their businesses with a new buyer in mind. They often expect the buyer to make them wealthy—that which they were perhaps unable to achieve through the business themselves. It is human nature to want it all. But do we need it all *at one time?* Be wary of sellers "bearing gifts." Be quick to conclude discussions with sellers who are inflexible—they cannot be made to do what they choose not to do. Do not "reach" for a *brass ring*, but make the gold come to you . . . or pass.

    A debt retirement structure must be developed within the safety of existing cash flow being generated out of the acquired business. In "stretching" this scenario, payments to a seller might be kept small during the earlier years and then structured for larger payments, when certain preagreed target goals are met. However, do not be lured into fancy financing "footwork," which carries with it the strong possibility of immediate or longer-term cash flow burdens. In the long run, all acquisitions must pay for themselves—or you are much better off passing on that purchase. Working for naught cannot be fun. Neither overestimate your strengths nor underestimate your courage. No one is truly a fool, but some of us get fooled. I am uncomfortable with the connotation of the word fool; however, an old saying fits the bill, "fools walk in where angels fear to tread."

5. Fails to view cash flow in pessimistic and optimistic light. Plan for the worst, and hope for the best! Expect that old equipment might

fail, that customer accounts might be lost, or that key employees might quit. Expect the unexpected, and factor these events into business plan and cash flow forecasts. Build a cushion into the schedule of debt retirement, and **negotiate these elements into the purchase contract.** When a seller expects payments that are beyond the level of existing cash flow, plan to use private reserves, or better yet, pass on the deal. Where would the "deal" be if you were to lose your shirt?

6. Fails to assess and deal with key personnel and customers. Frequently, the retiring seller represents a key element in the success of his/her business. This is especially true in the smaller company structure. When the founder or owner has chosen to "go-it-alone," he/she comprises the only true "cog" of knowledge and functional power in the company. Remove this person and a tendency to remove the business occurs. Take the necessary time to fully explore, understand, and plan how your own skills fill the void left when the seller vacates his/her company. Decide which skills you lack, and develop a plan to hire outside consultants or educate yourself to fill this void. Price out the cost to accomplish the task, and factor the expense into the cost of doing business for the new venture. Companies need direction and organization. This involves delegation of responsibilities to the lowest possible and capable level in order for the enterprise to effectively grow.

   There is the risk that employees and customers will not react adequately to the new owner. Largely, people are creatures of habit and do not react very well to change. Special care needs to be exercised with key and long-service employees, to assess both the capability and the transferable loyalty that might exist. Stories abound about the "hatchet" effect often taking place after acquisitions. Employees worry about their jobs and security. When employees are aware of a pending sale and the process of selling takes much time, fear of the unknown will quite often encourage capable employees to search for new work. Customers become edgy and worry about continuity and, particularly, the dependability of service or product under a new owner. *Fear of the unknown* is an important human motivational element that both buyer and seller must guard against and be prepared to appropriately handle, if the transaction is to smoothly proceed. The wiser course of action is often to maintain complete privacy and secrecy of sale prospect.

Granted, this is not always possible. As Abe Lincoln said, "Once you tell another person a secret, it is no longer a secret." The more time that the selling process takes, the greater the chance of disclosure. When disclosure occurs, it may be advisable to take into confidence personnel and customers who are most vital to the business's continued success. The ideal pattern would be to maintain complete privacy during the process, and then both buyer and seller in a joint effort announce the closing of sale. People are not as naive as we might sometimes like them to be. When a new face is seen repeatedly visiting with the boss, behind closed doors, employees will start guessing and conjuring up all sorts of rumors. Nip this at the gate, and use *plausible* explanations if you choose not to disclose all the facts.

Sometimes a fresh, energetic management will be necessary to produce the desired motivation in employees and to expand the customer base. Even in such a case, present employees and customers will be needed for some time until the new owner becomes familiar with the operation.

Somewhere during the discovery process, it will become necessary to talk with key personnel and, at least, major customers. Rightfully, the seller will express concern over this proposed undertaking. In a failure to complete the transaction, he/she might well be left with a "can of worms." Buyers will have equal concerns and could be exposing themselves to liability through a premature disclosure. A convenient way to handle the process would be to make this eventual necessity a condition of the purchase contract. At that point, both seller and buyer have contractually agreed upon the major issues, which customarily involve price and terms and all but, perhaps, financing contingencies and discussions with these key players. As a condition of purchase, the buyer is then protected should he or she discover improper representation on the part of the seller. When talking with these key individuals, "in your opinion" is always a wonderfully engaging way to open discussion. You may be surprised at the response. Such an opening sets the stage for good human relations and recognizes that their opinions may be of value to you. In talking with customers, find out what they like best about products and services. New ideas for promotion may come from the answer to this question. What changes would they like to see occur under your management. Problems or obstacles may be discovered, which can then be turned around. Find out why they chose to purchase from this business. Answers to this question may shed light on the decision-making process that other customers or clients go through. Ask if competitors are doing anything they would like this company to do, or if there is a product or service they would like provided. In talking with employees, what are their gripes and points of happiness. What changes would they make if they were the new owner. Some of the most valuable improvements to a company's success have come from front line workers. A great failure in some companies has been not to ask. Successful entrepreneurs recognize that both their front lines of defense and that of innovative change will many times be found in the bottom ranks of their enterprise. Opportunities exist at this juncture to learn important features about the business, which numbers simply do not reveal.

7. Fails to evaluate the effect of competition on the marketplace. Research! Research! Research the competition and marketplace. Visit a competitor business wherever possible, and make mental notes of his/her strengths and weakness. On what specific competitive "edge" do they appear to trade? What can you do to counter or compete with this edge? Remember that price, quality, or service is all that you have, and never more than two at one time. Customers buy on motivations of gain, need, desire, and embarrassment of not having—that's it!

When acquiring this business, where will you fit in? Plan how you will counteract competition, because the competition will certainly be doing the same toward you. If a business is to move ahead, it will require organized planning and other measures to counteract the effect of competition. Do not underestimate the potential strength of even the smallest challenger. Remember the Avis Rent-a-Car motto, "We're number two, we try harder."

Exploration of the industry at large is too often overlooked or underresearched by prospective buyers. Obtain industry periodicals and news releases. Examine closely all projections for growth in the industry. Even a successful business in a dying industry may not be a worthwhile purchase. However, some will usually survive and even grow. Take the industry "temperature," and direct a course of action to combat this element over which you have little or no control.

Even the best run companies will stagger for a while under new and inexperienced management. Build into your business and purchase plans a deficit cash flow factor to accommodate the effects of competition and industry while you become accustomed to the new reins.

8. Fails to consider purchasing receivables. Receivables frequently represent a major part of a company's working capital. Sellers will often expect to remove receivables and other liquid assets at the time of sale. While this has the effect of lowering the initial purchase price, it also starves the new firm of valuable operating funds—particularly during the first few months after purchase. Purchasing business receivables can be an important source of secondary financing and should not be casually overlooked, even to the extent of increasing the purchase price by a similar amount. The removal of the receivable asset also sets up a psychological imbalance: that of interruption in continuity and/or confusion within the rank of customers. The purchase of receivables can be risky business. Thoroughly examine *each* customer account for age and history of payment. Bear in mind that, for example, in a 30-day collection cycle, those accounts uncollected for 60 days or more are increasingly difficult to obtain. Buy only those that are current, and require the seller to warrant all accounts outside the terms of the regular cycle, which he/she expects a buyer to assume. Some may obviously not be worth purchasing. Lacking personal collection experience, an accountant can bring particular value to the evaluation process.

9. Fails to negotiate "achievable" payout. Rather blunt but to the point, acceptance of unrealistic payout schedules almost certainly will force the buyer into bankruptcy proceedings. Anxiousness to obtain the maximum price, payback terms, etc., does not serve the seller's purpose, although he/she frequently tends not to recognize this fact during the negotiating process. If the buyer loses when the seller is financing some part of the deal, then the seller will ultimately lose as well. Bear in mind that any price ultimately paid for a business is fair, but only as long as *existing* cash flow will pay for the purchase over a reasonable length of time. (This is the golden rule of business purchase.) Only giants such as Fortune 500 companies have reasonable assurance of continuity of business. Smaller companies, including those with sales as high as $50 million, are at risk and have little or no guiding control of the

market economy outside their enterprises. Pricing and buying a business, other than giants, on *future* earnings is an incredibly risky and adventuresome purchase decision. The wise and more successful entrepreneur will not chance his/her future and that of his/her family to this kind of unknown.

Worth noting again is the fact that it is not uncommon for sales to decline during the first year of the new operation. Getting acquainted with the new business will take time, and planned events tend to fall behind schedule. Using all of a buyer's personal cash toward the down payment is risky business as well.

10. Fails to consider alternatives for financing. *Before* executing the purchase agreement, take particular time to consider and evaluate financing alternatives, including the needs for lines of credit as working capital. Some form of "back up" financing will often be required, at least in the first year of the new operation. This secondary need for cash is too frequently omitted during initial acquisition planning. There are frequent situations where the purchase price is reasonable, but total financing terms doom the venture to failure. Use caution in dealing with the seller who expects to siphon his/her cash out of the deal too quickly.

Possibly, when the purchase price is reasonable in comparison to assets being sold, the seller's bank may be interested in participating in all or some part of the deal. Their experience with the previous owner and business provides detailed awareness to particulars, which may seem vague and difficult to comprehend for a new bank. Even in cases where the previous owner has historically operated outside of expectation, the seller's bank should be approached. They could be eager to protect their loan and welcome the new management on board. Sometimes the current bank, plus an additional bank, will be willing to underwrite financing for the proposed acquisition. Regardless of how cash requirements are addressed, there needs to be provisions for working and expansion capital lines included in the original loan request. Proceed with extreme caution if these are unavailable at that time. Unless you have an excess of personal cash waiting in the wing, you must, for your own safety and survival, negotiate these into the original contract. Lack of "operating" funds is quoted by the Small Business Administration to be among the top three reasons for small-business failure. If you cannot obtain lines of credit in an initial package, chances are real that you will not be able to obtain them at all. Where will these funds come from 6, 8, 12, or so months from purchase? You may increase cash flow to qualify at a future date, but then again, you may not. Protect your flank—you're the only one watching that end!

The SBA guaranteed loans have improved the conditions of conventional bank financing. However, federally subsidized programs are not always available when you need them most. They too have been burned and are becoming more cautious in their standards of acceptance.

The application process can be painful in terms of paperwork and time, but as long as the borrower performs in accordance with contract, life after financing will model that of working with a conventional source. The SBA often expects to see "lines of credit" included in the original request.

Business finders can be a resource for financing from outside of conventional institutions. These include private placement, offshore placement, venture capital placement, and other companies who specialize in financing business acquisitions. Unfortunately, recent market economies have made this form of financing quite "pricey." When you turn to these sources, an excess cost of capital needs to be factored into the deal.

I wish there was a nickel for the times that "sugar daddy" money is brought up! When you consider money from a friend or relative, think back on your own children's requests of you for cash. How tiring it becomes when time after time they come back to the "well!" This, moreover, is an undependable source of funds. Perhaps, when this method is considered, it may make sense that the parties incorporate their agreement into a legal and binding format.

11. Fails to make proper use of professionals. Bringing these professionals on the scene too early is a common decision of the novice buyer. Use of your accountant or attorney is never wrong, and only you can decide when they are needed. It is important to recognize several concerns over their use. First, their "meter" starts running even with short conversations. Costs can mount up on those businesses you eventually choose not to buy. Second, if you need their preliminary assistance for each offer presented by you, then perhaps you are best advised to continue working in

your customary trade. It is hard to realize success where financial, marketing, and general business skills have not first been obtained. Third, they are highly trained specialists and rarely have "hands on" experience at "running" operating concerns. To be most effective, their expertise should be focused upon questions and concerns that *you*, through your skills, have uncovered, and their expertise should add a wealth of knowledge to the overall discovery process. Most will never expose themselves to the final purchase decision, which is yours to make alone. The successful entrepreneur will possess or develop the necessary skills to operate a business, before engaging in an actual purchase. The successful entrepreneur will wisely use professional experts at appropriate times. Only the prospective buyer can decide when to bring in an advisor. A prudent buyer will never "play" lawyer or accountant to themselves.

Both professionals in the course of their business represent various types of clients. They may or may not have particular experience with the business transaction. While the nature of their education has exposed them to all aspects of law or accounting, this alone does not make the expert. Before engaging their service, ask about the relevance of their personal experience in handling a similar situation that you are about to buy. Business finders or brokers can usually provide sample purchase agreements for "roughing" in prior to meeting with attorneys and may be helpful in the discovery and purchasing process. However, bear in mind that most brokers represent sellers and are contractually responsible to this party alone. They generally *do not* represent the interests of buyers; although, there has been an emerging wave of "buyer brokers" who appear to increasingly fit this need. The final decision is yours. Do not depend upon others to carry the ball over even the last five yards!

12. Depends too heavily on others in forming a business plan. Creating an independently structured business plan conceived out of facts from the existing business and detailing what a new buyer expects to do about future changes and growth is paramount to successful acquisition financing and the new operation. Several important issues happen in the process:

   a. The buyer is forced into thinking, really thinking, about the planned purchase.

b. The buyer is compelled to look hard at what needs to be accomplished, considering his personal skills in the process.

c. The act of working and reworking the numbers can be very revealing, to the extent that realism creeps in and questions of how, why, when, and where raise their heads, demanding explicit answers.

It is both a thought-provoking and a structuring process. Properly executed business plans form the basis not only for obtaining best available financing and an "edge up" on the marginal deal but also for longer-term operating plans as well. Success and growth rarely come accidentally and require planning for their eventual occurrence. It is hard to grasp overriding evidence that this important aspect of business purchase is so often entirely ignored or, still worse, farmed out to others, such as accountants and brokers, to perform. If the prospective buyer is unwilling or unable to envision a plan, then commit it to writing; perhaps he or she is ill-advised to be purchasing at all.

Rashomon by Akira Kurosana teaches us, "There may be more truths to an event than all of us who observed it can supply."

"Bankruptcy changes a man's nature. I feel as though every person has lost confidence in me . . ."
> Henry John Heinz
> Heinz '57

"The first step is recognizing that conflict and confrontation are a part of the job. Acknowledge that fact, but don't view it as an insurmountable barrier. In truth, conflict and confrontation are more like obstacles in a running course. View them as hurdles to be leaped over."
> Lawrence D. Schwimmer,
> *How to Ask For A Raise, Without Getting Fired*

"If you would win a man to your cause, first convince him that you are his sincere friend."
> Abraham Lincoln

13

Preparation for Sale of a Going Concern

Planning for the eventual sale of a business starts the day one buys or starts that business. Enthusiasm, motivation, and prudent management are all very necessary to maintain and grow a small business. They are just as necessary to sell a business.

Described more fully in Chapter 8, the vast number of small businesses purchased are lifestyle ventures, such as restaurants, motels, grocery stores, etc. In fact, sampling studies indicate these types may well represent as many as 70% of all small business in the United States. Long-range **personal goals** simply **may not be obtainable** through the **first business purchased.** But each business, when carefully planned for, can provide a "stepping-stone" to the next level toward meeting ultimate personal goals. *Long-range personal goals must always be the focal point during purchase and sale of the privately owned and controlled enterprise.*

With this in mind, each of us enters the purchase with a degree of pride in ownership and joy of being free of whatever else we had been doing. Anticipation and motivation, more than likely, are as high as they will ever get. This is the time to add a new personal goal. One of selling at some given point. This is the time to decide to manage the business as if it is always for sale. This is the time to *decide to always maintain "paper trails" for each and every financial transaction.*

A cardinal rule that nearly always confronts sellers is that you "can't sell what can't be proven beyond a reasonable doubt." A wise and several-time buyer once said to me, "If those numbers he claims existed, did exist, then the seller has already received a large part of the sale. I'm not going to pay for it again."

Now, I believe that the majority of owners appropriately report their business activity, and I am not suggesting they don't. I am, however, citing the following to accentuate a point. If I took my profits out through not reporting revenue or through inflating expenses, then I have enjoyed a large portion of yield already. I may have "crippled" my financial statements to the extent that both *value* and *financing capability* for a new buyer are no longer there to support a high sale.

Think about what has just been reflected. Think about the likelihood that a ready, willing, and able buyer may approach your business today or at any time. Do financial statements reflect an accurate picture of business health at all times? Can a legitimate paper trail for actions taken to reduce taxes on business activity be provided?

Simple arithmetic on the 1993 year of ABC Company used in other chapters reveals that the owner enjoyed well over $200,000 of earnings and perquisites but paid only $18,000 in corporate taxes and continued to show $42,000 in profit. We learned in Chapter 10, through reconstruction of earnings, that Mr. ABC actually had $320,131 available at his discretion for personal salary, taxes, depreciation, and interest payments.

Whether one plans for sale at the time of purchase or later during ownership, *the plan for a sale must be well in advance of actual marketing activity.* In the case of ABC, I used only three years for analysis, but many financial analysts prefer five years. This aids in establishing a precedent for how far in advance the business owner should formulate his or her sellout plan. When an owner operates his or her business as if it was always for sale, puts all receipts in the till, and utilizes IRS-approved capital shelters for reducing net taxable income, there is considerably less planning required.

It is none of my business as to how an owner chooses to operate his or her business, and I apologize for using examples so steeped in the negative. But I think in so doing, the message comes out loud and clear. **Impulsive decisions to sell one's business will cost hard earned dollars, unless the plan to sell was initiated well in the past.** Prudent financial management on a daily basis is the only assurance of securing the best possible price. And it can be done by owners, by themselves, and for themselves.

THE PROCESS OF SELLING A BUSINESS

The following list details the process of selling a business:

1. Start with *attitude*. The process of selling often requires more time than anticipated. Maintaining a proper frame of mind may prevent the business from going downhill. Assume that the business will *never* sell, and keep operating as if that fact is true.

2. Allow plenty of time. It takes an inordinate amount of time to sell a company. Minimally, begin with the following steps:

   a. Gather together at least the past three years' tax filings. Array sales by *month* for the preceding 24 months, and show year-to-date comparisons for months in an incomplete year. Spreading monthly expenses along with sales information is preferred; however, if not available, thoroughly examine annual costs. Anticipate! Anticipate! *Anticipate the questions by prospective buyers.* Put on the buyer's hat. What questions would you be asking about the business sales/expense information? Answer these questions through anticipation. You will be one "leg" ahead of the competition! Be prepared to inundate the prospective buyer with *explainable* financial information. Suspicion breeds from secrecy. Buyers disappear when extracting information becomes like "pulling teeth." All the rest is essentially unimportant, unless a seller can get over the financial hurdle.

   b. Establish a fair market price for the business. This can be accomplished by owners, their accountant/financial advisor, or by skilled and experienced business finders or brokers. Obtain information on tax implications relating to the sale.

   c. Write a *job description* of owner duties being performed. Highlight the top one or two skills most required. Outline which skills might be desired to carry the business to a next level. Describe elements that you as the owner might wish had been handled differently.

   d. Write a brief but thorough history of the company. Include information about previous owner operation and changes currently accomplished. Cover weaknesses and strengths. Describe competition and suppliers. What is the company's *mission statement?* To what degree has this mission been accomplished? What remains to be done? Include a brief statement covering any legal situations of the past, present, or anticipated future.

e. Decide how marketing the business will be accomplished. If a business finder or broker is to be involved, selection from a final one or two candidates can be enhanced with the assistance of an accountant or attorney. If marketing will be "homegrown," decide how the prospective purchaser will be contacted, screened, contracted, and closed. Bear in mind that shortcuts tend to be costly to owners in the long run.

3. Prepare the "plan" for selling the business. View the sale as an investment. And yes, your sale is an investment in your own future. Identify those attributes about yourself that you feel will be necessary for a new owner to win in your business. Put these characteristics down on paper, bearing in mind that you will most likely be expected to finance a portion of your sale. With this picture of your ideal purchase candidate, you will be amply prepared to screen prospects for the business. Be sure that you understand *what* you are selling *before* you offer the business for sale. Establish a price for the business that is in line with the market. If you really intend to sell, then do the appropriate things necessary to make it sell. Time is money, and much time and energy can be lost in attempting to market overpriced merchandise. At this point, there is merit in viewing your business as if it were merchandise on a shelf. If you prefer a higher price than value determinants indicate, then perhaps you will need to continue operating the business until you reach sales and profits that justify that value.

When merchandise, or a business, does not sell, it has to do with *price, quality, or service,* nothing more. And there is never a time that one can have all three in distinct advantage simultaneously, not if planning to stay in business. Therefore, in the marketing plan, be conscious to trade on the one or two items most indicative of strength. Take, for example, the attributes of price and quality. If the business is in immaculate condition and possesses great buyer appeal (as in higher demand businesses, such as manufacturing), the price might be set at a higher-than-value indicator level. The reason for this is that there rarely are sufficient manufacturing businesses for sale at any given time to meet market requests. Supply and demand will tend to raise the "market" value over the "cash flow" value of the business. Caution in pricing should be exercised in this instance, because even "market" value will disappear when a price reaches some inflated level. This is an example of "subtle" factors influencing the price/market strategy. *Experienced* business finders or brokers, more often than not, are the best source of information for dealing with subtle pricing factors. It would serve as valuable consideration to balance "finder" opinions of value with those opinions of your own financial advisors. The broker or finder is no more than an extension of you, along with other advisors—your team. If teamwork and specific cooperation cannot be achieved, get another broker or change advisors. There will be enough emotional frustration attached to selling the business . . . and that's a plain and simple fact most owners endure!

4. Enlist professional help where required. Selling a business can create major consequences in life after sale—both positive and negative. Be sure that each element is understood *before contract and sale*. Inform the accountant and lawyer as early as possible of your pending decision. Ask them to join you in selecting a finder or broker, if you choose to go this route. Cooperation and teamwork will be necessary to effectively complete a transaction. However, trust *not* your ultimate decisions to anyone else but yourself. An old saying states, "The only person that you will never lose is yourself."

5. Prepare a "confidential" offering document on the company. Include such items as company history, industry trends, survey of competition, survey of production facilities, list of furniture, fixture and equipment by age and condition, marketing strengths and weaknesses along with ideas for improvement, past financial statements (reconstructed for extraordinary and personal expense items), a possible forecast statement for a new owner, attribution of purchase price (all with supporting rationale), and a disclaimer statement that cautions the prospective buyer to conduct further discovery. Add photos of various elements of the business. Photos sell! Pertinent data on the business should be immediately available in one concise document for presentation to prospective buyers. Include the asking price and proposed terms.

Never, never send your offering document out on telephone

inquiry alone. Buyers cannot buy from afar. Until prospective buyers sit with you in person, they are not buyers. They are just lookers! Unless prospects are willing to invest time and money in a trip to view the offering, they remain lookers and dreamers. It is simply American to want to be in business for ourselves. We all dream of this possibility, but less than 5% of us actually have the mental stamina, fortitude, and financial wherewithal to make the transition. Save energy and anticipation for committed prospective buyers. Learn to discern the difference, or engage a finder or broker to help with this important task.

6. Consider third-party approach to locate buyers for the company. Working through an intermediary, such as a business finder, broker, lawyer, or accountant, means premature disclosure is less likely to occur. Bargaining positions can be weakened unless the timing of disclosure is managed. Premature disclosure can put continuing sales, customers, and employees at real or emotional risk. Many owners do not understand the full impact that they, as individuals, actually bring to their businesses. Unfortunately, some have not taken the necessary steps toward planning for a transition of ownership. Too much risk at this stage can undermine the ultimate price that will be paid by a buyer. Though rare, premature disclosure can leave the business in such a depleted condition that even the owner may not want to continue beyond its effect. No one can guarantee that such disclosure will not occur, but experienced, third-party mediation is the most reliable assurance of maintaining privacy in a sale.

   In the event of untimely disclosure, direct denial and/or comic forwardness may be the best policy to follow. Direct denial might be, "I am *absolutely* not for sale!", while comic forwardness might be, "I'd sell anything I own for a million, or two million." The personality of the owner determines which posture he or she, with conviction, might assume. Nip all rumors in the bud, while they are fresh and occurring!

7. Consider the risk/reward dilemma. Every offer entails its own set of risks. Do not allow enthusiasm generated out of visions of retiring or leaving the business get in the way of evaluating each deal. Seek opinions from advisors, and require that they define "gray" areas in which you can make decisions. Carefully weigh the pluses and minuses of the offer. Structure all counter offers

within the reality of each prospective buyer—or pass! Ridiculous counteroffers have a way of getting around and may linger to exacerbate a deal that is ultimately sought. The buyer and seller's wants and needs will always differ. Learn to discern and work for the achievable within the framework of each individual buyer. Don't waste time on a fastidious buyer who may be attempting to steal away your value. At the same time, don't pass up the prospect for a reasonable deal. Buyers for businesses are not in plentiful supply.

8. "Fairness" reduces risk. It is far from prudent to attempt to get the largest down payment, highest price, and highest interest, if an owner is serious about selling. Out-of-balance transactions tend to put all parties at risk. Entire cash deals are rare, if not impossible to achieve. Few of us can get our cake and eat it too. As an old saying goes, "Bulls and bears make money, but the hogs don't."

9. Be open, and listen to alternative methods of purchase. Sometimes the best sale considerations surface through unique features in a specific buyer. Try to stay open-minded, until the proposal fully unfolds. When temperament and personality of a seller might get in the way, third-party mediation can often increase listening skills. There often is opportunity provided through listening.

10. Seek compromise, and the *way* shall become clear. Successful sales of companies, netting appropriate prices, terms, and conditions available, involve a fair amount of give and take during negotiations. It is with constructive thinking, creative actions, and compassionate willingness that owners and buyers complete transactions and live happily on to tell about it. "Win-win" attitudes create healthy compromise solutions.

Troublesome Mistakes Owners Can Make in Selling

The following list describes mistakes made in the selling process:

1. Begins process "overpriced." A "fair" market price is usually one that provides return on a prospective buyer's investment and one that recognizes the market value of assets being sold. A fair price

includes reasonable consideration of both the past earnings and the potential for future earnings of the company. Bear in mind that the "value" of *future* earnings belongs to the person who owns and operates the business at the time they occur. It is risky business to purchase an income stream yet to occur. A buyer's advisors *will* eventually inform them of this fact. Count on it!

Establishing a fair price is understandably hard for owners who have spent much of their lifetime building their business. Often it is as much a part of them as a son or a daughter. For this reason, they can feel that the business is worth much more than it actually is. Sellers can find themselves placing a "psychological" value on their business, which often sets the stage for tremendous letdown as they spend inordinate amounts of time and money in the process.

2. Poor timing of sale. The best time to maximize the selling price is when *business is good* and when the *operation is growing*. Selling on the upside insures a fair price, while attempting to sell on the downside almost always decreases the yield. Timing is everything, as an old saying goes.

3. Establishes offering value through rule-of-thumb ratios. Use of illogical rules of thumb or frequently quoted industry standards oversimplify the answer to value. They can, however, serve as useful, broad-gauged yardsticks when in the hands of experienced valuators.

Two often-quoted examples might be that a motel is worth 3–5 times gross or that a restaurant is worth 1 times sales. Selling or buying a motel or restaurant on these oversimplified ratios can, and usually does, produce unsatisfactory results. Rules of thumb do not recognize expense management, nor the time required to make corrective changes where necessary. A business can be "lost" in the time frame of change.

Business worth depends upon many factors and is not limited to the following examples:

a. Asset condition and current value. (Some assets carry an "in-place, in-operation" value that can be recognized, although not financeable, in the deal. Replacement reserve must be built into the value equation.)

b. *Sustainable* level of sales.

c. Level of historical profitability.

    d. Forecasts for growth. (Confirmed industry and company data.)

    e. Competition in the particular industry.

    f. Condition and age of inventory. (Almost all inventory has "whatnot" gathering dust.)

    g. Production and delivery schedules. (Interruption by sale process can raise havoc with continuity.)

    h. Customer profiles, contracts, duration of purchasing, etc.

    i. Competitive value of the business. (Of all businesses available, how does this one stack up?)

    j. Reputation of the business and years in business.

    k. Ability to retain key employees, their skill levels, years with this business, their ability to maintain and bring in new business, etc.

    l. The new buyer's operating cost structure. (New debt and working-capital requirement versus seller's present condition.)

    m. Buyer's cost of money. (This feature affects value by much wider margins than most sellers recognize.)

    n. Buyer's skill level.

    o. Buyer's expected rate of return on investment.

    p. Enthusiasm and appeal that the business or product generates in the mind of the buyer.

    q. The marketplace in general, etc.

The process of determining a fair market value for a business is much greater than simple use of gross or net multipliers or the application of a book value. Always an overriding consideration is the question of "will the business being acquired pay for itself over a reasonable length of time." Market value is found somewhere in the balancing of asset value to a historically justified projection of cash flow, when encumbered by the debt retirement schedule, return on investment for the buyer, and provision for a "living" wage for the new buyer.

  4. Unrealistic down payment demand. Often, companies being sold have utilized much of their depreciation schedule, and for tax considerations, the transaction is best structured as an installment sale. An installment sale frequently creates "jitters" for the seller.

Knowing the likelihood that some portion may be trapped in seller financing, the seller is blinded with security jitters as well. In any event, requests for large down payments have a very real tendency to *lower* the overall selling price. With exception of a cash out, high purchase/sale prices generally produce the greatest risk to a seller when supportable cash flow is in question.

Large down payments can deplete otherwise available working capital and present risks in reaching sufficient profitability such that the buyer can make payments to the seller. The seller may want to be cautious about taking all of the buyer's available funds in the form of a down payment.

Both parties will eventually lose where working capital is excessively strained and where the buyer becomes financially "strapped" in his or her efforts to continue building the business.

5. Wants two dollars for one dollar of collateral. Available security is often no more than the assets of the business being sold, and this security is frequently reduced to "second" position behind a bank. The most predictable security is in knowing the buyer. Learn all that you can about their education, needs, expectations, stick-to-itiveness, past payment practices, etc. Rarely do owner-financed sales contain the hammered out clauses obtained by banks. When seeking owner financing, the mindset of buyers is oddly different. While 100% leverage seems a concept of the past, there still remain sellers who seek too much security, which may break the deal. Consider requiring life insurance on a buyer.

6. Payout period to amortize debt. It may be a useful exercise for the seller to theoretically put himself or herself in the buyer's position, as a final "test" of the deal. Could the seller make forecast monthly payments out of the cash flow of his or her business? Would the seller be able to "survive" on his or her own cash flow and still have enough reserve for emergencies? It is simply unreasonable to expect the buyer to use other sources of income to support the purchase. An intelligent buyer will require the purchase to be self-sustaining, on its own financial merits. Financial and legal advisors will usually fight to see that this occurs. An uninformed buyer may "swallow the hook," but the seller may lose the "catch." Beware of balloon payments shorter than five to seven years. Short-term balloon financing can be a disaster waiting to happen.

7. Wants to have their cake and eat it too. A seller often wants to take with them all of the cash of the business, accounts receivables,

and even some important equipment. Removing these assets serves no useful purpose to the buyer or the seller and may in fact lead to a subsequent loss for both parties. Price it and leave it, or negotiate these items, openly, out of the purchase price. The seller best knows his or her business strengths and weaknesses. As increased assurance of payment, it is to the seller's advantage to leave the business in a "going concern" condition.

8. Auction to the highest bidder. It is only human to want the sensational price for a company, but check what else comes with high price. Those that remain to venture forth with high offers may not, in fact, be good risks at all!

9. Inadequate records. When a seller resists in making available all appropriate data for an informed purchase decision, it is usually the seller who ultimately suffers. Loss of the prospective sale as well as issues of liability can occur. The qualified buyer has every right to complete and honest information. The courts will protect and enforce this right in cases where misrepresentation occurs and where buyers have been misled by incomplete or inaccurate statements from a seller. On occasion, a seller will make the statement that "the profit and loss statement does not properly reflect operation because of ways that money is taken out of the business." Watch out for this one! This is a lawsuit waiting to happen or, minimally, an invitation for the IRS to enter upon the scene. Remember, the IRS no longer needs to identify itself when probing for suspected tax fraud.

   Sellers or their accountant should "reconstruct" financial statements for the legitimate fringe benefits they remove from the business. This will provide the picture of available cash flow for purchase and financing decisions. Good records, a sale price closer to value, and honesty of description seem the prudent way to go. To a seller, this will provide reasonable assurance that he or she may keep the proceeds . . . in peace.

10. Targets a "dream" market. Industrial giants rarely buy companies producing a few million dollars in sales. They simply are too big to be interested in companies with modest sales unless the offered company produces a completely unique item necessary to their business. Be realistic in establishing a target buyer market. Look to the individual buyer when selling a small business and to a similar size corporation when a medium size business is being sold.

Venture capital and acquisition-oriented limited partnership buyers have very little interest in businesses with sales under ten million dollars unless those businesses serve a distinct or "niche" marketplace. Many trade on "cash outs" and will not pay close to the asking price of a seller.

11. Understates business requirements for a new owner. Whereas many businesses are sold due to the age of a principal or lack of working capital (often caused by a profit deficiency), the seller may be advised to prepare and present a schedule forecasting the capital improvements that a buyer will likely be required to make. All too frequently a seller has not made major improvements in his or her business for many years. Here again, misrepresentations have a nasty way of plaguing the unsuspecting seller. The buyer must improve what the seller failed to improve. Physical depletion effectively decreases the ultimate selling price.

    Prudent sellers, particularly where owner financing is involved, will work with buyers to assure reasonable cash flow for sustaining and improving the business. A seller's security is found in the nature of the financial and psychological wherewithal of the buyer.

12. Win-win scenario. Undoubtedly, the most successful transactions are those in which sellers and buyers, with empathy, cooperate with each other. Not an easy task for a seller who rightfully wants all that he or she can get for their business or for a buyer who seeks to purchase as low as possible. No formula works here. It is the human element of being open and willing to negotiate in good faith . . . and for both to win with reasonableness of purpose.

    Each proposed deal must be viewed on individual merit, and not all deals will be right for both parties. When it feels "right," a bit of empathy goes a long way toward providing safety and security for both and providing a transaction that stands the best chance at staying "closed."

13. Unmanaged use of professionals. Lawyers, accountants, and other professionals should always be consulted for their areas of expertise. However, the final business decision is the seller's alone. Overdependence on professionals is as inappropriate as is an underutilization of their skills. Do the legwork, obtain and scrutinize their advice, and then thoroughly examine the facts and the "gray" areas that they point out. These are the seller's dollars on the line—not the advisor's dollars. Professional service fees can

mount up rapidly when not managed closely in the selling process.

An experienced *intermediary* can help determine a fair and equitable selling price, define affordable terms and methods of payment, assess the tax consequences in allocation of assets, and mediate the psychological requirements of both the buyer and seller. He or she may be the best source to bring necessary financing to the transaction.

Finally, check references on professionals unknown to you, *before* you engage their services.

14. Bilked by a "smoothie." Look beyond the individual to see if there are both ability and security behind the buyer. *Evaluate* your *investment* in the buyer. More often today, companies are sold in a combination of cash and notes—in effect, an investment in a new company (the buyer). Except in all-cash transactions, the financed sale proceeds from this investment in the new company. In such context, take a hard look at the buyer and his or her overall capability. Experience in this business has taught the seller just what it takes to make it run smoothly. Check on the buyer in the same fashion that one would a new employee.

15. The best way to avoid surprises is to make all appropriate information available to a qualified buyer in advance. Anticipate his or her needs, and react in timely fashion to requests. Withholding pertinent information can cause great consternation at times when perhaps least expected or wanted. Repossession has proven far too often to be the result of poor judgment on the parts of sellers. The exercise of good and cautious planning, along with a reasonable approach to the sale, becomes the best "no fault" insurance that a seller can obtain.

Surprise turns buyers off! Surprise causes buyers to ask more and more questions.

Surprise brings more advisors on the scene for the buyer. Surprise ultimately kills deals.

Openness elicits confidence that, in spite of some negatives, the deal may still be worthwhile.

There never has been and never will be the perfect deal.

Those who sell wisely stand the best chance of *keeping* and enjoying the proceeds of their deal.

"Grasshoppers never get anywhere." Chinese Proverb

"If you rely just on 'thinking big', all you'll ever be is a big thinker."
David J. Schwartz, "The Magic of Thinking Big"

"Every bit of human progress . . . our inventions big and little, our medical discoveries, our engineering triumphs, our business successes . . . were first visualized *before they became realities."*
David J. Schwartz, "The Magic of Thinking Big"

Appendix A

17 Tips for Negotiating

PROLOGUE

Most happenings between people occur without significant incident. However, sometimes a disagreement, dispute, or misunderstanding can arise that tends to block further communication between parties or between the parties and third parties. While many people view **mediation** as separate from **negotiation,** the wide-ranging successes of the American Arbitration Association, a long-established national group, cannot be overlooked for its capacity to effectively utilize negotiating tools and to resolve disagreement.

The mediation process is simple because it can be accomplished without lawyers . . . so long as the *parties agree to work* toward resolution of differences. It must be understood that while mediation is not always successful at resolving a dispute, it can be a critically needed process when ultimate agreement is required of the parties, when agreement is in the best interest of parties, or when there is a strong *desire to agree* between parties. Mediation has a chance at resolving disagreement when participants can agree to "stay at the table of negotiation," regardless of all overriding feelings. If one or more will not, or cannot, invest in the *process,* then there is little likelihood of mediated or negotiated resolution. In this context, at least the psychological elements in mediation and negotiation can be similarly applied. Neither mediators, negotiators, nor principals can bully their beliefs into the resolutions of differences. We might, therefore, look at resolving negotiation as a sensible solution providing "win-win" scenarios, through give-and-take.

While the following in no way reflects the precepts of the American Arbitration Association, I certainly am influenced by personal experiences in dealing with them and their years of successful practice.

17 Tips for Negotiating

1. Select a single spokesperson for each side or viewpoint . . . or choose an uninvolved, jointly paid third party. Involve only necessary people in meetings to reduce incident and magnitude of disagreement; allow spokesperson to focus on specifics of concern.

2. Establish an agenda prior to meetings. Critical points and valuable time can be lost when there is no established agenda. Using this outline as a guide, differences can be identified and compromises negotiated, so long as the *intent to pursue* on both sides remains intact.

3. Prepare for the meeting. Failure to research the company, and opposing principals, greatly reduces the likelihood of a successful conclusion. Strength is fostered through an understanding of issues being presented on both sides and in thoroughly understanding what each person really wants. Never wait for something to happen; *make* it happen through *persuasive* presentation! Do it now! Try to contain each meeting to two hours or less.

4. Deal only with primary decision makers. Only a principal decision maker can negotiate from strength. Staff people such as lawyers, accountants, and finders may be used to define "gray" areas and present possible alternative solutions. A proposition will "cool" very quickly, if made to wait for decisions from outside of the meeting. Lawyers have no license on the field of negotiation. A few are trained and become skilled in mediation of the intricacies of business sale contracts. The *art* of gentle persuasion is mostly a selling skill and a field unto itself. For example, the American Mediation Association, perhaps the largest so functioning group, is comprised mostly of businesspeople who specialize in settlement negotiation. Few major union contracts in America are negotiated by members of the legal field. Ever present, however, are lawyers and accountants to advise in the deal. Business finders or brokers have at stake their entire payment of wages or commissions in such negotiations.

Yet, not all such people are good negotiators. Only principals have "chips" on the table. Principals must be present, seen, and "touchable" at all stages of the negotiation. When the ball is on the one-yard line, don't risk a fumble; *carry it over yourself.*

A note of caution: Few deals are actually struck at the bargaining table. Moreover, fine details are bargained for outside of meetings and "hammered" into reality by third-party spokespeople. At first this may appear to be a contradiction to the above. The art form of negotiating is in fact an art or subtle skill—a drama being played out to achieve an advantage, on a point-by-point basis. Sometimes this plays out as "cage rattling" at the table and "feather soothing and stroking" while behind the scene. This skill is best categorically depicted in union/company negotiations for major union contracts and perhaps is the leading edge to the development of negotiating skills employed in our society today. Lawyers, brokers, and occasionally accountants serve useful purposes in this third or go-between role. Principals, however, must always remain in control. For maximum effectiveness, do only what you do best, and let others do the rest.

5. Success begets success. Don't waste time telling people what you are doing or what you are going to do. Results have a way of informing the world. "Success comes to the person who brings emotion to a world starved for emotion," stated an unknown author. "True success is overcoming the fear of being unsuccessful," observed Paul Sweeny.

6. Establish strength of priorities. Prioritize issues, while bearing in mind that it is very difficult to obtain more than one or two major concessions. In getting this far along, the time for "wish listing" has disappeared. Concentrate on the major points that must be overcome. Establish the argument; then repeat these points as often as required to make your position understood. Emphasize favorable points, minimize negative issues, and be honest. *Strength in negotiation comes from a true willingness to lose it all.* It's pretty hard to beat a "mind-set" of being free to walk away. Inexperienced negotiators have a tendency, in their enthusiasm, to *tailgate* each other with "one-upmanships." Enthusiasm is contagious . . . but don't over sell. Establish each point independently, and then listen to feedback. Care must be exercised that, inadvertently, one does not lose what one has gained.

Wants can dilute the effect of strength. What we want *too much* of can rarely be obtained! Establish reasonable expectations, and hold fast to the goal. Confidence in a purpose can be convincing evidence of a person's determination. Confidence telescopes "boundaries" and builds on the framework, in which we wish the negotiation to be contained. To accomplish an objective, first you must begin. Second, concentrate exclusively on the project at hand. Third, don't stop.

7. Self-contain all *personal* feelings and emotions. When "going it alone," act emotional only when self-control can be exerted and when it comprises *planned acting* deemed essential to gain an advantage for a particular point. Emotional outbursts can permanently sever negotiation. The drama that is often employed in the negotiating process is best left to experts. Knowledge of timing and the art form employed take years to perfect. Negotiating can parallel the actions of players in a good game of poker, where "bluff" rules king of the land. Never give any indication or hint that reflects the draw of a card. The time to display the cards is *after* the deal is done. Good bluffers know their players as well as their odds. Calm discussion, in lieu of drama, may be the prudent choice for many.

8. Document the proceedings. Commit each point promptly to writing, when agreement on that point is reached. It may be suitable to work from a flip chart, outlining and checking off each point when consensus is reached. Principals can signal their consent by initialing each agreed upon point. Tear sheets can then be used to draft a resolved contract. An important psychological benefit takes place as principals engage in this process. Their acceptance of the final contract occurs gradually, thereby decreasing a natural resistance to signing at a later time. Handling minor points early in discussion fosters an ongoing impression that progress is being made. Such strategy can ease the discussion of major points later in the negotiation and when the parties have gotten into the "swing" of agreeing.

9. Act considerately, but exercise caution. Unfortunately, while engaged in negotiations, even husband and wife can be on opposite sides. It is the *attempting* nature of negotiation for one side to take advantage of the other, whenever they can. While it may be best to negotiate in an amicable environment, opposing views of-

ten tend to fan the fire of discontent. Care needs to be exercised and boundaries established to avoid the prospect of one side taking unfair advantage of the other. It must be remembered that both sides have certain select responsibilities to themselves and to others on their team. Remain on guard, and stay alert, but act fairly. The golden rule serves all parties well. The gambler's motto "easy come, easy go" has this unique tendency of finding its mark in all walks of life. Protect your interests, consider your instincts, proceed with caution, act with confidence, but try to examine each item from the other side's point of view, especially when formulating an opposing response. The ugly head of animosity serves no useful purpose in negotiation. Concentrate on long-term, permanent solutions rather than stopgap measures.

10. Don't superimpose a better deal, unless . . . you really have one. This is a common error made by inexperienced negotiators and, perhaps, shuts down more buy/sell conversations than those obvious points of contention. How can you continue to walk, without a limp, once you have shot yourself in the foot? Such a statement, without absolute truthfulness, puts one *forever* at a major disadvantage in all future negotiation. Never compromise your integrity—for anyone or anything.

11. Don't exaggerate. Exaggerations or promises made during negotiation, and not later fulfilled, are often the source of numerous problems after the marriage is consummated. Be open with answers and slow to make promises, unless they can in fact be kept. Exaggerations will tend to occur when "overtalking" a point. When a point is scored, learn to stop, and then proceed to the next point. Don't be tempted to take the easy way out. Have the self-discipline to do the right thing, rather than the instinctive thing.

12. Listen carefully. Important settlement issues are often subtle and may be hidden. Listen fully to opponents views, and they will respect you for your acts. Marriages, relationships, and negotiations fail because the parties don't pay enough attention to each other. Listening establishes a willingness to negotiate. Focus your efforts on the crux of the problem. Don't expend energy on peripheral issues that are not crucial to producing results.

13. Let silence work for you. Silence can work effectively and powerfully in negotiation. Silence can both convey the message, "I am

thinking about what you just said," and when extended, can create mild anxiety in an opponent, worrying that their request could be rejected. Planned use of silence can effectively keep an opponent off guard and afford opportunity to quiescently glide over minor items that otherwise might have been requested.

14. Never rush the discussions. Push too hard, too quick and the answer will almost always be no! Let circumstances dictate your priorities; let priorities determine your actions.

15. Always negotiate on a friendly, good faith basis. Consider an old saying, "angry people are losers." No matter how hard we try, without the act of physical force, it is impossible to *make* another person follow our will. We can only coax them along. The cardinal rule in salesmanship is first to make a friend of your customer. Don't try to be all things to all people. Learn to say no politely and pleasantly, but immediately and firmly.

16. Thank the participants. Regardless of outcomes, show appreciation for their courtesy and the time spent. If you "played" responsibly, you will most likely meet again!

17. Do not linger after the meeting. The atmosphere usually becomes relaxed and guards go down. The deck has been played, and all cards are down. Avoid premature celebrations. You're not through until you've dotted all the *i*'s and crossed all the *t*'s—and the check has cleared the bank!

"People don't care how much you know about them once they realize how much you care about them."

Harvey Mackay, "Beware The Naked Man Who Offers You His Shirt"

"If you are determined to play together, then you'll stay together."

"Indecision is the seedling of fear! Indecision crystallized into doubt, the two blend and become fear! They germinate and grow, without their presence being observed."

Napoleon Hill, "Think And Grow Rich"

"Show the way to others and you'll discover the way yourself."

Appendix B

22 "Jump-Start" Thoughts about Buying or Selling a Business

INTRODUCTION

Be certain to understand the reasons behind buying or selling a business. To understand reasons *why* can be critical to productive negotiation and can aid in structuring the deal, financing and planning for management succession, etc.

Gain, need, desire, and embarrassment-not-to-have are the only motivational factors that cause any of us to react to a proposal. Determine which of these elements are present in the task ahead, collect appropriate guiding information on the issues, and build a purchase or sale plan to fit the given situation. Without understanding of the reasons for a sale or purchase, there is little hope for successful trade-offs necessary to complete transactions. Psychological factors break, or make, as many deals as do the numbers, especially in the smaller businesses, where lifestyles are at stake or at risk in each transaction.

22 "Jump-Start" Thoughts about Buying or Selling a Business

1. Purchasing a job. This might at first appear to be a foolish first reason. However, consider the many 50-plus individuals laid off from work and who have very little real chance of becoming re-

employed at their previous level of capability or salary. There are very talented people who fit into this category of buyer and who are very willing and quite financially able to buy a business. A large number are interested for job security reasons alone. Many businesses were purchased for this reason during the downturn of the late 1980s and the early 1990s, and it is frequently the most viable option for the venturesome coming from this group of displaced employees.

2. Increase personal wealth. This is perhaps the most significant reason for individuals to purchase a business. It is very difficult to become wealthy while working for someone else. Through ownership of all or part of a growing business, a very real prospect exists to substantially increase personal net worth. An employed individual enjoys reasonable security in their job; however, this all but disappears in small-business ownership. Therefore, the risk is high, and so must be the returns. This sets up a major conflict between seller and buyer . . . both want to become wealthy through their transaction. In the opening remarks, it was pointed out that fewer than 20% of small businesses succeed beyond the tenth year. Both buyers and sellers must bear in mind these statistics; however, they can also be encouraged by the fact that small-business ownership can and does produce wealth.

3. Independence. The third most compelling reason for individuals to purchase a business is independence. Many people feel that through owning a business they will have the freedom to do as they wish, when they wish, with their lives. They want to tie their earning power to their own personal efforts.

4. Family employment. While stories abound in recent articles suggesting that families are falling apart, there remain an amazing number of prospective buyers who want small businesses that can provide employment for the whole "family."

5. Boredom. Many small businesses do not readily provide appropriate growth and challenge for their owners. Most simply cannot be developed as fast as owners might have themselves developed. Boredom creeps in, and the owner becomes ready to move on to a greater challenge. The business may have been a stepping stone for the present owner, and it can represent a solid new path for entry by first-time buyers.

6. Lost cause. Highlighted in the dedication portion of this text, it was noted that as many as 80% of small businesses fail because of weak management. Some of these present challenging opportunity, while many more are doomed to extinction because of ill-conceived ideas or products or are just beyond hope or salvation. Bear in mind that financial difficulty is embarrassing to most of us, and subsequently, we frequently do not ask for help until it is too late for that help to be cost-effectively employed. Bank work-out departments and bankruptcy court systems are good sources for locating business purchase considerations within this category. Businesses falling into this group are of considerable risk to novice or inexperienced buyer/operators.

7. Vertical integration. Although much can be said about focused specialty, there are times when in-house technology can produce savings and/or needed efficiency for operations, expediting production or delivery, and cost control.

8. Diversification. Spreading the "risk" across dissimilar product or service lines can stabilize cyclical sales, production, and subsequently, profits.

9. Eliminate duplication in a shrinking market. Two or more marginal companies can sometimes be merged and, thereby, create a profitable operation. A better selling price can occasionally be warranted where consolidation of two or more operations reduce competition. More often, however, the consolidation of production or plant facilities can make a significant difference toward eliminating duplicate cost, while building capacity and profit.

10. Reduce marketing and distribution expense. Many smaller companies utilize "reps" or networks of salesmen and/or dealers. Often, these independents handle more than one company's products. Selling and distribution expense can occasionally be lowered in a "target" company when merged with the efforts of the acquirer.

11. Market penetration. Expansion of market shares is a problem common to well-operated, but small, lifestyle businesses. At some successful point, sales increases are limited through saturation and slowed to the creep of population growth and consumer-tolerated price increases. Purchase of a growing "clone," outside of existing markets, may be a wise alternative for accelerated growth and profit.

12. Retirement. Some feel that there is more assurance of a retirement "nest egg" through ownership of small businesses. Retirement can also be a reason for sale.

13. Tax reasons. Tax shelter of income is an attractive benefit to some individual buyers. The purchase of tax losses or carryovers has become less significant since December 31, 1985. Nevertheless, this can still be reasonably attractive, when other considerations also prevail.

14. Leverage. Both individuals and companies look to trade on a company's net worth. They reason that this equity-asset value can then be used as the down payment to purchase that business. Leverage buyout has been significantly impaired by the economy of recent times and by high bank failure rates of the 1980s and 1990s. Banks have dramatically changed how they look at deals and often seek 25–30% down payments in cash before they will even open discussions with prospective buyers. Nevertheless, a few leveraged purchases continue to take place each year. Leverage, combined with "earn out" purchase, can become quite value productive to the seller with vision who picks a bright "rising star" buyer.

15. Improved capital position. Purchasing firms with strong balance sheets can improve financing for both purchase and growth. Sellers and their advisors are quite aware of this feature and often price the businesses accordingly. The cash stream may often control value to the extent that hard assets can be acquired at or below market value. While still a form of leverage, this thought is included to suggest a middle ground use.

16. Investment. Individuals and companies occasionally have excess and/or unproductive capital, and they simply prefer business acquisition over more conservative investments in stocks, bonds, etc. Also a source of small-business venture capital for some types of purchase.

17. Optimistic adventure. Many of today's buyers have not personally experienced bad economic times. While the recession of the late 1980s and early 1990s has etched caution in the minds of many, there exist those who are much more entrepreneurial and want to grow through buying businesses. The younger and more educated the buyer, the more apt this is to be true. Entrepreneurial education has become "big" business for even *elite* colleges and uni-

versities. Many well-educated young people are being developed specifically for small-business ownership.

18. Competitive advantage and growth. A key reminder is in "reducing," not eliminating, competition to the extent of trading on monopolistic practice. Much can be said for an old adage, "If you can't beat them, join them!" Or buy them! Lifestyle businesses can find much growth and savings by joining or purchasing a competitor. True monopolies rarely develop in the realm of smaller businesses, but "captive" markets can be achieved so long as unfair trade practices are not implemented.

19. Ease and cost of entry. Purchasing a business with developed expertise and production of a new product or with unique market area penetration may be less costly than to "reinvent the wheel" internally.

20. Consolidating R&D facilities can frequently result in lower new product costs, where R&D efforts are similar in the entities under consideration.

21. Technology. This element has been a persuasive factor since the advent and substantial progress of the computer. Robotics now replace much repetitive work, and "paper" residual once housed in large buildings is now stored and retrieved from units no larger than a child's desk. Yet, we are just on the cutting edge of technological change. During the next ten years, incredible changes in how we do business will occur. Some persons will bridge the gap . . . some will not. Some business owners cannot afford technological enhancement, although technology might substantially reduce the cost of their doing business, make the business more competitive, and provide new markets. Much opportunity will be available to those who learn and adjust to technological development.

22. The American dream. I seriously believe that we Americans, by the age of 40, all have experienced several passing thoughts about small-business ownership. When we are critiqued at work, when we don't get the pay increase we want, or when our vacation does not occur as we wish, the thought simply creeps up naturally. Granted, not all can make transitions successfully. The challenge lies in *vision* and *attitude*. With proper attitude and respect, both buyers and sellers who build vision for the other will enjoy the most long-term success for themselves.

"Even the blazing sun can't burn a hole through paper, unless its rays are concentrated on one spot."

"He who has a limp vision remains impotent forever."

"It will not be a chore but an adventure if you bring to it a sense of the glory of striving . . . if your sights are set far above the merely secure and mediocre."

David Sarnoff, the "Father of Television"

Appendix C

Text Material Application to Real-Life Cases

INTRODUCTION

Plaguing me for several years has been the apparent weakness in day-to-day applicability of large numbers of business book materials to real-life scenarios. Why? For several very good reasons:

1. Authors tend to present data from a singular viewpoint, which is their personal belief system and perhaps a major and unique reason why their book is published.
2. Often, presented general or generic experiences and examples relate to the mathematical deficiency of averaging averages or a "mock-up" in support of the particular belief system, therefore, making it difficult for the reader to find specific help for his or her real-life situation.
3. Business authors, particularly by their very astute nature, tend to utilize the *intellectual* versus *commonsense* approach, which dilutes an ability typical to fiction writers, to allow the reader to enter the head of the character (in this case the author), which often creates huge voids caused by writing assumptions that a certain body of knowledge pre-exists within the reader.
4. Markets for business books are not nearly as monetarily handsome as fiction and much other material and, subsequently, the ultimate audience for the book is often less clearly defined.

5. Business authors either openly or subconsciously strive to appeal to both the academic as well as their presumed audience . . . after all, it is a business task to scrutinize what appears to be a better "mouse-trap," and the educated elite will surely review the work.

An incomplete list, these no more than pass at reality and are not intended to represent criticisms, because on the more positive end of the spectrum, each does serve serendipitous enlightenment, encourage appropriate exploration and assumption of risk, and challenge individual thinking to improve what has been or what is in practice or what might be considered worth challenging. But, as U.S. Ambassador to the United Nations, Madeleine Albright, said recently, "Words are cheap, actions are the coin of the realm."

For at least some of these reasons I thought it useful to cite several cases where my "preaching" has been applied with successful results.

Disclaimer

Consulting can be a strange world of events. You may perform successfully for a client in a particular industry, and many times at association meetings he or she will pass your name to others in that industry. Before long, your clients within a given industry grow out of proportion in your practice. You find yourself confronted with the prospect of specialization. On one front, specialization can be a blessing due to valuable accumulating knowledge and a greater ability to obtain useful compiled data from industry associations. On the other front, specialization can be restricting in the services you offer. While my company endeavors to remain the "generalist," we do tend to engage more frequently with clients in several industries, although we remain careful about containment. We have a number of clients whereupon their story is similar to these in print. To protect local anonymity and to insulate the author's responsibility to protect client rights, case scenarios presented herein are taken from the travails of clients located not closer than 150 miles from the author's home in Wells, Maine.

The Case of Successful Financing for a Service Business That Was Previously Turned Down by Several Banks

In existence for 30 years and owned by the present individual for five years, the business had grown in sales by nearly 170%, or an average of 34% per year during his tenure. Accounts receivable and payable were steady at a good two-to-one ratio, and profits had risen appropriately with the level of sales. The company's reason for loan request was simply to retire a "ballooning" note from the previous seller . . . not to increase debt. No additional *bank* debt existed. Current and future business conditions looked good. At first glance it might be puzzling as to why they were rejected several times for a loan. *Examination of previous documents used in bank loan applications indicated a lack of assiduous analysis, correlation of fact, and mounting crescendo to the story being told.* Bear in mind that a business plan is a *story* about the utilization of labor, machines, and money in a specific situation. The only acceptable assumption is that the audience does not know this story. Told with enthusiasm, in chronological order, and supported by fact, a well-operated business will secure appropriate financing.

As many recognize, the service business sector is growing more rapidly than all others together. A major financing situation presented to most successful, smaller service businesses is lodged in the imbalance between hard assets and cash flow (see Figure 1, Chapter 10). Conversely, this low-capital investment, high prospect for yield is often a compelling reason for purchase and ownership of a service business. After all, if we can limit our investment/debt in hard assets and make an acceptable living from cash flow, isn't this a good name for the game? *The dilemma presented to many in the service sector, including this case example, is framed in the lack of hard asset collateral to pledge for borrowing to fund both business purchase and business growth.* I don't recall if I heard the phrase from others or coined it myself, but **banks don't finance "fluff,"** and neither will the SBA. In small business we can build all the right ratios and do all the right things in forming a business plan, but the whole package is lifeless until we answer, *beyond a reasonable doubt,* the question, "Can the loan be paid back as contracted?" Validation that sufficient hard asset value exists to cover most of the remaining loan balance in the event of failure must also be provided.

In some respects, the vast number of times I have watched commercial bankers scramble through pages of business plans, only to zero in on the debt-to-worth ratio, is amusing. A local banker recently coined a descriptive phrase "assets are too skinny," which quite often is the answer received by the service business applicant. Venture capitalists traditionally are not interested in the small service business venture, and private money is normally just too expensive for the enterprise to survive this type of debt load. Unless the owner has a "sugar daddy" relative or friend, what can he or she do to get a loan?

In our case example, as for most of my clients, we look to build the "beyond reasonable doubt" scenario. Bear in mind that faking it won't make it. Commercial bankers are not generally naive, although they may get hoodwinked occasionally during their careers. They have learned to be acutely on guard for the unsure, unsteady, and unreliable.

Our case owner had an impeccable technical background earned through both education and previous experience in a larger, closely similar public company. Work habits established during his five-year tenure were consistent with other entrepreneurial success stories. We capitalized on **personal** features and habitual characteristics of the owner, making them *seen as significant "assets,"* and/or minimally, as stamina insurance to the loan officer that the bank would be paid back. *Coupled with a credit report on both the individual and his business, showing history of prompt and reliable pay back, the commercial banker agreed to look more closely at other elements relating to his concern over safety of the bank's possible loan.*

Next we turned to *industry sources.* National data compilation resources were unable to provide the specific information we needed. We contacted the national headquarters of the specific industry association and obtained much valuable "benchmark" information. For example, we learned that of approximately 1,200 members, our client enjoyed a "niche" market advantage. He could by education, training, and state certification offer a fully engineered design service, while many other competitors were limited to off-the-shelf, pre-engineered products. We learned that average national company size, by sales and other criteria, was considerably smaller than that believed of the client by the banker. We learned that our client's operation measured above industry performance in many categories and at least equal to the remainder. What we also learned was that the owner's sales/profit forecast two years out, if achieved, would place him in the upper quartile of association membership. Finally, we learned how both existing and proposed federal and state governmental statutes played favorably into the growth of our client's on-going business. We capitalized on these data, quoting industry spokespeople frequently.

We completed a size/performance study on local competition. Examining rejected "bid" information for a preceding three years, we were able to ascertain categorical reasons why our client failed to achieve each job and which competitor did obtain that work. These elements were correlated with data from bids contracted and compared with known *strengths* and *weaknesses* of our client's company. A tightened list of strengths and weaknesses were prescribed, and an assessment of ability to overcome weaknesses were made. Some were cost-effectively achievable . . . some were not. Worth mentioning at this point is that "dwelling on positive elements" is key. List possible negative features, but **accent** the positive . . . no person or company is expected to be perfect. From these data, we tailored the marketing approach to capture more business based on strengths. A *weighted* bid specification questionnaire was developed, permitting our client to more fully assess probability of obtaining a particular job. When their prospective customer highlighted contract requirements largely outside areas of strength, completing the bid process could be passed up for concentration on potential customers where strengths provided reasonable assurance in securing work. This study provided a series of benefits, including a refinement of the sales approach and the selling strategy, much clearer understanding of competitor strengths and weaknesses, and a prospect of working more harmoniously with competitors in establishing a referral network. This referral network might particularly benefit our client where fully engineered systems were sought. In our client's primary, secondary, and tertiary market, this design capability was threatened only by one larger, higher-priced firm. An expanded marketplace was outlined, and targeted goals for penetration were established. Strengths and weaknesses were restated and pro/con rationale developed for each. The marketing plan included estimated total market potential and quantified client market share prospect.

Consolidated on one page, five years of historical financial information was presented in a reconstructed format. Reconstruction involved removing amounts for debt service, depreciation, extraordinary and one-time expenses, and owner salary to obtain an unobstructed picture of levels in cash flows. Sales by product mix and profit contribution were segregated to reveal historical skills of this owner to focus and develop profitable business.

The balance sheets presented a dilemma that had to be overcome in order to secure financing. Because of the balloon note coming due in the year of the loan application, the balance sheet revealed a "whopping" current liability problem. However, this could be simply explained as the purpose for the loan and handled by reconstructing the balance sheet under "assumed" and new financing terms. The overriding situation, and one somewhat more complex in handling, lay in *negative* owner equity created by accumulated deficit earnings in each of the five years. Simple arithmetic teaches us that when even a positive number is divided by a negative number, it leads to a negative end product. In this case, and especially concerning a lender, the product results in **negative net worth.** *A condition of too few hard assets, when coupled with negative net worth,* *should scare off any prospective lender!* Vis-à-vis, it was the source of several loan rejections for our client and the principal obstacle necessary for us to overcome.

Upon the continuing advice from an accountant, the client elected to employ tax loopholes to legitimately avoid paying corporate taxes in each of the five years. Carried forth to the balance sheet each year, these grew to a significant *negative* net worth. Although it is not my place to criticize this practice, I do have my own opinion: *As a standard operating principle, I believe that it is always prudent advice to maintain at least a small bottom-line profit, and pay some taxes—if for no other reason than planning for the eventuality of requiring borrowed funds in the future.* Statement reconstruction, for a privately held enterprise, is widely accepted within the broad financial community. The existence of this acceptable practice is, perhaps, the guise under which so many financial advisors recommend tax minimizing to their clients. In some instances, however, it forces the funds-seeking entrepreneur into the costly and time-delaying maneuver of engaging outside help to complete the process. With some profit, some taxes, an established banking relationship, and other things being equal, often the businessperson can obtain loans without the reconstruction process or a business plan. In our client's case, reconstructed earnings provided the vehicle to explain that reported negative earnings were, in reality, positive. This was accomplished by cross referencing company paychecks with his personal IRS reported earnings. Owner earnings for these periods were then compared with prevailing industry owner-compensation ranges to show that he had not received excessive salary for the purpose of corporate tax avoidance.

Average sales growth of 34% per annum required funding, which this owner chose to allocate from internal cash flow. A sufficient number of expenses directly related to sales expansion could be identified, and their composite completed the picture for reconstructing positive cash flows.

When seeking a loan, always bear in mind that a negative balance sheet will become a significant "red flag" to the lender. Unless this condition can be *legitimately* defused by fact, chances for obtaining a loan become quite bleak. In my experience, it often seems that the proverbial 80/20 principle holds true in many lending decisions. If so, then 80% of the decision rests with the quality/quantity in historical performance and 20% with the quality/quantity in forecast performance. This being possible, then perhaps the importance for particular efforts in telling the "what *has* been accomplished" story are emphatically underscored. Action has its subtle way of speaking louder than words.

The most current balance sheet was restated, new financing terms assumed, and five years of accumulated earnings under a "what if the owner had allowed some profit to trickle down" scenario were incorporated. Current ratio, quick ratio, ratio for gross margin, sales/receivable ratio, day's receivable ratio, cost of sales/payable ratio, net sales/working capital ratio, cost of sales/inventory ratio, and day's inventory ratio were calculated from these reconstructed statements. Measured to industry ranges, an analysis of our client's performance was completed. Highlighting this part of the plan was a positive outcome, direct performance comparison to a larger, distant, but similar service-capable company.

Following guidelines explained in Chapter 3, a break-even study, spanning historical and forecast periods, was completed, and these benchmarks along with healthy excess margins were interwoven into the business plan. The break-even study also provided answers to the client in regards to adding and compensating a road salesperson in a start-up territory. Questions about what additional amount of sales must be achieved to pay the base rate and what commission percent could be justified without diluting historical earnings were answered. A targeted sales goal was established for the salesperson, with performance evaluation criteria included. These were interwoven into both the marketing and financial plans where appropriate.

At this point, we were able to factually conclude through both visual and analytical observation that our client safely operated his business within industry ranges, continued to experience healthy and predictable growth, and exercised capable management control over operating expenses.

One essential chore remained to be completed before forecasting future years of performance. The process of visualizing likely conclusions for one, two, or more years into the future have a tendency to develop into acts of "wild" guessing, with layers of vagueness and unreliability, until constructed upward from component days, weeks, or months of performance leading to period endings. Also, projections are enhanced, and much more likely to be acceptable, when forecasts have their foundations built out of historical roots. The task, therefore, is to explore best available periodic, or shorter-termed record keeping, which has been maintained for each previous year used in the plan. In the smaller company, this is many times nonexistent as a formal or informal record and may necessitate desired periods reconstruction directly from deposits and payments recorded in company checkbooks. As described in Chapter 4, forecasting begins with estimating sales expected by month, for each of the years being projected.

Bear in mind capacity when estimating. Forecasting must be tempered by reality in meeting production needs through labor, machinery, and money . . . those elements of **capacity.** When a sales forecast might be greater than present capacity accommodates, a provision for attendant expense to reach the new capacity must be included in the expense forecast. **Early months of the first year forecast can be supported with booked work-in-progress and through bids outstanding.** Greater reliability and believability to a lender might be gained when these categories' percentage relationship to the historical period sales supports the logic of the forecasted condition.

In our client's case, we chose sales by month as a reliable forecasting index and proceeded to examine two month-by-month, past years of actual experience for both sales and expense. Subsequently, the first forecast year became a composite of monthly projections, rather than an arbitrary percentage growth for the whole year. A case was built in support of the forecast by comparing the levels of work-in-progress and bids outstanding at the end of each of the three previous actual years. Discernible cost elements from the new marketing plan were overlaid into appropriate expense categories as projected to occur. Percentage improvements confirmed by historical period performances set the stage in support for increasing sales by logical amounts. This sales forecasting process continued until three future years were completed. As a final reality check, it is wise to review the final forecast year total in the context of the sales year just completed. If you had completed sales at this future level today, how would your company capacity react under the strain? Based on your previous drive, do you *personally* have the tenacity to meet these goals? If the answer is yes, then the task is simply to complete forecast profit and loss statements. If no, then adjustments should be made to sales estimates that reasonably accommodate beliefs.

Historical cost of goods sold and operating expense percentage relationship to sales formed the basis for preliminary estimates in these categories. Anticipated price increases were factored into each major element when expected to occur, rather than spread equally across the whole period. One-time charges, such as insurance premiums and anticipated extraordinary expenses, were plotted in months where expected to occur. This may all seem like an inordinate amount of detail work; however, this process not only serves useful for the forecast but also produces an *operating cash budget* for the year ahead. The cash budget is more fully described in Chapter 5. Forecast years two and three were similarly constructed, applying essentially the same reality checks and balances.

Changes to balance sheets incorporated traditional accounting for depreciation, debt treatment, equipment acquisition, etc., and the profit/loss performance from each forecast completed year. While atypical in many small-business plans, we did include a "sources and uses of cash statement" to show how our client planned to retire part of his debt earlier than contracted. In this case it was a personal choice, but so doing added a nice touch, considering asset value to loan and net worth.

The business plan concluded with opinions and recommendations rendered by us to the client and included examples of simple worksheets that might improve daily control over operations. The client signed a consent to implement agreement and provided his endorsement for the accuracy of information contained. He participated fully in every step of the business plan construction.

No consultant is wise enough to get into the head of the client. The final document must be the product of a client's capability. The document must reveal *his or her* story, told in *his or her* reality. The consultant's role can be summed up in a statement by Akira Kurosana's *Rashomon,* "There may be more truths to an event than all of us who observed it can supply," and in a statement by Johann W. von Goethe, "Everything has been thought of before, but the problem is to think of it again."

Our client reapplied to one of the five rejecting banks and, when coupled with SBA guarantee, the loan closed without a hitch late this past year. Neither the client nor his business had changed . . . no magic or miracle, just a change in *how* his story was being told.

Owning and operating a successful business takes certain amounts of enthusiasm, dedication, and courage. Include several exciting victories, and tell the "real" story from the gut! Blend with careful analysis, mix well, add problem solving through anticipation, and the loan will be yours to keep, enjoy, and grow.

> *"Telling a story is one of the oldest methods of conveying a message or promoting an idea. A story entertains as it sells. It goes deep into the reader's subconscious mind. It sells ideas and promotes action."*
> John Caples, "How To Make Your Advertising Make Money"

The Case of "No Available Operating Records," and the Leverage Purchase of a Twice-Bankrupted Restaurant

Buyers, operators, sellers, and business brokers quite often stagger under the resistance by banks to finance restaurants. All with good reason. Quite contrary to naive belief, restaurants are high on the scale of the most difficult businesses to successfully operate. A close relative spent many years in this industry and, along with many other young cash-strapped college students, I toiled long hours as dishwasher, line cook, and finally, waiter. Arranging the *capacity* (labor, machines, and money) of this simple enough seeming business into operating harmony is no easy task.

My father, with all his years in that industry, near the end said, "If I have learned one major thing about the restaurant industry, it would be skills as an industrial engineer may be much more important than those of being a cook . . . a good cook can be hired, but engineering the process of food preparation to table-side delivery calls upon more commonsense knowledge than most of us intuitively possess. Learning this element on-the-job more often does not develop quickly enough to survive." How well a particular waitstaff person appears to deliver service is not nearly as important as knowing how many tables can be effectively handled by that person during rush periods. Soft, plushy carpets may be great for the customer, but not for staff. Soft carpet attacks the legs, particularly the calf, and encourages serious fatigue, subsequently entering the possibility of paying for eight hours but gaining fewer hours of output and/or intimidating service attention. Food requires various preparation durations and can be kept warm and succulent only so long. Strategy from order taking through the kitchen and back to the table with an "oohs and ahs" encore requires more than cooking wherewithal. It all comes together with a well thought out customer menu, knowledge of preparation times, understanding of portion control in the kitchen, and a proper application of the capacity of staff. In a sense, it is the professional who becomes frightened by the multifaceted *odds,* and the novice who unsuspectingly believes that whipping up great home brews will lead them to be successful restaurateurs.

Please bear with me through this momentary sidetracking dialogue, but it is important criteria in this particular story, because quite frankly, the pre-existence of professional restaurant operating skills plays a significant part toward obtaining bank participation in most restaurant financing.

Our client's proposed purchase involved valuable oceanfront property, situated within a cluster of fine cuisine-delivering establishments. The area, because of its natural panoramic scenery, had developed from the early 1800s as a unique tourist magnet. The shortest tenure of competing operators was 12 years, and all had developed an established, repeating clientele. Frequent state traffic/demographic studies were conducted for the area, because of the influence of this concentrated location on overall state tourism information. Competitor business flourished, while the subject business failed twice during the past eight-year period. Why? It was determined that questions about previous failures must be answered before proceeding with the construction of any business plan. Our clients and prospective buyers were skilled and experienced restaurant owner/operators, but, we were told, so was this bank's foreclosed client. What then precipitated these two failures? Standing firm under conditions of "lender liability," the bank refused or was unable to provide us with financial and operating histories on the facility.

Subsequently, the process became no different than the task of building a business plan for a start-up company, with a twist of being exacerbated by the history of failure. Before committing excessive client funds, however, we needed reasonable assurances that traffic existed to support this additional restaurant. Obtaining knowledge of available competitor seating, typical seat turnover ratios, and traffic volume, we quickly discounted this as a potential problem. One other important fact was learned in the process: because of incredible evening volume, no competitor offered breakfast, and only one offered a lunch entree. This might provide an opening niche for our client.

Examination of the physical plant provided answers to much of the failure story. The kitchen was too small and poorly laid out for effective service volume, and equipment was outdated and inadequate for competitive meals. Serving stations lacked essential logic in their location, and a rather attractive hostess station showed zeal in design from previous ownership, but it also showed a serious lack of understanding regarding the importance of traffic control. Exacerbating customer service and convenience was the awkward positioning of a lounge at the rear in the dinning room. This necessitated lounge patrons to wind through a tightly woven maze of seated dinner customers to reach their destination. Strategic photographs were taken for later reference. Many factors influence the proper layout and design for restaurants, but one very important consideration must be the factor of serving volume. Balancing for service volume lies somewhere between design for maximum peak volume and practical economic sustaining volume. It is psychosocially unwise and equipment cost inefficient to have too many tables vacant for great blocks of time. Being unable to seat a few customers occasionally can actually be good advertising. Knowledge coming from experience, not guesswork, provides the essential ingredient for a proper balance in configuration. With some finesse, and a bit of luck, we learned from a competitor's employee that during the height of tourist season, their restaurant seated and served as many as 600 customers per night. From these preliminary observations, we had our cause/effect hypothesis regarding events leading to previous failures. The cause was design/layout, and the effects were inconsistent food quality and unacceptable service. Consistency of quality, quantity, and service is critical in the restaurant business. These were at the heart of failure. Now we have the task of proving our hypothesis.

Detective work is needed at this stage. Our client collected menus of each competitor and thoroughly analyzed entrees for price, complexity in preparation, and table delivery timing. Local purveyors were contacted for raw product costing, and National Restaurant Association expense data were applied to round out a picture of approximate profit per entree meal. Without going into detail, we quickly proved that the subject's facilities could not cost-effectively compete without retrofitting. We engaged three persons with related experience, armed them with structured questionnaires, and sent them out to observe competitor practices. Their reports provided valuable information and added the prospect for interviewing a competitor-vacated chef, now head chef and buyer at a larger, distant enterprise. Seating capacity was confirmed. In-season lunch patronage averaged 180 meals, representing 3.0 seat turns, and in-season dinner patronage averaged 150 meals, representing 2.5 seat turns. This was said to be the maximum capacity for their kitchen, and owners expressed no concern that people were routinely turned away during the peaks each year. The bar/lounge in-season would always average three to four patrons deep. Average entree price from the lunch menu was $8.17, and from the dinner menu it was $17.16. Average annual head count was 71,176 patrons. Individual lunch checks averaged $9.97, and for dinner, $21.36. This competitor is situated adjacent to the subject property.

Our hypothesis is confirmed. Failure by an experienced person was determined to be a product of undercapitalization and not having relevant experience fitting the size and volume potential of this facility. The other became overwhelmed and lost heart and investment. With exception of the kitchen, redesign of service footpaths and the customer area had been an inexpensive process. The kitchen was functionally obsolete, and only curable with substantial investment. Our client proceeded to redesign the facility, and we continued work on the plan.

Detailing results from this homework assignment supplied the cornerstone for overcoming the first step in financing resistance. These data reinforced a need to highlight particular skills existing in our client/buyer . . . skills learned through previous work assignments, particularly those that were directly applicable to handling facility and operating shortcomings. Résumés were redrafted in the form of short case scenarios, outlining problems encountered, solutions presented, and their actual results. A "strategic objectives" section was developed to summarize the subject's problems, to recommend corrective solutions, and to forecast results likely to occur. Incorporated into this section were complete re-engineering design with transparent traffic pattern overlays, specific equipment positioning, calculated rationale, time table to complete, and detail costing supported by purveyor quotes.

Using competitor menus as guides, the next task was to construct a proposed subject menu and cost out delivery of service. This was entirely accomplished by the client and then compared with National Restaurant Association data to support authenticity in forecast. The client planned initially to offer three meals per day. Although his forecast for the breakfast meal suggested profitability, little information about "morning" tourist movement patterns were available to support more than a best guess level of sales. Nevertheless, breakfast even as a loss leader would get customers back on the premises.

Applying data supplied by the relocated competitor chef, and believed to be reliable, in-season sales could be estimated at $327,552 and off-season at $232,518, for total revenue of $560,070, or average sales per seat of $9,334.50. These estimates were felt to be conservative. From the menus of other direct-proximity competitors, data were similarly correlated to estimate their sales. All were then compared with the actual operating results of two restaurants situated approximately one mile away. Being of less densely trafficked locations, these two operations could provide support for our "downside" forecast. Reliable sampling techniques have a lot to do with skills, of course, but *availability* of critical local information more often results from strategically accumulated data banks. This is a valuable addition that assisting consultants should be able to provide.

A first-year forecast now complete, low, median, and high probability of occurrence were then benchmarked. Proposed debt service held as a constant, the lowest level of operation would cover debt service, provide a livable owner wage, and accommodate modest reserves for working capital. An enhancing level of authenticity was brought to the forecasts through the ability of our client to provide recent operating statements from his previous restaurant. This is not always available and not always important, but in this case, it is of significant psychological value. Bear in mind that proposed is a highly leveraged purchase from bankruptcy, which is exacerbated by on-the-blink prevailing economy. This, in our opinion, necessitated establishing above average credibility for the buyer. In the traditional cash-on-cash down payment scenario, this feature might not be quite so essential; however, it certainly will always help. The remainder of business plan construction followed essentially the format outlined in text material.

The client secured a contract on the property, pledged unencumbered oceanfront property as down payment collateral, obtained a construction/equipment loan, a $50,000 working line of credit, and closed the purchase. He and his family rehabilitated the facilities as proposed, added to the kitchen, installed appropriate equipment, opened on schedule, and have operated a full season. Revenues exceeded median forecasts by 110%, and cost of goods sold, along with operating expenses, have tracked very close to forecasts presented in the business plan. Both he and the bank are quite happy with first-year results.

Was our service an expensive process for the client? Yes! Was it worth doing? He thinks there was no other way. Some business plans will be expensive and will involve incredible time and effort. Some will not. Cost/benefit depends upon how one views cost/work in its direct relationship to successful attainment of goals and the prospect for living out personal dreams.

> *"It's a funny thing about life, if you refuse to accept anything but the best, you very often get it."*
>
> W. Somerset Maugham

A Special Case, a Special Need

Life journeys will periodically bring each of us into contact with opportunities for undertaking projects where humanitarian interests may become as strong as the need for monetary reward. Such was the case for me in accepting a very recent client assignment.

A debilitating industrial accident, coupled with repetitive motion injury, cut short during midlife the client's advancing industrial career. To some this presents complacent and quiescent retirement, but to others it represents a staggering blow to self-esteem and worth. In his opening statements, I found the particular criteria I personally require for accepting any job. With conditions explained, he provided the unlocking key . . . motivation . . . "I'm a workaholic. I need to work."

This person was focused on clear objectives, had collected amazing amounts of market information, and had thoroughly researched equipment for completing production requirements without exacerbating a permanent physical limitation. This convincing evidence lacked only organization, financial forecasts, and study for possible success . . . and a business plan for the bank. Recorded in his mind lay most of the story. The bank referred him to me, and they were anxious to do business with him.

During his life, the client has completed a long series of courses that will contribute to success in this new endeavor. Since the injury, special education in the use of adaptive equipment via robotics was undergone to explore adverse effect in limitations and to research safe work options. Nine years of related industrial employment, coupled with supplemental experience producing products for sale in his wife's business and in other businesses, formed the basis for his résumé and added an important overture to prospects for success.

Where do you begin the process when a proposal for a new venture involves a single-employee operation and the client has debilitating obstacles to overcome? First, bring the obstacles into perspective. What can and cannot be done? In this case, the client had already researched and solved the question of what could be accomplished and which type of equipment could be safely operated. Documentation was all that remained. Professional verification of injuries and medical endorsement of proposed equipment use were included in the report. This plan development required special attention to the *physically possible,* along with conventional elements.

Shuffling stacks of paper into some semblance of logical order can seem quite overwhelming at times. Organized into smaller parts, the project will appear less threatening and will become more possible. For example, I use a large three-ring binder, divided by tabs that are labeled in much the same fashion as chapters in the text. It then becomes relatively easy to sort pages of material into their respective slots, to determine what I have and what remains to be done.

With formulated ideas in hand, and much homework complete, our client was stumped when the bank required a written plan before further consideration of his loan request. This is a frequent reason that many clients engage our service. Referenced often in my text, broad financial wherewithal is uncommonly found in the initial makeup of budding entrepreneurs. Successful operators learn what they need to know along the way. The client knew what he would do to organize, operate, and grow the business, but did not know how to translate this information into language acceptable for loan review.

Although he had researched several manufacturers and received their encouragement, he did not have solid commitments for proposed sub-contract work. Projects he might complete for his wife's business and others would not forecast sufficient cash flow to cover machinery purchase debt. Subsequently, an early chore was to obtain letters from prospective customers that might contain as strong language as possible regarding their needs and potential use of his service. This responsibility in the project was assumed by the client. Working in his distinct favor was the fact that the major piece of equipment he would purchase could set him apart from local competitors. We directed our attention to exploring the industry at large.

Much can be discovered about operational characteristics of the larger, privately held company, but it can be incredibly difficult to obtain much information on the single-operator shop. Business failure rates at this level of entry seem incurably high, and those that do succeed tend to grow into the larger category, while an even greater number become merely recorded in fatality statistics. Great companies such as Digital Equipment and Boise, however, have their founding roots stretching back into this one-employee level.

While we had little accumulated experience in his industry, we nevertheless did have a good friend with the business of a larger company. He, in turn, introduced us to a national industry consultant . . . one that specialized in the growth of the smaller company. Between these two individuals, the rest of this part of the client story became relatively easy to construct. Not only did we obtain criteria of successful operation but we also were provided key elements where failure seemed imminent.

Working together, the client and I developed a list of strengths and weaknesses, outlining those items that could be initially handled, and established a longer-term marketing plan that addressed those elements that would take time to cure. Several letters obtained from potential customers were definitive enough to suggest excellent opportunity for viable work. Those traditional questions of how, why, where, and when were answered in the marketing plan.

The financial plan stole the "when" of the marketing plan and translated these data into period-occurring sales. Early cash flow could be forecast from sales to his wife's business, and sales coming from other similar shops were estimated based on his own past experience. While not justifying costly machine purchase, this particular product manufacturing would serve in familiarizing the client with use of the new equipment and provide some initial cash flow. The plan called to phase out this production as principal jobs were phased in. Cost of goods sold involved mostly his labor at cost and cost of the material used in production of products for his wife. Principal jobs would involve performing skilled work on materials supplied by the customer, therefore, labor-only cost. Expenses were refined from known facility costs, and others were estimated from an insurance agent's quote, equipment manufacturer's estimated power consumption, transportation cost factors, etc. To these were added a contingency expense to cover estimating error, and the completed forecast then compared with industry range. Three years were projected into low, median, and high probable growth categories. Debt service remained a constant in the analysis. First-year breakeven was forecast to take place during the ninth month of low probable sales, or in the sixth month of median attainment sales. A cash flow budget and a balance sheet were constructed for year one only. Some bankers may want these completed for all three years; however, I find it difficult to put much stock in more than one year out, particularly in a single-employee, start-up business, unless breakeven cannot be counted on in the first year. Although *educated guesswork,* much about any new-beginning business is still just a guess. That guess can usually be made quite focused for a short period, but the "what if" variables make the ride wild and woolly as one moves out in time. A refinement process is costly, and the banker is more often content with longer-term sales pro formas and with reviewing the year forecasting breakeven.

The client was approved by the bank for his loan. This story does not have an ending for now. Equipment is ordered but has not been delivered.

My hat goes off to this particular client for a number of reasons. His homework prior to meeting with me was far more complete than most whom I initially see. What impressed me the most was his character and steadfast purpose. He could well have remained a number among worker-compensation statistics, but he chose to remove himself . . . to become gainfully self-supporting once again. He deserves a great deal of credit for his tenacity and for the search to regain a self-esteem so vital in American society today. He well deserves encouragement and support along his path to success in this endeavor. His depth of research is convincing evidence to me that he will eventually fill voids in knowledge and be counted among a fortunate few start-up operators who do survive and grow.

"People are always blaming their circumstances for what they are. I don't believe in circumstances. The people who get on in this world are the people who get up and look for the circumstance they want, and, if they can't find them, make them."

George Bernard Shaw

Overlooked Source of Information on Very Small Businesses

Business brokers are a resource too often overlooked by both the financial community and by individuals. These brokers are on the front line of selling much of "Main-Street" American business. The corner store, the small diner, the neighborhood hardware store, the local computer store, gift shops, apparel stores, drug stores, liquor stores, florist shops, advertising and printing businesses, etc., fall within their mainstay of daily business. Much information about the *mom and pop* business is at their fingertips. Some business brokers are adept at financial management, and some are not. But, in some format or other, all business brokerage offices have financial records of the businesses they have listed and/or sold. Their major network organization is the International Business Brokers Association (IBBA), 11250 Roger Bacon Drive, Suite 8, Reston, Virginia 22090-5202. Another network is the Institute of Certified Business Counselors, P. O. Box 70326, Eugene, Oregon 97401. Thomas L. West, Editor, *Business Brokerage Press,* P. O. Box 704, Concord, Massachusetts 01742, a founding charter member of IBBA, is a storehouse of small-business knowledge. Tom has spent much of his life in the industry and either founded or cofounded two large franchise business brokerage firms. He is a consultant to brokerage firms and may charge a fee for information or might direct the inquirer to an appropriate compilation service traditionally used by business brokers.

Example of Conducting Market Research

Several years ago we were engaged by a small community economic development commission to assist them in attracting private enterprise to locate in their community. Work completed to entice one particular candidate may provide insight into a process of employing market research options to tame or eliminate prospects of the word "no."

The candidate target was a major chain superstore grocer. Their annual report emphatically stressed future development as limited to large stores within a distinct shopping territory. Gains from property tax income and provision for employment of hundreds of local residents made this candidate particularly attractive to the community group. "No, just too small a community," was the response they received from initial inquiry.

Short Course in Sales Psychology

When shifting from the world of finance, to work on sales and marketing issues, I always give myself a quick shot of psychology . . . a four-point refresher course in motivation that helps keep my eye on the ball: GAIN, NEED, DESIRE, and EMBARRASSMENT NOT TO HAVE! These are the four horsemen of motivation. From training in psychology, I no doubt could write a book for each category, but this is completely unnecessary because no matter how each are expanded upon, their sum total is still just gain, need, desire, and/or embarrassment not to have. What do you or I stand to *gain* from a decision? Do we *need* what is being considered, or do we just *want* it? *Keeping up with the Joneses* has certainly been a compelling motivation for extracranial purchases. To cause another to react favorably to a proposal necessitates **overcoming the objections** to that proposal. *One of the best ways to overcome a possible objection is to anticipate its existence and to provide positive answers for it in an initial approach.*

When given the assignment, provided information was the target's annual report and their response that the community was considered too small for a superstore. The group felt this chain store was superficially underestimating potential for locating here, but they did not know how to go about proving it. Although assertively pursuing new store openings, it became apparent that initial site-selection criteria by the company precluded what appeared to be the makeup of our community.

The annual report listed total number of stores in the chain, total housing square footage, and total annual sales. Also listed were the number of superstores presently opened and that apparent preferred size of these grand stores was 33,000 square feet. Reducing total company sales to average sales per square foot, this product, when calculated on 33,000 square feet, produced estimated sales the chain might expect from new locations. The task now became one of ascertaining sales potential within the community and the close-proximity territory.

Market research frequently is a collection of fact, sometimes minimally available; educated guesswork, requiring some experience; and quite often, a large dose of finesse, which is anybody's game. I don't say this to be critical of the process, but to underscore the fact that information being sought is usually quite personal and, therefore, quite particularly protected from the ready grasp of researchers. Market researchers, however, have become very adept, with unusual accuracy, through use of scientific sampling techniques in their guesswork. A good market researcher is, by any standard, first a good detective.

We visited three different superstores in the target chain. This part of the project involved counting the number of check-out registers being used and the number of cars in the parking lot at various times of the day. For comparison, we conducted the same study of two potential competitor locations. Total sales reduced to sales per register can produce a useful benchmark for interpolating sales by another. Granted, this benchmark will be enhanced when starting with confirmed, rather than estimated average sales. However, in this case, more precise information is unavailable. Remember, they said no, and we must provide compelling reasons for their reconsideration of a location in the community. Benchmark information would be useful toward estimating sales produced at local stores within the community territory. Important additional data for this part of the guesswork was readily obtained from our own data bank of operating small and larger grocery stores. Sales were estimated for community stores and plotted on a map drawn for that purpose. Included were estimates for the two more distant, larger stores.

United States census data were obtained on the community, as well as on the secondary and tertiary market. This information was also plotted on the map. Applying local store sales estimates to census information, it was determined that per capita purchases made within the town were under $400. If our conclusions were correct, $400 per person per year would represent an abysmal contribution to overall local food purchase and consumption. According to census data, this community's median household income exceeded $40,000 per year, which established the town as having above average buying power. Primary and secondary population were determined to be slightly under 42,000. Sales coming from the tertiary market might be more difficult to predict, because the distance of two large stores, when compared with location in this community, appeared only to give that population another choice in where they could shop. The two stores were both situated in larger, more industrialized towns. Parking lot volume/time, supported by number of store registers open, provided some insight into shopping patterns. Coupled with to/from work migration, it was concluded that a tertiary population night be inclined to shop in our community for reasons of ease of entry and/or point of purchase pricing. Traffic in our town was fairly consistent and specifically not exacerbated with spurts of shift employment changeover. Further study could pinpoint the conditions and likelihood of attracting from tertiary markets; however, the town group felt satisfied with this preliminary information and would now prefer us to concentrate on local study.

Where was major shopping being carried out? A weighted questionnaire was developed, ten local housewives were hired and appropriately trained, and then they conducted a "street press" survey of 500 community residents. The outcome revealed patterns in higher income householders to shop with a chain competitor located 18 miles to the south and mid and lower income householders to shop with a chain competitor located 12 miles to the west of the community. Both groups shopped with local merchants when convenience between major shopping trips prompted.

The demographic overlay to information collected provided sufficient compelling evidence for the chain to reasonably expect attainment of superstore sales requirements.

Desire can be considered a component of need when gain is established to exist. To outdo the Joneses can be turned into outdoing competition. Neither competing chain store had reason to build in this community—they had their share from current locations 18 and 12 miles away. However, the closest location for the target chain store was 50 miles away.

After reviewing a report, the target company answered, "YES, we will look closer at your community." After confirming report information through their own discovery process, they purchased land and built a local superstore. Six years later they are more than content with GAINS. The town's tax base rose, and local unemployment has precipitously dropped. A "no" was turned into a "yes" by providing alternative answers to anticipated objections, all of which caused the objector to act positively and decisively on the town's proposal.

> *"Change starts when someone sees the next step."*
> William Drayton

Market Research in Use with Relocation and Business Plan Production

A well-known physician elected to relocate to another state. He asked for help in screening specific communities and help in identifying group practices within that community for him to consider joining. As a well-known, established geriatric practitioner, he wished a reduced-pace lifestyle and more time to study and write about his experiences with an aging population. Relocation affect to personal economics must be a consideration in his decision.

Historical accounting and selected patient statistics were provided, as was a detailed description by the physician of his specialized study-target goal. Office location must be within commuting distance of an acquired home and of a key hospital. Pinpointing the community, of course, would necessarily be a beginning task.

Background data were gathered from the American Medical Association, Harvard studies, and specialized geriatric groups. United States census information was assembled on each target community. Practice data were correlated with professional association information and with national experiences of physician absorption into new locations.

Before delving into our study, however, it would prove useful to review characteristics of professional practices. There are both similarities and differences between a small business and a professional practice. Several characteristics that can be broken down into five categories distinguish it from other small businesses:

1. The practice is primarily a service business.
2. There is necessarily a relationship of trust and respect between the patient and the doctor and/or employees of the practice. The patient must rely on medical expertise that they themselves are not fully capable of understanding or evaluating.
3. The practice and practitioner relies upon a referral source or sources as mainstay and business growth.
4. Practice requires a specific college degree, and rigid standards of credentialing must be met for most specialized medical practices.
5. A medical doctor must be licensed in each state where practicing.

The distinction between medical practices and certain kinds of service businesses may be fine-lined, at least for some of these characteristics; however, trust and respect factors must be underscored as crucial to a doctor's personal success. *Trust and respect are chief reasons why "goodwill" relates strongly to each individual practitioner.* Subsequently, "group practice goodwill" must be evaluated on individual goodwill basis.

New patients more often choose their doctor on the basis of referral from a friend or another known medical source. Fingers walking through the yellow pages rarely is a precipitating cause.

Location of a practice has a substantial impact on potential revenue. Some communities are good "family" towns and provide wider avenues for family practice, while nearness to a ski area might serve best for an orthopedic specialist, etc. Socioeconomic make-up of a community impacts both levels and timing in revenue generation. When location is a condition by choice, areas that contain strong and vibrant economies will generally afford larger returns.

These were some of the industry elements that had to be recognized during our study. Some readers may not be aware of the value that can be extracted from data provided through U.S. Census Centers. Therefore, the information on page 211 is exhibited to show ranges for possible use in market research and for assistance with likely scenario forecasting.

There are additional demographic statistics that can also be purchased in categories by town, county, state, and the United States. These data are widely used by commercial researchers for market, pricing, location, and a whole bevy of probability studies. These data are so frequently used by my firm that we have computerized census information into extensive cross-reference files. When indexed with specific industry data, much stronger justification can be presented, supporting or rejecting a proposition.

The search was narrowed to two likely communities, with detailed community histories compiled and an overlay primary, secondary, and tertiary market established for each. Distance of patient migration to a medical specialist can largely be determined by knowledge of distance from other competing practitioners. Highly specialized practices are dissimilar from general practice in this particular respect. In the client's case of restricted geriatric specialty, age in the defined market population, coupled with number and location of competing practitioners, became an essential ingredient leading to our final recommendation. Many factors influenced the doctor's ultimate decision, but he did choose the community that we believed suited him best.

Locating a possible group for him to join was handled much like the one time-fashioned by executive recruiters in the "headhunting" game: identify groups, establish practitioner service offered, look for a void/asset to service offered, and make a "do you know of" situation phone call. Three interested group practices were found within the target community, contact names were provided to the doctor, and he made his own choice.

Demographic Information on Selected Towns
(All data as of 1990 census unless otherwise noted)

Town: _____ Pop: _____ Med. HH Inc. $: _____

Age Categories

Under age 5	_____
5–15	_____
16–20	_____
21–24	_____
25–44	_____
45–54	_____
55–59	_____
60–64	_____
65–74	_____
75–84	_____
85 and up	_____
Median age	_____

By Sex

Male	_____
Female	_____

By Race

White	_____
Black	_____
Ind/Esk/Ale	_____
Asian/Pac I	_____
Other	_____

Population Growth

1960	_____
1970	_____
1980	_____
1990	_____

Rents

Less than $250	_____
250–499	_____
500–749	_____
750–999	_____
1,000 or more	_____
Median	$ _____

Household Characteristics

Persons in households	_____
Persons in group qtrs	_____
Institutionalized per	_____
Total # households	_____
Married-couple family	_____
Female HH, no husband	_____
Nonfamily household	_____
Live-alone HH	_____
65 and over	_____
Male	_____
Female	_____
Persons per household	_____
Persons per family	_____
Persons per sq. mile	_____

Housing

Detached unit	_____
1 unit attached	_____
2–4 unit	_____
5–9 unit	_____
10 plus unit	_____
Mobile homes	_____
With 1.01 or more persons per room	_____
Vacant housing units	_____
Rental vacancy rate	_____
Homeowner vac/rate	_____
Value of house unit	
Less than $50,000	_____
50,000– 99,999	_____
100,000–149,999	_____
150,000–199,999	_____
200,000–299,999	_____
300,000 or more	_____
Median	$ _____

Five years have passed. The physician is quite happy in the community group practice and has written two books, and in supplemental benefit, I have gained a good friend and sailing cohort.

> *"Decide what you want, decide what you are willing to exchange for it. Establish your priorities and go to work."*
>
> H. L. Hunt

The Case of Arbitrating a Business Value

Unusually tumultuous conditions in a pending divorce precipitated our employment by a superior court system. The contested value of a jointly owned manufacturing company, doing 3.5 million dollars in sales, was at the heart of purpose and reason for our engagement. Discord between the couple was rampant on many fronts and had prevailed for an unfortunate, extended period of time. Dissenting parties employed qualified business evaluation experts, representing individual sides in the case. Each expert presented compelling reasons for his or her stand on value. Resolution and settlement were stymied, with wide disagreement over value of this asset. Mediation for a middle ground had been unsuccessfully tried.

A review of Chapter 10 reminds us that worth is nothing more than perception, and we each bring to the evaluation process our own ideas on what the "right" perception is . . . that's what makes the process of analyzing the concept of a business's value so interesting. The process of evaluating worth is a process of **sophisticated estimating,** no more, no less. Even experts can honestly disagree over perception of worth. The conclusive test to value perception occurs only in the marketplace, when actual buyers and sellers *close* transactions. When transpired, there no longer exists need for valuation service. However, root data taken from results of actual transactions must, wherever possible, provide the "yardstick" for measuring estimates in value, or too much of the process can become a guessing game.

Experts in our case had done their homework, and I could understand how each had arrived at their conclusions. Having been in their predicament myself, I could also understand the psychology in positioning their opinions as they did. Working for two bosses, a client attorney and the client, is always more difficult than working for one. I enjoyed a unique advantage by serving just one master—the Judge!

Although I am not high on *rule of thumb* as essential in business valuation, there can be a clear assistance from their occasional use. No one approach, one formula, nor one expert can represent all things in all value assignments. Cohesive data from the business, cohesive external information by comparison, and comprehensive analysis usually lead to the best forecast for expected results. When information is vague, essentially unavailable, or the price to complete appropriate study is objectionable, rule of thumb can be a worthwhile recourse. Rule of thumb can also add support to findings in the detail study.

The company in point owned substantial hard assets (virtually without leverage), enjoyed a niche market, produced a unique product, and was rewarded an incredible cash flow. It was not hard to understand reasoning in the discord over dividing this community asset. But it will always be hard for me assuming responsibility as a possible deciding factor affecting livelihoods. The key rests in humanitarian impartiality. I mention feelings here for three reasons:

1. My education/experience in both psychology and finance was a specific reason why the court picked me for this case.
2. Belief that this criteria may be required to resolve.
3. Both reasons 1 and 2 did play a significant role in the ultimate resolution.

The mystery in perception unlocks itself when one understands oneself. Although easy by standards in most valuation tasks, this may have personally been my most difficult assignment.

No directly comparable closed sale data were discovered, but similarities found in functional operation afforded projection of rule-of-thumb value. Defense of this projection was built, using each expert's assigned value and then working through buy-out scenarios. In effect, the attempt was to change points of view from focussing on splitting whole value to focussing on dividing this asset by value in cash flow. As suspected, the lower value was considerable "giveaway," and the higher value violated prudent investment principals. The obvious answer was somewhere in between— but the task was how to resolve it!

Returning to facts about the business itself provided key ingredients to understanding other elements of the discord. First, day-to-day engineering know how was required to operate the company. Second, research and development of patentable new products was essential in future company growth. The wife held an engineering degree, founded the business on the basis of a product that she designed and patented, and remained the major R&D contributor. The husband, entering the business two years after its inception, became a significant contributor to sales. Day-to-day financial affairs were handled by an unrelated employee, and major cash decisions were shared between the couple. Fact: the business contained in the wife a critical and perhaps unique skill not easily replaced. Fact: the wife wanted to continue in and was needed in the business, but the husband wanted out after the divorce. Both believed that sale prospect for the business rested in major growth of sales, to a point that a large company could be interested. Uncommon requirements at this point of development suggested that finding an individual buyer might be like "finding a needle in a haystack." This issue was not fully considered by either valuation expert. These conditions on the table raise valid questions. Is value of this particular business as simple as turning a faucet on or off— value or no value? Is value beholden exclusively to the skills of one employee?

I think consensus answer would be no! But I also believe that experts will agree that highly specialized skill of an owner plays a role in overall value, until some size or point when the business employs others to replicate that skill. To some considerably lesser degree, most smaller businesses suffer under dilemmas presented through personal owner involvement. Defense could be built for unequal value in our case, but pure logic is often blind when anger rules. Selling this concept to the parties would require repetition of fact and a good deal of salesmanship.

Line-by-line agreement was negotiated as each affected item was reconstructed, where appropriate, in profit and loss statements. Joint agreement over cash flows was reached for each of the years examined and used. Item-by-item agreements were essential to any thought for agreement on the whole. With rule-of-thumb value recalled and traditional terms applied, a new possible settlement value was offered. Although still in disagreement over price, one vital aspect of perception had changed: there were both agreement and understanding of the rather simple logic used in arriving at a new value.

Effective salesmanship teaches us that questions framed to cause a series of yes answers build walls behind them that make it difficult to return our answer with no. An agreement was also jointly reached that it may take several more years for the company to reach its sale potential. This provided a choice for the husband: stay with the company to that point or consider accepting a lesser value and be done with it. The door to possible joint resolution opened upon his question, "What is lesser value?" A question not easy to provide a *defensible* answer. In fact, one that may defy any resemblance to precision in quantitative answer!

Finesse, in poker, is often nine-tenths of a game. These were intelligent people, and no matter how I chose to propose an answer to the husband's question, it must involve logic in the finesse. Perhaps any number of thoughtful approaches would serve the desired result, but I elected to build my case through the value of employment. Benchmarked from American Management Association Executive Compensation Surveys, cross-referenced with opinions from two local employment agencies and an executive search firm, we came to agreement on what typical heads of companies this size might earn. We then asked both parties to agree upon an exact number of future years for the company to grow to sellout potential. Irrespective of right or wrong assumptions, both were convinced that a complete sellout right now could be costly to both—a key psychological advantage for leveraging some form of agreement. With the game plan not fully exposed, I told them that it really didn't matter what the number was but that a specific number of future years required must be agreed upon. They agreed on three years. I used external compensation data, rather than actual individual earnings, simply to keep logic on an impersonal note. The wide difference in expert values proposed represented considerable money, but their median of value turned out to be 20% *below* the rule-of-thumb value I had been using. "You both are intelligent people and fully recognize that neither the high nor the low numbers will fly . . . what if, for a moment, we assume that value is as I propose and that we imbalance that number by three years of the wife's employment," I offered. Before the afternoon was over, agreement was reached on the *logic,* but there was still disagreement on settlement. The proposal was reduced to writing, and the couple was sent away to think about it for two days.

This epilogue served to break the larger perception into two smaller elements for individual consideration and addressed the wife's unswayed contention that *any and all* value in the business was her doing. It was her doing . . . but the husband repetitively contributed to growth and value, also providing her with much essential time for R&D. His job could not go unreplaced, and an outside employee might not be so effective overall. In different ways, both had created value together.

The situation did not resolve immediately, but the focus of the argument evolved to the factor of number of years being used versus whole value, and an agreement on settlement value was eventually reached. One and one-half years versus three years became the criteria for discount.

I present this case history not so much in its merit for experience at learning valuation, but more to highlight the issue of *perception* in worth. Worth of any business most often hangs in the balance of its ability to pay for itself over a reasonable period of time. "Ability to pay for itself" can be quantitatively interpreted and confirmed. However, "reasonable period of time" is a product of perception, and opposing sides usually bring different perceptions to the table. As explained more fully in Chapter 10, opinions of value will simply be unilateral until factors swaying perception are effectively handled.

> *"People seldom* buy *an idea without* buying *its author in the process. When they sense that they are treated as equals, all working together in the search for the right course of actions, they eagerly join in discussion with good will, even if your idea is repellent."*
>
> Henry M. Boettinger

An Overview of Perception/Worth Reality Influencing "Overpricing" Occurrence in Business Price Setting (Composite of Many Case Experiences)

Most small-business owners, comprising a group in which I include myself, experience varying degrees of emotional conflict when reaching the point of considering sale of their businesses. Conflicting feelings can, and do, quite naturally grow out of *comfort zones* established through *time* in relationships with family, friends, community, and business. Time and types of experiences accumulate by no accident to play significant roles in decisions affecting personal lives. It is human nature that some life experiences will benefit and provide essential protection to well being and that some will condition reality from being readily seen. We all know this . . . we really do.

I believe that a most difficult relationship encountered everyday is the relationship we have with ourselves. Each man, woman, and child is somehow taught, or otherwise learns, to wrestle the "who" we are with the "what" we are expected to be. Men experience particular difficulty separating their personage from that of marching to drums beat by others. We men tend too quickly to view our whole *worth* as relative to holding down jobs. Business and professional women easily get caught up in this whirlwind fantasy as well. He's a doctor, or she's a company president . . . versus he's a man, or she's a woman. Our *major* worth, as seen *both by ourselves* and by others, is also too precisely measured by *what* we do for a living, rather than consentingly measured by our individual, sometimes very personal, need to be unique human beings. We all know this, too; however, many of us still continue avoiding its recognition.

Perhaps we can aptly shorten these thoughts by saying that we can *allow* ourselves to get out of touch with our own reality, and that *this is* sometimes okay. Inventions and other great happenings more often come from people who leave bodies of reality to dream, imagine, plot, and plan the unexpected and to capture the surreal.

However, where we most need reality, and where we become crippled from its absence, is during decisive moments leading our daily lives, vis-à-vis, planning events unlikely to occur and then inordinate daydreaming about farside outcomes. Debilitating mantras or gratifying adventures can result. There are many stories told about money, and it's back to the old job/worth syndrome. "The love of money is the root of all evil." "A fool and his money are soon parted." "Money cannot buy love, but it can help fake it." "If I had the money, I could do this or that." Money, wealth, and *worth* walk side by side on the same path in the views of many who attempt to "judge" and, frankly, pigeonhole us by *their* opinions. We can just as easily pigeonhole ourselves. A wise man once said, "Wealth, to me is not measured in money. It is the ability to do what I want to do, when I want to do it, and as often as I want to do it." From his statement, it sounds as if he knows the value in his own personal worth. We all know and possibly experienced these things, too.

What relevance does this psychosocial rambling have to do with business valuation and/or value in sale? It has to do with necessity of "balancing" reality in transactions for both obtaining and enjoying proceeds. You and I—we are the *who,* and importance is stated in its context of important to us. With realities in check, the *what* can be summed as understanding future value of dollars obtained now versus present value of dollars obtained at some future time. In effect, following reasoning in an old adage, "A bird in the hand is worth two in the bush."

Ensuing information may help broadly to serve description of a tangential marketplace. Over the past 14 years, it has been my experience that evolving changes in buyer attitude have been mostly evidenced by their *increased* search effort to locate *quality* business purchases. Skills required in their search effort have greatly improved. Higher initial cost of businesses, decreased ability of people to save money, increased average education of prospective buyers, and availability of professional services may have a great deal to do with these changes. Much of the following data are provided through the courtesy of Tom West, *Business Brokerage Press,* and past Executive Director of the International Business Brokers Association. While lacking authenticity of impartial, controlled sampling technique, I do believe this information is reliable. Brokerage companies derive earnings exclusively from commissions, only *when* businesses they have listed are actually sold. To them, total market awareness is critical to future business planning and for benchmarks on market shares.

Using SBA guidelines, Tom West was able to determine that there are approximately six million businesses in the United States with one or more employees. In further breakdown, 89%, or 5,340,000, are considered very small, with fewer than 20 employees. Nine percent, or 540,000, fit a category of small, with between 20 and 100 employees. The remaining 2%, or 120,000, businesses are considered medium to large, with greater than 100 employees.

Other data provide that approximately 55%, or 3,330,000, of the total number of businesses have individual gross sales of less than $500,000. Seventy-four percent, or 4,440,000, have individual gross sales of less than one million dollars. Interesting information, but what does this mean to readers? I hope that the wide picture helps focus the data that follow.

For any number of very practical reasons, the government has had little apparent interest in keeping track of businesses being offered for sale and not much justification for corralling and compiling data on businesses being sold. Subsequently, we must turn to the business brokerage trade for help in understanding what takes place in the market. No need to run through the criteria that Tom West used to arrive at his conclusions, except to say that his positioned expertise has become the funnel through which passes much information about industry happenings. I have learned to trust and respect him as a great body of reliable business brokerage knowledge. He concludes that about 300,000 businesses, of all sizes, actually sell in a given year. Along with other broker's practical experience, he suggests that only one out of five businesses listed and offered will actually sell in a given year. With this prospect in mind, 1,500,000 or 25% of total businesses are on the market during the year.

Once again using SBA guideline, 255,000 out of 300,000 businesses sold might fit the category of 19 employees or less. If the SBA guideline estimates that 55% will have under $500,000 of sales are accurate, then 165,000 of these businesses sold fall within this category. As many as 222,000 will have had sales under one million dollars, and 78,000 will have had sales over one million dollars. In a 1992 study conducted by the *Business Brokerage Press* (Tom West's company), an average business sale price was calculated to be $227,000. Through another industry data service, that average sale price was found to be approximately $175,000 during 1994. Without sampling correlation in these last two separate collections, it is impossible to come to any specific conclusion, except in smallness of average business sale price. It has been estimated that business brokers are the precipitating cause of approximately one-half of all businesses sold in the United States. Direct owner sale, acquisition intermediaries, and investment bankers appear to account for the balance.

In one of West's recent publications, he coins a phrase that well epitomizes sentiment of those working with buyers and sellers, "Sellers never change! And buyers are a product of their own fear. The foreign buyer is a valuable buyer, but can be difficult to work with due to different customs and language barriers."

On another front, a four-year study of businesses listed for sale with values over one million dollars concluded that when the primary reason for listing a business was for financial gain, and possibly fraught with greed (55.6% of reasons for listing in the total sample), that 94.8% had not sold within the time frame of the study. The liquidation rate, however, stood at a staggering high of 52.1%. When the purpose for listing was disagreement, health, and inappropriate owner mesh, the percentage of businesses sold increased to 50%, and liquidation was nonexistent for those still unsold. Quoting Tom West, "The more sincere the reason for sale, the more likely that something will happen."

Perhaps I lean too much on the "implied" in these numbers, when I draw assumptions that reasons of financial gain and possibly greed, as the purpose for listing, suggest overpricing, but perhaps not. Due to sample preponderance in liquidation, it might be indicated that many had no choice but to attempt to clear debt and to outrun pending foreclosure. One fact not implied is that 94.8% did not sell. Without additional information, it is impossible to discern whether the remaining 5.2% obtained price in their sales or made precipitous change in conditions that promoted those few sales.

As with the example garbage business in Chapter 10, buyer appeal for a small business can have a great deal to do with its ever selling at all. As pointed out in this chapter, however, high cash flow conditioned by lower price will almost always find its mark in buyers. Price is a concubine of King Cash. *Price, in its relationship to verifiable cash flow, is by far the most predictable indicator for why businesses do or do not sell.* Reconcilable price, coupled with an ingredient of wide buyer appeal, improves chances for sellers to obtain maximum yield. Marketing experts can dress up existing features and benefits, but they cannot undress buyer knowledge. As mentioned earlier in this section, a fool and his money are soon parted . . . and part with his money he can. But SBA statistics published in 1992 suggest that over 75% of small businesses sold are to some greater or lesser degree financed by sellers. A Maine broker's study indicated 83% owner financing prevalence in 1994 businesses sold. What then is the implication for sellers? Without seller-assisted financing, many, many businesses simply will not sell.

Another informal study of buyer files revealed that as high as 80% of smaller-business sales are completed by *individual* buyers versus buyout groups. One-third sought manufacturing companies, 20%, service companies, 10%, nonfood retail, 9%, food and lodging business, and 5%, other categories. *One-quarter of prospective business buyers were unsure of what they wanted.* Several interesting thoughts might be offered through examination of businesses sought when compared with the backgrounds of those seeking purchase. Nine percent of the 31% seeking a manufacturing business had a manufacturing-related background, while 21% of prospective buyers had backgrounds in food and lodging, but only 9% of the study group was seeking that type business. In the manufacturing category, one may see implications to financing, whereas in the food and lodging category, one may see implications of exodus from that field. Twenty-seven percent of the study group came from backgrounds in finance, insurance, and real estate, and 15% came out of sales and marketing. The balance of these buyers studied came from varied backgrounds and experience. The approximate 25% buyers unsure of businesses sought can be a particularly good category from which more general and/or distressed and less-structured enterprises are sold. Some in this group are there simply because of newness in the purchase marketplace.

Establishing an offering price must include appropriate attention to all available factual and *subtle* criteria. Subtle information may often develop high on the list of events effectuating a sale. Market research can be as productive in predicting business sale as it is in forecasting sale of products and services. Seasoned business brokers, without regard to varying levels of financial expertise, can add real value to owner strategies by providing forecasts for probable sale in any given marketplace and through balance in formulating initial offering prospectus. The first 90 days of a marketing scenario sets the stage for progress and formulates opinion in prospective buyers that becomes difficult to change. Initial market positioning can be an asset or liability, affecting both time and event of sale.

Owning and working in a business is for many similar to growing up with a spouse or child. We can become dreadfully attached and swayed in our visions! We each have a human right to enjoy the fruits of our successful labor. We have a right to be proud of our achievements. We have rights to reasonableness and fairness in all that we do and in that which may be done to us. These human rights, however, are appropriate for *both* buyers and sellers alike. The closer that an offering is to honoring rights of both parties, the greater is the chance that the business will sell. The converse effect quite frequently can be an event contemplated but not ever achieved. Serious intentions call for serious reality, and we each can make a choice—we really can. We really should . . . when sale is more than a casual thought.

Inextricable market reality points to a salient fact: when desired earnings cannot be obtained while running a business, then expecting to glean them from a business's sale is likely to be a dream on the farside.

An Example of Terms Exacerbating Sale

Insulated by its physical location, a metropolitan neighborhood store competed effectively with several chain giants. The store prospered through years of utilizing professional management, giving attention to customer needs, filling unique product voids, and maintaining good employee relations. Sales and profits climbed to levels that afforded ownership's choice in personal hours of work. Both a manager and an assistant manager were engaged, and the owner has enjoyed several years of working less than 15 hours a week. Takeout for the owner still exceeded $150,000 per year. Age appropriate retirement was his stated reason for sale.

The business was listed by several brokers during the span of over two years, with the initial offering price appearing somewhat high. The owner was perplexed that his viable business was so difficult to sell. He was frustrated that brokers did not bring more potential buyers through the business itself, believing that upon seeing the operation, more individuals would be interested to buy. The owner's call to me was prompted out of social friendship, established years before when I lived in his neighborhood. Perhaps I'm unduly suspicious, but I find that calls from friends and relatives for professional advice tends, in reality, to be a request for endorsement of their own beliefs. A telephone conversation with his broker provided a needed balance to the story.

Booked assets and historical cash flow suggested that the current offering price might be in order. Several listing price decreases had occurred to this point in the marketing plan. Comparing hard asset value with asking price suggested a transaction scenario calling for blends of bank *and seller* financing. Highlighted through conversation with the broker, sale resistance point number one came in the form of an owner demanding all cash at closing. This was perhaps seen by the various listing brokers as a dilemma that all cash sales tend to create. Sale resistance point number two appeared in the form of a cash down payment requirement for not less than $150,000.

Grocery stores in general, through a customary operating nature, are seen as long-hour, seven-day-per-week work commitments by prospective buyers. *It is in the very nature of a vast majority of candidates more capable of sizable purchases that they will be unaccustomed to and unwilling to invest in labor-intense businesses.* In addition, by its nature, grocery store ownership cannot be counted upon to create life-work excitement to people with means.

Why this reasonably attractive business had not sold was partially answered through examination of its positioning in regards to maximum numbers of most-likely buyers. Offering price was fair, but the owner's demand for all cash forced the down payment/financing requirement out of reach for a majority of persons who comprise a segment of most-likely buyers. In regards to the issue of initial appeal, grocery store businesses might represent steps down in status to white collar buyers but could represent upgrading moves for hardworking blue collar buyers. Stockpiles of readily available cash accumulate more slowly from the customary pay scales offered for blue collar work. *Appeal for a business's makeup is necessary to cause potential buyers to consider looking at its operating data.* In this owner's case, he critically forgot conditions that caused him to enter the business and focused only on conditions as they now exist. Granted, in some respects the business currently represents a proverbial "cash cow," but priced thus . . . this is true only to him, while he is there! *Factors of appeal are partially overridden when purchase price offers large amounts of potential cash flow, but appeal still weighs heavy in decision.* To maximize sale probability, he has a choice of dropping price consistent with investment principals prevailing of white collar buyers, which serves to open that market or holding price and focuses marketing on the more-probable blue collar buying sector. Class ordering, for purposes herein, references nothing more than its colloquial, governmental use to describe economic habit formation, and which use underscores a very real feature inhibiting sale.

Inclusion of debt financed by sellers can effectively serve to reduce down payment requirements. In turn, lower down payments open gates that permit larger numbers of buyers to compete for the purchase. Owner financing does involve risk to a seller. Price financing is the sum product of hard assets, cash flow, buyer credit strength, and terms. Lenders encourage seller involvement, because a vast majority of businesses being sold simply do not present adequate collateral for sole bank participation. To sell at all, many owners are confronted with lowering their price to accommodate levels of bank financing or holding their price with debt coverage provision. Assuming credit/risk factors of a buyer are appropriately met, seller financing can add a possible tax benefit through installment sale provisions and provide interest payments that increase value received above the original sale price.

In our concluding remarks to the seller, it was suggested that the current offering price for this business should remain unchanged. Prevailing bank practice guided a recommendation for financing strategy, which was to blend institutional and seller debt. An amount for cash down payment was suggested, and criteria for screening credit worthiness in candidates was presented. A target profile of the indicated ideal buyer was given to both the owner and his broker. Guidelines for handling variations in actual candidate capability were also provided.

Issues involving safety of principal are matters of credit/risk evaluation of buyers. Institutional lenders are professional credit researchers. That they may participate in a deal lends some creditability to an owner's safety of principal as well. However, owner participation is *always* in *second* position. It will be wise to have an accountant review the whole package, before signing on the dotted line.

This owner has struggled for better than two years in attempts to sell his business and still had little future prospect for a sale. What good is a dream that can't be spent? He clearly had choices. He could forgive some value and reduce the price or provide financing and roll dice that he would be paid a greater amount. Irrespective of "luck," positioning the sale as he had, forecast only that prospects for the sale would be unpredictable, based on his particular marketplace. With seriousness of purpose imminent, profiles for most likely purchase candidates should be among seriously considered criteria that lead decisions on setting initial asking prices, terms, and conditions for any proposed business sale.

It is not important which of the two routes this seller chose to proceed, because sale resistance could be freed with either one. The business was put under contract and closed a few months later.

Price Is Often a Culprit

Knowing how we each learn to perceive value, in its comparison to prices we personally become willing to pay for various things, I am continually amazed over our ignorance in empathizing with the other person's similar view. However, in spite of acute awareness, I am no exception to falling into price/value traps periodically as well. Price must necessarily be established in accordance with (a) quality and/or (b) service of a product, for that product to be *predictably* sold. Because each person does independently assess price/value, seldom will a mass-buying public allow repetitive hoodwinking or be willing to participate in continual purchase of overpriced merchandise. Value systems may simply go on the blink when personal involvement cannot be separated from rational thought.

The reaction of business owners during price setting can evolve to threaten personal self-esteem. Again, that rascal personal worth gets all rolled up in the process. If by example I paid $100,000 for a business six or eight years ago, and I'm told its value is only $80,000 these years later, I will be certain to question the value of my own personal worth in the equation. Irrespective of prevailing conditions beyond my control, how do I explain to friends and family that six or eight years of work provided no contribution of my life to value? I am quite normally embarrassed! This is an affront to my person . . . an *insult* to my personal *worth! At this point in feelings, qualitative fact is not being considered. Until I might overcome emotional questioning by locating justifiable reason, I would most often be blinded from any logic presented through fact.* So powerful are issues involving these questions of personal worth that they remain unresolved through bankruptcy proceedings for many unfortunate business persons.

For a bevy of logistical and self-preserving reasons, traditional marketers most commonly direct their reasoning for price changes to that of a focus on fact. When price change efforts are ineffective, the business and/or product tends generically to be classified as "overpriced." *Real* selling efforts within a marketer's organization then become focused on moving *better* priced merchandise. Occurrence of a shifting work effort may be more predominant where sales forces derive personal earnings from straight commission. Subsequently, the questionably priced business or product may be disadvantaged to prospects for "luck would have it" sale. This is not a very pleasant thought but, in fact, a market-driven reality.

Although the following section does not directly address concepts for handling businesses referenced in an earlier survey, as believed overpriced through motivations of financial gain and greed, to some degree it really will. Emotional values in perceptions of personal worth may still be the causing factor. Realities in marketplaces are promoted by factors of supply and demand. Although much truth prevails in a commonly heard adage, "There are just too many good buyers, chasing too few good deals," small-business buyers rarely throw hard-earned cash into ominous winds. Therefore, common ground for price-setting rationale can usually be found by the discovery of belief systems revolving around issues of personal worth.

Many people personally do not understand how subtle and sequential learning affects their own mind play on worth in decision. No one is precluded its essence, and we all become confronted periodically with questions concerning personal worth. Where price setting seems out of proportion with fact, count on attitude of personal worth as a real culprit. Anticipate its existence, and first handle emotional affronts, before expecting numerical logic to have meaning. Overcoming an emotional obstacle encourages hope for change.

Reactive thought (when identified by its principal motivators: gain, need, desire, and embarrassment not to have) is a good place for most of us to begin attempting change in value outlook. For the owner of a financially distressed business, *need* will most likely be the principal cause fostering sale. Factors in gain, desire, and embarrassment are certainly present, but these really are only secondary to his or her pressing need to financially survive. One does not need to be a mind expert to recognize this owner's propensity to agonize and question personal worth.

Solutions forecasting relief from emotional duress in financially troubled businesses are often discovered through examination of events leading up to the condition. For example, we all know the affect that a giant competitor choosing to locate in our "backyard" can usher. That a particular small store may no longer be able to survive in this territory may in fact no longer represent *personal* failure, because *all* smaller competitors are being threatened the same way. Debt holders, usually banks financing the business, will just as quickly become keenly aware of profound risks to repayment of many loans. With the first news of a giant's planned onslaught, local lenders enter into frenzied review of "reality levels" in their secured collateral covering loans to these customers. While foreclosure may become their sole long-term recourse in some cases, a few business owners may develop niche markets and survive the onslaught. Which ones will survive? All will most likely experience cash strains short term, and which, if any, proposal can the bank safely support?

Overpricing, when existing in a distressed business, is commonly the result of an attempt to outdistance debt, made overwhelming through decreased operating efficiency. Without prospect for niche survival, a business from the competing-giant scenario stands little chance of being predictably sold, and unfortunately, some will most always eventually fail. We know that there are still selling choices for this business owner. Businesses in such tenuous condition no longer have cash flow values. They do, however, continue to have value in "hard" assets. These assets often represent the collateral taken by banks in extending loans. When outstanding loan balances exceed appraised value of hard assets, the third party or bank's need must be negotiated into line, or the debt impasse preventing sale cannot be overcome.

Lender liability notwithstanding, bankers are acutely aware of "hammer" value in their collateral being held. Contrary to some popular belief, banks do not want any business or its assets accumulating in inventory. What they specifically want is their cash! Facts that evidence a bank's new risk can provide an avenue of hope toward changing outlooks from a contractual and profitable GAIN, to that of a self-preserving NEED. There will always be fierce and legal resistance to any redefinition of loan amounts owed.

When hammer and appraised values in collateral *exceed* loan amounts, the bank's outlook most likely cannot be changed. If these secured loans are not repaid, the bank will foreclose on assets. Where weak functional capability in current ownership may be a problem, and where future prospect for the business itself is generally good, some hope for eventual salvation can be obtained by negotiating time from the lender to locate someone more skilled. Affronts to owner's personal worth in troubled businesses are often beyond help of marketing experts, but to some degree, pride and self-esteem can be returned to them by selling the business and affording these owners a prospect for getting out reasonably intact. Effective selling requires openness with lenders, cooperation in pricing by the owner, and very directed objectives.

I recognize this section to be far less text applicable, but I've done this for several reasons. First, mechanical aspects of valuing business are widely studied, widely understood, and broadly applied through a proliferation of experts. Second, my particular approach and process neither adds to nor detracts from the science itself . . . there simply is no one best or singular right way to estimate business value, and a very large collection of available formulas can do the same job. Third, many useful texts written by skilled, experienced authors compete effectively with anything I might mechanically add. Fourth, the prospect for bragging self-esteem "great-ness" versus providing useful comparison blocked my several attempts.

What I have attempted to add by this section is an element that I find critically missing from most, if not all, mechanical presentation. That is the *rest* of the story unfolded by samples of personal struggle involved when pricing or selling a business. We all know the fragile nature of this human processing . . . we really do. Therefore, my sole hopes for reader benefit come from my own need for occasional reminders to be humanly human and to be encouraged toward constructive versus destructive per-ception involving the business value problem. In my sometimes dyslexic survey of a business/finance problem, I find that solving for X is often not nearly enough. Trust and respect are two scarce commodities. I can think of no surer way to obtain these from clients, except through early recognition of both my own and their human need. And after all, it is from the human side of enterprise that most things really get done.

"The meeting of two personalities is like the contact of two chemical substances: If there is any reaction, both are transformed."
C.G. Jung

"When a man seeks the pride of his heart he does not count horses."
Wallace Black Hawk

As Business Individuals, We Each Have More Resources Than We Often Recognize

Mind over Matter

For starters, I am sure that you have all heard the story about the half glass of water. One person looks at the glass and proclaims it half empty. On seeing the very same glass, another views it as half full. Both conclu-sions are correct; however, viewpoints are quite different. Positive or neg-ative thinking is no more than a matter of how we look at things.

Onsets of minor illnesses can represent another good example of positive/negative thinking. For years, upon waking and feeling mildly ill, I would say to myself, "Better stay home, I might get worse." I consistently missed several workdays per year because of this negative thought conversation with myself. Eight or nine years ago, I attended one of those well-advertised "self-motivation" courses and was taught a new way to converse with myself. I learned to say, "Better go to work, might get better." It took practice and time to get into the swing of consistently acting out this new philosophy, but I found that it worked with remarkable results. I have not missed work due to minor illness for more than seven years; I work longer hours than many, stay much more focused in what I do, and still have plenty of energy at the end of a day for home projects.

I once heard my partner's consistently positive attitude described in a rather unusual way. Bear in mind that the person illustrating his character was a farmer. He said about my partner, "____ is a person who walks into a field seeing wonder in all that he surveys. While many will see *cow pies* for what they are, ____ would pick up one and exclaim, 'Look at the beautiful yellow streaks!'" He is focused on and dedicated to what is important in his life. Married for more than 40 years, he and his wife can still be frequently seen, quiescently strolling hand in hand along the beach. Though in his 60s, he continues to enjoy a high energy level, and he is a top producer in his field.

Strength of conviction and attitude often weigh heavy in whether we gain or lose. I have had at least two recent clients, disorganized and fumbling with various conventionally accepted processes, who nevertheless went on to achieve considerable success with their dreams. Their convictions and attitudes were so strong that they overwhelmed obstacles that blocked their paths. Commonsense logic was incredibly well developed, and they focused on specific purpose. For example, I have an uncle who with no more than an eighth grade education took his business from a small takeout affair to a chain of 90 restaurants. Mr. Alan Crock bought a 15¢ hamburger joint on a California beach to become the giant McDonald's. His background was similar to my uncle's.

America abounds with stories such as these, and although I believe that formal education is extremely important, close examination of individual successes nearly always reveals that the key to exceptional progress is steeped in positive attitude and a clear focus on goals. It takes down-to-earth common sense to implement the intellect's ideas. Some very intelligent people simply do not have the common sense necessary to implement all that they dream, but success stories as those told above will usually involve elements of both. With a focus on purpose and a positive attitude you can achieve what you set out to do. You really can . . . anyone can.

Mind over Matter in Business

Each individual mind is an incredible storehouse. Regardless of background, or who someone may be, the brain has stored information about a service or a product that others would be willing to pay for! Maybe it's something you do differently in cutting and shaping a dress or something you do in your free time in your shop. Or maybe it's something you do in your business or with your product. Just as with fishing, what we are looking for here is a "hook." Look for things that you think about, or do, that get you particularly enthused. Remember, enthusiasm begets enthusiasm! When you are enthused about what you are doing, you create excitement in others around you. Combine this with your expertise on a subject and people will pay to learn more about developing their own excitement.

Several years before the vegetarian/health frenzy, a chef friend of mine hit upon a way to expand advertising impact *and to get others to pay for his advertising*. There was nothing fancy in his idea—just instructing a seminar, adding the "twist" of healthy meal preparation. Vegetarian menu planning and concepts for healthy eating were all that he brought new to the seminar process. He capitalized on the time-proven marketing standby "how-to . . ." and brought students to his class and new customers to his restaurant in droves. At first his recipes were given free to students in his class. Later they were bound in a pamphlet and sold locally. Eventually his recipe book became published and sold nationally. "This Old House" and similar TV programs exhibit more well-known examples of the "how-to" benefit in marketing. Stand before a public, present topics you know very well and are excited about, and your perception as an expert will grow and grow.

Think about the last time you and friends were *sitting* in conversation. Ever notice how the tone of conversation changes when one party *stands* up? Regardless of the nature of conversation, attention will shift momentarily to the standing individual. Speaking as he or she stands, the group's focus on this person's subject becomes much more concentrated. The act of standing and speaking to a seated individual or group makes use of a subtle form of *intimidation*. Mind you, the word intimidation can be interpreted as "that of being intimate." Unless made negative by *tone* of voice, intimidation can be a positive action. Public speakers, salespersons, and many business people learn effectively to intimidate their audiences into taking specific action on something they present. Add enthusiasm, positive attitude, expertise, eye contact, focus, and honesty in fact, and the presenter is virtually assured of convincing even the most doubting participant. View intimidation as a positive tool in your bag of business skills, and use it to your advantage every day.

The point to this whole scheme of discussion is simply *increasing public perception* of an *expertise* that the particular person or business has been an expert at doing for some time. What a wonderful way to build a business . . . just *teach* other persons *what you already know,* and better yet, get paid for your knowledge while you build business!

You can't think of something to teach others? I'll bet you really can! This book is my own personal example of teaching and attempting to capture a larger share in the market through the how-to scenario. Housewives working outside formal business structures have developed home economics, day care, parenting, single-parenting, craft, cooking, exercise, and many more useful classes that they are paid to conduct. A few have written books and have become TV personalities. Professionals isolate specific topics in their fields and bring state-of-the-art, concentrated technical knowledge within learning grasp of a lay public. As a general populace, we buy literally tons of this type of information every day, and presenters get paid well for their ideas.

Electricians, carpenters, auto mechanics, collectors, accountants, lawyers, physicians, etc., all have information that can be directed to the how-to marketplace. Each and every person knows something, some skill or process, better than an average population, and it is more than likely that a general audience will pay to learn from someone with more specific expertise. Using an electrician for example, he or she can teach concepts in basic home wiring. Both correct methods and potential for hazard could be taught in the course. Handy persons attempt these simpler jobs quite frequently without an electrician, and therefore, no contract work is really lost. However, the electrician teacher becomes the *last-seen expert* and may well be the first one employed when the homeowner runs into trouble or has a major task. New work or no new work, he or she has been paid for classroom time and probably for parts of a job he or she might not have gotten anyway.

How Do I Put This Information into Practical Use?

Let's say that you own a carpet store. What a competitive business selling carpet can be. It seems as though there is an outlet on every street corner, in every large and small town. Color, density, ease of cleaning, etc., are usually some of the features causing people to initially buy carpet. Pretty hard to find a "hook" in these features alone to draw customers to trade with you versus any other competitor. *In the carpet business, the hook, or competitive edge, is found in installation of the product.* We all know what an unsightly seam can do to our enthusiasm in getting a new carpet. Skills in an installer develop slowly, and they are frequently paid on piecework as subcontracted employees of the store. In other words, quality-controlled installation is difficult to facilitate by store owners. Now let's assume that you have a highly skilled and effective installer, and one that is especially adept in minimizing yard goods necessary to complete jobs. You now have two hooks, or selling edges: great installation and effective utilization of costly material. If you have been in business for awhile, you can collect written *testimonials* from satisfied customers of previous work completed. We now have proper conditions for a positive use of intimidation.

A selling scenario could begin with leading statements such as, "You know, Mr. and Mrs. Customer, the key to long-term enjoyment with your new carpet is assurance that everything about the finished job will make you feel content. Our installers are the best in the business, and we guarantee a perfect installation. These letters from other customers point out our ability to excel in getting the job done. Anybody can sell carpet, but the key is installing it without unsightly blemish, don't you agree?" The intimidation in this presentation is found in the last sentence. Anybody, meaning competitors, and the subtle suggestion that others, meaning competitors, might not do quite as good of a job.

An unsung hero in this story, if an installer is really good, is the ability to maximize use of yard goods. This can translate into squeezing a bit more profit out of a job. Although carpet buyers will usually ask about price per square yard, their real question is what will the whole job cost. The job price is a product of carpet, pad, installation, and tax. For the most part today, carpet is manufactured only in 12-foot widths. This presents a challenge in, for example, a 14 × 14 foot room, where 2 × 14 feet fail to be covered by manufactured size goods. Do we buy another 12 × 14 piece, with considerable waste, or is there some other method to handle the void? Since the arithmetic solution in our story is unimportant, let's just assume you will take my word that an additional piece, 12 × 3 1/2 feet, can be skillfully "chain-seamed" into the void with virtually no waste. Not all carpets chain seam inconspicuously. In this case, the challenge is to steer the customer into selecting goods that will seam acceptably, minimize fabric utilization, and thereby, contain retail customer costs at a minimum. This allows you as the retailer to obtain maximum profit per square yard sold and still be competitive at bidding the whole job. Years back, in my own retail outfit, I cannot begin to count the number of times that this single layout feature gained the benefit of winning very profitable bids away from even our lowest priced competitor. This store, incidentally, was one of the businesses I purchased out of bankruptcy and sold at a handsome profit a few years later.

Expensive paint is another of highly competitive products that necessitate marketing "hooks." Price is more often the major hurdle preventing a sale of topline, expensive paint. Expense in paint's manufacture is a combination of the product's ability to hide what it covers and how much coverage it provides per gallon. Old-time professional painters used to measure value in a gallon of paint by its weight. Partly, this was due to its content of lead that, in reality, only provided paint with an ability to hide what the customer wants to cover over. Lead, of course, has been replaced by less toxic hiding additives; however, these chemicals are quite expensive for the manufacturer to include. It is a proven fact that less expensive paint does not contain equal levels of these chemical additives that are found in expensive paint. Subsequently, less expensive paint neither hides, nor covers equally. The *feature* about paint in general, which causes people to use any paint product, is to hide something they no longer want to see. The hook or edge in selling the more expensive paint is found only in its *benefit* of hiding more thoroughly in single applications. It is a consistent and proven fact that cheaper paint requires more product and more applications to hide. A customer seeking paint in a store does not have to be convinced to buy paint . . . that's why he or she is there. When aghast at the price of my gallons of paint, I focused on benefits through one-coat hiding and reduced labor. I would move the discussion into time for clean-up between coats and lost use of rooms in disarray. In effect, while describing technical clean-up features present in **all** competing products, I subtly reminded them how purchasing my expensive paint would be cheaper in the long run. During the sales presentation, I continually reminded them that while my product cost more, less product is required to hide and less time is required to do the job and clean up, which resulted in earlier enjoyment of their finished project. As more convincing evidence, I made a display of one-coat application of light colors covering dark subjects and vice-versa; using several less expensive competitor products, I then compared these samples to hiding qualities in my expensive paint. I continued to stress how personally good it usually feels to get the job done with the least amount of work. Features, benefits . . . features, benefits!

What proper academic right does all this psychology and selling mumbo jumbo have in a text written about financial tools? Frankly, it has to do with success . . . my assumption about your success. What comes first, the horse or the cart? In a more general business sense, accounting and finance serve only as features, until products and services that you render are converted into benefit by customer consumption. At this point, however, efficient record keeping becomes a tool by which you can control expenses and, perhaps, even squeeze more cash to the bottom line. In my opening remarks in this book, I commented that few persons enter the world of small business because of their great skill in finance and accounting . . . it is usually product or service and/or selling skills that precipitate their entry. As individuals, you each have powers within yourself to be great winners at what you do. I want to help you win. It requires trust in me for you to have any degree of confidence in what I present. While I can never know everything about business, or about your special endeavor, I do believe that trust and respect for my knowledge may be enhanced by displaying that I've personally been in your shoes . . . and walked with you on the proverbial tightrope in small-business ownership. That's why I end this text on a rather different note. Why at the end? That's simple. Those of you who have read this far already have a positive attitude, an appropriate enthusiasm, and a focus in purpose. You are winners, before picking up the book. I can do no more than expect to be helpful to people who help themselves.

> *"Find something people want, advertise it in a small way, show a profit, then do it in a big way. Most people skip the two middle steps."*
>
> Richard Thalheimer, Founder of The Sharper Image

Shalom,
Great speed and continued success.
WMY

Index

About the NAM

The National Association of Manufacturers (NAM) is the nation's oldest and largest broad-based industrial trade association. Its more than 13,000 member companies and subsidiaries, including 9,000 small manufacturers, are located in every state and produce approximately 85 percent of U.S. manufactured goods. Through its member companies and affiliated associations, the NAM represents every industrial sector, 185,000 businesses, and more than 18 million employees.

The NAM's mission is to enhance the competitiveness of manufacturers by shaping a legislative and regulatory environment conducive to U.S. economic growth in a global economy, and to increase understanding among policymakers, the media, and the general public about the importance of manufacturing to America's economic strength and standard of living.

The NAM is headquartered in Washington, D.C., and has regional offices across the nation. For more information on the NAM, call 202-637-3000.